ANIME PARABLES

366 Daily Devotions

Sam T Rajkumar

INDIA • SINGAPORE • MALAYSIA

Made with ♥ on the Notion Press Platform
www.notionpress.com

Anime Parables: 366 Daily Devotions

Welcome to "Anime Parables", a unique devotional book that explores the spiritual lessons and themes found in anime. As one of the most popular forms of storytelling in the world, anime has captured the hearts and minds of audiences with its richly drawn characters, epic narratives, and stunning visuals. But beyond its entertainment value, anime can also provide profound insights into our lives, our faith, and our relationship with God.

Through almost 350 different characters from over 115 anime series, this devotional book draws on specific scriptures to reveal the spiritual lessons inherent in each character's story. Additionally, each devotion includes a quote from the anime series to inspire reflection and contemplation throughout the day.

Parables are uncomplicated narratives in the Bible that serve to communicate ethical and religious teachings. Jesus utilized parables in the Gospels since numerous individuals during that period could not wholly comprehend and grasp the significance of his message. In today's society, we often fail to acknowledge and appreciate the never-ending love of God that supports us every day.

My hope is that this book will help you to discover the spiritual depth of anime and inspire you to grow in your faith. As you journey through these anime parables, I encourage you to take your time, reflect on the scriptures, and allow the lessons to penetrate your heart and mind.

My prayer is that through "Anime Parables", you will encounter God in a new and meaningful way and that this book will enrich and strengthen your walk with Him.

May you find Christ in the little things just as I did with Anime!

Your Senpai,
Sam T Rajkumar

Acknowledgments

Firstly, I would like to express my deepest gratitude to God for the inspiration and guidance that He provided throughout the writing process of this anime devotional book. Without His blessings, this book would not have been possible.

I would like to thank my Mom Grace Devasudar, Dad Samuel Devasudar and Sis Shiny G Deborah for their unwavering love, support and encouragement.

I extend my wishes to all my friends and anime nerds who have been a constant source of motivation and inspiration.

I am also indebted to the creators of the anime series that served as the inspiration for this book. Their creative works provided a rich and meaningful source of material that I was able to draw from.

Finally, I would like to express my gratitude to the readers of this book. It is my sincere hope that the insights and reflections contained within its pages will inspire and encourage you in your own spiritual journey.

January 1

Be kind to one another, tender-hearted, forgiving one another, as God in Christ forgave you. Ephesians 4:32

Hero of Konoha

(Naruto)

Naruto is a person who always yearned to be accepted by the people of Konoha. However, the villagers despised, feared, ignored, and never loved him due to the Nine-Tailed beast inside of him. This is probably why, in his childhood days, Naruto always did something mischievous to seek the attention of people from his village. However, despite everything, Naruto remained optimistic and cherished every bond he formed, even with those who had initially rejected him.

Ephesians 4:32 encourages us to show kindness, compassion, and forgiveness to one another, just as God has forgiven us through Christ. This verse is taken from the example of Jesus Christ, who forgave those who hurt him and was considerate of people who felt miserable and lonely.

Naruto's dream of becoming a Hokage, despite the lack of support from those around him, shows the importance of persevering towards our goals and trusting in God's plan for our lives, even in the face of adversity. Through his journey, Naruto learned to accept others and to forgive those who had hurt him, which is a powerful message of love and forgiveness towards our neighbours.

We can learn from Naruto's example to show love and compassion towards others, even when it may be difficult. We can also strive to forgive those who have wronged us, knowing that we ourselves have been forgiven by God. Like Naruto, we can pursue our dreams with perseverance and trust in God's guidance, knowing that He will always be with us.

"When people are protecting something truly special to them, they truly can become as strong as they can be."
- Naruto Uzumaki

January 2

Refrain from anger, and forsake wrath! Fret not yourself; it tends only to evil. Psalm 37:8

Icelandic Explorer

(Vinland Saga)

Thorfinn from Vinland Saga is a character who struggles with anger and a desire for revenge. Following the death of his father by Askeladd, he becomes obsessed with avenging his father and makes it his life's mission to kill Askeladd. Thorfinn's anger and desire for revenge lead him down a path of violence and bloodshed, consuming him to the point where he loses sight of everything else in his life. His obsession with revenge ultimately causes him to lose sight of his original goal, which was to find Vinland and live in peace.

Psalm 37:8 advises us to release our anger and avoid becoming wrathful, and not to worry or be troubled by the actions of those who do evil. It teaches us to have faith in the Lord, to do good, and to patiently wait for Him to act, because holding onto anger can lead to undesirable outcomes, and it is best to let go of it.

The story of Thorfinn in Vinland Saga demonstrates the destructive nature of anger and revenge, and how they can lead one down a path of darkness. It also emphasizes the importance of forgiveness and letting go of our anger to find peace and happiness in life. Thorfinn's journey is characterized by his struggle with anger and the destructive impact it has on his life. As he confronts the negative consequences of his choices, he begins to question the path he has chosen and seeks a life without violence and revenge.

Thorfinn's journey emphasizes the importance of controlling anger and finding positive ways to channel emotions. It can be difficult to do so, especially in the face of great injustice, but the Bible tells us that God is just and will ultimately bring justice to those who do evil. By trusting in God and letting go of our anger, we can find peace and hope in the midst of difficult circumstances, just like Thorfinn eventually did in his journey.

"What's the point of living, if all we do is hurt each other?"
- Thorfinn Karlsefni

January 3

Do not look on his appearance or on the height of his stature, because I have rejected him. For the Lord sees not as man sees: man looks on the outward appearance, but the Lord looks on the heart. 1 Samuel 16:7

Humanity's Strongest Soldier

(Attack on Titan)

Levi from Attack on Titan is not someone who can be judged based on his appearance alone. While he may come across as cold and unapproachable, his actions reveal a much deeper and more complex character. Levi is a skilled fighter who has had to endure many hardships, including losing his entire family at a young age. Despite his tough exterior, he cares deeply for those he considers family and will do whatever it takes to protect them.

There is a striking parallel between Levi from Attack on Titan and the message of 1 Samuel 16:7. The biblical verse stresses the importance of looking beyond physical appearances and recognizing the true character and deeds of an individual. Similarly, Levi's outward demeanour may not portray the qualities that make him an exceptional leader and warrior, much like David, the son of Jesse who was initially rejected in 1 Samuel.

However, just as God saw David's heart and appointed him as king, Levi's comrades have come to appreciate and respect his heart, despite his rough exterior. This highlights the significance of not judging others solely on their appearance, but instead evaluating their true worth based on their actions and character.

Levi may not fit the mould of what we expect a hero to look like, but his heart is pure and his intentions are noble. We can learn from his example of dedication, loyalty, and courage in the face of overwhelming obstacles. And we can be reminded that our worth is not determined by our outward appearance, but by the content of our character and the state of our heart.

"So, just do the best you can and choose whichever you'll regret the least." - Levi Ackerman

January 4

Live in harmony with one another. Do not be haughty, but associate with the lowly. Never be wise in your own sight.
Romans 12:16

Explosive Dynamight

(My Hero Academia)

Bakugo's attitude in My Hero Academia is characterized by competitiveness, aggression, impatience, and a tendency to become quickly angry. He often speaks harshly and critically to those around him, making it challenging for him to work collaboratively with others. Bakugo also has a strong desire to win and be recognized as the best, which sometimes leads him to belittle and mistreat his classmates.

In Romans 12:16, the apostle Paul urges believers to live in harmony with one another and not to be haughty, but to associate with the lowly. Bakugo's attitude is the opposite of what Paul is instructing in this verse. Instead of living in harmony and treating others with kindness and respect, Bakugo is often confrontational and belittling towards his peers. He is haughty and holds himself above others, not associating with those he deems beneath him.

Despite his abrasive personality, Bakugo possesses a fierce determination and an unyielding spirit. He is willing to push himself to the limits to achieve his goals, and his strength and tenacity often inspire those around him. As the story progresses, Bakugo's character undergoes some growth and development, and he learns to work better with his classmates and become a more effective hero.

The attitude of Bakugo thus serves as a cautionary example of the dangers of pride and arrogance. It reminds us to strive for humility, kindness, and respect towards others. By doing so, we can live in harmony with one another, building strong and healthy relationships that bring glory to God.

"If all you ever do is look down on people, you won't be able to recognize your own weaknesses." - Katsuki Bakugo

January 5

For he is God's servant. But if you do wrong, be afraid, for he does not bear the sword in vain. For he is the servant of God, an avenger who carries out God's wrath on the wrongdoer. Romans 13:4

Chain User

(Hunter x Hunter)

Kurapika is a character who has undergone tremendous suffering and grief. His entire clan, the Kurta, was ruthlessly slaughtered by the Phantom Troupe, a gang of robbers who sought after their distinct crimson eyes. Fuelled by a powerful thirst for retribution, he dedicates his life to tracking down the members of the Phantom Troupe and bringing them to justice.

Scripture states in Romans 13:4 that government authorities are God's servants, agents of wrath to bring punishment on the wrongdoer. In the case of Kurapika, he takes it upon himself to serve as judge, jury, and executioner for the members of the Phantom Troupe. His desire for revenge and justice is so strong that he is willing to take extreme measures to achieve it, even if it means sacrificing his own life.

Kurapika's journey in Hunter X Hunter also highlights the dangers of vengeance and the toll it can take on one's soul. As he becomes more consumed by his desire for revenge, Kurapika begins to lose sight of his original goal and becomes increasingly ruthless and isolated. This serves as a reminder to us as believers that we are not called to take justice into our own hands but to trust in God's justice and mercy.

The circumstances which Kurapika faces in his life serve as a cautionary tale about the dangers of revenge and the importance of finding a balance between justice and mercy. As believers, we are called to seek justice and hold wrongdoers accountable, but also to extend forgiveness and show love and compassion to those who have wronged us.

"Some people keep talking because they have nothing to say. Some people keep quiet because they have too much to say." - Kurapika Kurta

January 6

Let your heart therefore be wholly true to the Lord our God, walking in his statutes and keeping his commandments, as at this day. 1 Kings 8:61

Electric Mouse

(Pokémon)

Pikachu is a beloved character from the anime series Pokémon who demonstrates exceptional commitment and loyalty to his trainer, Ash Ketchum. This Pokémon's devotion is evident throughout the series as he always stands by Ash's side through various challenges and obstacles, whether it's battling tough opponents or traveling together on their journey. The commitment and loyalty that Pikachu displays to Ash in the Pokémon series is a powerful example for Christians to follow.

In 1 Kings 8:61, the verse stresses the value of wholehearted devotion and obedience to God's commandments. Despite facing many challenges and obstacles, Pikachu remains dedicated to Ash and always seeks to help him in any way possible. This level of commitment is a reflection of the kind of commitment that we should have towards God.

Pikachu's dedication and loyalty serve as a reminder of the value of faithfulness, perseverance, and steadfastness, which can inspire us all. It encourages us to stand by those we love through all circumstances and to always value loyalty, dedication, and perseverance in all areas of our lives.

In today's world, where there are so many distractions that can easily steer us away from what truly matters, Pikachu's unwavering loyalty serves as a reminder of the importance of being fully devoted to God and to those we love and care about. By emulating Pikachu's example and remaining committed to the things we believe in, we can overcome challenges and achieve great things in our own lives.

"Sometimes friends have to go away, but a part of them stays behind with you." - Ash Ketchum

January 7

And let us consider how to stir up one another to love and good works, not neglecting to meet together, as is the habit of some, but encouraging one another, and all the more as you see the Day drawing near. Hebrews 10:24-25

Fiore's Strongest Guild

(Fairy Tail)

Fairy Tail is a community of mages who band together to complete missions and protect each other. The guild is built on a foundation of mutual respect, trust, and loyalty, and its members come together to support one another through difficult times.

Believers are urged in Hebrews 10:24-25 to encourage each other to love and do good works, and to continue gathering together and not abandon this practice. This reminds Christians of the importance of community and the role it plays in helping us to grow in our faith and become better people. In the guild, members work together to complete missions, support each other in battles, and celebrate their victories together. They also hold a strong sense of loyalty to the guild and its members, as well as a desire to protect and defend their guildmates.

Like the members of Fairy Tail, we are called to support each other through difficult times, to celebrate each other's victories, and to work together towards a common goal. Whether we are facing trials or celebrating blessings, we are meant to do so in community with others.

Similar to how the Fairy Tail guild helps its members to develop into stronger and better versions of themselves, the Christian community is intended to aid us in growing in our faith and becoming the individuals that God has intended us to be. By coming together regularly to encourage and uplift one another, we can create a strong and supportive community that helps us to navigate the challenges of life and grow in our relationship with God.

"Comrade isn't simply a word. Comrades are about the heart. It's the unconditional trust in your partners."
- Mavis Vermillion

January 8

Be strong and courageous. Do not fear or be in dread of them, for it is the Lord your God who goes with you. He will not leave you or forsake you. Deuteronomy 31:6

Thunder Breathing Slayer

(Demon Slayer)

The character Zenitsu from Demon Slayer starts off as a timid and fearful person who struggles to overcome his own insecurities. However, as he continues to fight alongside his companions and witness their bravery, he begins to find the courage to face his own fears and fight for what he believes in.

Deuteronomy 31:6 reminds us that even in times of fear and uncertainty, we can find strength and hope in God's presence and promises. Zenitsu's journey highlights the importance of perseverance and endurance in the face of challenges and trials. As we face our own personal battles and struggles, it can be easy to become overwhelmed by fear and doubt. However, by trusting in God and relying on His promises, we can find the courage and resilience to face our challenges head-on.

Zenitsu undergoes a transformation from a timid and fearful person to a brave and determined warrior. This transformation can serve as a reflection of the Christian faith, where believers are called to put their trust in God and find strength and courage through Him. Zenitsu was also able to find courage and support through his companions, who encourage and uplift him throughout his journey. Similarly, we are called to gather together and support each other in our faith, spurring each other on towards love and good deeds.

Therefore, we are called to be brave warriors in our own right, empowered by the knowledge that God is always with us, providing strength and support every step of the way. Like Zenitsu, we can learn to overcome our fears and persevere through our struggles.

"Don't ever give up. Even if it's painful, even if it's agonizing, don't try to take the easy way out."
- Zenitsu Agatsuma

January 9

You therefore, beloved, knowing this beforehand, take care that you are not carried away with the error of lawless people and lose your own stability. 2 Peter 3:17

Anti-Heroic Detective

(Death Note)

Detective L, also known as Lawliet, is a highly intelligent investigator who has been assigned to uncover the truth behind the mysterious murders committed by the vigilante known as Kira in Death Note. Throughout the series, L makes a firm decision to remain steadfast in his pursuit of the truth, never allowing his own biases or preconceptions to cloud his judgment.

2 Peter 3:17 encourages believers to be on their guard against false teachings and not to be led astray by the errors of others. It also reminds us of the importance of being vigilant and discerning in our spiritual lives, avoiding anything that may lead us away from the truth. We must be on guard against false teachings and be willing to examine everything carefully to ensure that it aligns with the truth of God's word.

L's unwavering pursuit of the truth can serve as an example for us to follow in our own spiritual journeys. Just as he tirelessly investigates the Kira case, we too must be diligent in studying and understanding God's word, seeking the truth in all aspects of our lives. Furthermore, L's humility and willingness to admit his mistakes can also serve as a reminder for us to remain humble in our faith and acknowledge our own fallibility. As we grow in our understanding of God's truth, we must be willing to admit when we are wrong and seek to learn and grow from our mistakes.

Similar to how Lawliet utilizes his intelligence and analytical abilities to capture criminals in Death Note, we can also use our spiritual gifts and skills to discern the truth and pursue righteousness. By staying grounded in our faith and seeking God's guidance, we can overcome the challenges and obstacles that come our way, just as L does in his investigations.

"No matter how gifted you are… You, alone, cannot change the world." - L Lawliet

January 10

Only fear the Lord and serve him faithfully with all your heart. For consider what great things he has done for you.
1 Samuel 12:24

Bald Martial Artist

(Dragon Ball)

Krillin is a character from the Dragon Ball anime series who exemplifies a strong sense of devotion and loyalty to his friends and loved ones, despite his lack of physical strength compared to many of his allies. He remains dedicated to the cause of protecting his friends and fighting against evil.

In 1 Samuel 12:24, the people of Israel are urged to serve and obey the Lord with their whole hearts, knowing that God is dependable and will never abandon them. This verse underlines the importance of staying dedicated to God and striving to fulfil His desires in all aspects of our lives.

Krillin's unswerving loyalty to his friends and unwavering determination to do the right thing, even in the face of adversity, showcases the same qualities. His steadfastness can motivate us to remain committed and obedient to God's will, even during challenging times, as we seek to emulate his example in our spiritual journey. We are also called to have a strong sense of devotion and loyalty to our fellow believers.

The willingness of Krillin to risk his life for the sake of his friends demonstrates bravery and selflessness, providing a model for the kind of devotion and courage we should aspire to in our own lives. His unwavering faithfulness and loyalty also remind us that our strength comes from our reliance and commitment to serve God, not from our own abilities or physical capabilities. We can find comfort in knowing that, like Krillin, we are not alone in our battles, and that God is with us every step of the way, providing us with the strength and courage we need to overcome the obstacles that we face.

"I may not look like it, but I've seen a lot, so you'd better not underestimate me." - Krillin

January 11

It was fitting to celebrate and be glad, for this your brother was dead, and is alive; he was lost, and is found. Luke 15:32

Alchemist Duo

(Fullmetal Alchemist: Brotherhood)

The Elric brothers, Edward and Alphonse, are the main characters in the anime series Fullmetal Alchemist: Brotherhood. They are two brothers who performed forbidden alchemical experiments in an attempt to bring their deceased mother back to life. As a consequence, Edward lost his arm and leg, while Alphonse lost his entire body and his soul was bound to a suit of armour.

The parable of the prodigal son contains the verse Luke 15:32. In this parable, a son asks his father for his inheritance early and then goes and squanders it on loose living. When he is destitute and starving, he returns to his father's home and is welcomed back with open arms. The elder son, however, is angry at his father for welcoming back his rebellious brother.

There are some parallels between the Elric brothers and the prodigal son parable. Like the prodigal son, the Elric brothers made a mistake and suffered greatly as a result. They sought to make amends for their mistake but faced criticism and opposition, particularly from Roy Mustang, who, like the elder brother in the parable, was angered by their disregard for the rules of alchemy and the risks they had taken. However, in the end, the Elric brothers were able to find redemption and forgiveness for their past errors, and they were able to make a positive impact on the world around them.

The story of Edward and Alphonse reminds us that God's love and mercy are always available, no matter how far we may have fallen. We must always remember to turn towards God and seek His forgiveness, just as the Elric brothers did.

"We're going to be moving forward! If we move forward, we'll get stronger, both physically and mentally."
- Edward Elric

January 12

I sought the Lord, and he answered me and delivered me from all my fears. Those who look to him are radiant, and their faces shall never be ashamed. Psalm 34:4-5

Goddess of Water

(KonoSuba)

In the anime series KonoSuba, Aqua is a goddess who is worshipped by many, but she also has a deep fear of being forgotten or abandoned by her followers. This fear causes her to act out and seek attention, often causing trouble for the main character, Kazuma, and the rest of the party. In the same way, we as humans can also struggle with fear and insecurity, particularly when it comes to our relationships with others. We may fear being forgotten or rejected, causing us to act out or seek attention in unhealthy ways.

Psalm 34:4-5 reminds us that when we seek the Lord and put our trust in Him, we can be delivered from all our fears. Aqua often tries to take matters into her own hands and solve problems through her own power, leading to humorous and often disastrous results. While Aqua's fear may be played for comedic effect in the anime, it serves as a reminder of the very real struggles that we all face when it comes to fear and insecurity.

Just as Aqua's fear caused her to seek attention from her followers, we might also tend to seek validation and attention from others instead of turning to God. When we look to God and seek His presence, we can be radiant and free from shame. We can find comfort and security in the knowledge that we are loved and accepted by our Heavenly Father, no matter what fears or insecurities we may face.

Even in moments of fear and anxiety, we can always turn to God and find peace in his presence. We don't have to fear being forgotten by others because we are known and loved by the God who created us. Aqua's growth as a character reminds us of the importance of seeking a higher purpose and finding our identity in something greater than ourselves.

"Like they say, make the best of a bad situation." - Aqua

January 13

Repay no one evil for evil, but give thought to do what is honourable in the sight of all. Romans 12:17

Witch Student

(Little Witch Academia)

Atsuko Kagari, also known as Akko, is a character in Little Witch Academia who demonstrates forgiveness and compassion towards others, even those who have wronged her. At times, she can be impulsive and hot-headed, which leads her to make mistakes and unintentionally hurt others. However, she always takes responsibility for her actions and tries to make amends for her mistakes.

This is similar to the message in Romans 12:17, which encourages us not to repay evil for evil, but to do what is right in the sight of everyone. When Akko is mistreated or insulted by her peers, she doesn't seek revenge or hold grudges, but instead tries to understand them and find common ground. She also forgives her mentor, Ursula, for her initial deception, choosing to understand her motivations and work together towards their shared objectives rather than harbouring resentment.

Akko's example reminds us that showing kindness and forgiveness towards others, even when it is undeserved, can have a powerful impact and lead to greater unity and peace. As believers in Christ, we are commanded to forgive others as God has forgiven us. Although it may be challenging to release feelings of anger and pain, making the decision to forgive and strive for understanding can ultimately result in healing and reconciliation.

The journey of Akko in little witch academia serves as a reminder for us to uphold the importance of forgiveness, persistence, trust in God, and humility as we pursue our own purpose and strive to fulfil God's will for our lives.

"I'll work hard to become a witch who can make everyone smile. Because to me, magic is the most wonderful thing in the entire world!" - Atsuko Kagari

January 14

Greater love has no one than this, that someone lay down his life for his friends. John 15:13

Nakama Pirates

(One Piece)

The Straw Hat Pirates are a group of diverse individuals in the anime One Piece who are like one big family. They are a group of pirates led by Monkey D. Luffy, a young man who has eaten a Devil Fruit that gives him the ability to stretch his body like rubber. The crew consists of a diverse group of individuals with unique skills, personalities, and backgrounds, .who have come together to achieve their respective dreams and help Luffy become the King of the Pirates.

One well-known verse from the Bible is John 15:13, which highlights the ultimate act of sacrificial love that Jesus demonstrated when he died on the cross for our sins. Luffy's crew demonstrates this kind of sacrificial love through their loyalty and dedication to one another. They are willing to risk their lives to protect their crewmates and ensure their safety.

The Straw Hat Pirates are a prime example of the concept of Nakama, which in Japanese means companion, friend, or crewmate. This concept is not limited to just the Straw Hats but also expands to other pirate crews and even enemies who have earned the respect and admiration of the Straw Hats. The idea that someone can become a Nakama despite their differences is an essential part of the series, promoting unity and compassion.

The kind of selfless love and devotion shown by the pirate crew is a reflection of the kind of love that Jesus calls us to have for one another. As Christians, we are called to love one another, even to the point of sacrificing our own interests for the sake of others. The Straw Hat Pirates serve as an inspiring example of this kind of love and loyalty, and we can learn from their example as we strive to love others in our own lives.

"Being alone is more painful than getting hurt."
- Monkey D. Luffy

January 15

Whatever you do, work heartily, as for the Lord and not for men, knowing that from the Lord you will receive the inheritance as your reward. You are serving the Lord Christ. Colossians 3:23-24

Japanese Figure Skater

(Yuri!!! On Ice)

Yuri Katsuki, the main protagonist of Yuri on Ice, is a figure skater from Japan who faces challenges with self-doubt and anxiety. Throughout the series, Yuri works hard and dedicates himself to improving his skills as a figure skater and learns to overcome his fears and find confidence in himself with the help of his coach and loved ones.

The growth of Yuri in the anime series can be seen as an example of the principles set forth in Colossians 3:23-24, where Christians are encouraged to work wholeheartedly as if working for the Lord, knowing that their ultimate reward comes from God. This mindset inspires believers to give their best effort in everything they do, including the challenges they face. As Yuri pushes himself to become a better skater, he demonstrates the same level of dedication and commitment that Christians are called to have in their lives.

Yuri's journey also highlights the importance of perseverance and resilience, qualities that are essential for both figure skaters and us as Christians. Even when faced with doubt or discouragement, Yuri continues to push himself towards his goals, showing the same determination and tenacity that is needed in our own spiritual journeys.

The character of Yuri Katsuki not only serves as an inspiration for those who struggle with self-doubt and anxiety in their own pursuits but also serves as a reminder for us to approach our work with dedication and humility while also leaning on our faith for guidance and strength during challenging times.

"There's a place you just can't reach unless you have a dream too large to bear alone. We call everything on the ice love." - Yuri Katsuki

January 16

The light of the eyes rejoices the heart, and good news refreshes the bones. Proverbs 15:30

Sohma's Housekeeper

(Fruits Basket)

Tohru Honda, the main protagonist of Fruits Basket, is an inspiring character with her positive outlook on life, unwavering faith in the goodness of others, and ability to find joy in the simple things. Despite facing numerous challenges and heartbreaks throughout the series, she remains optimistic and seeks to find the good in every situation. Tohru is also quick to offer kindness and support to those around her, even those who have hurt her in the past. Her positivity and kindness have a profound effect on those around her, bringing joy and comfort to her friends and family.

The joyful demeanour of Tohru Honda can be seen as a reflection of the message in Proverbs 15:30. This verse emphasizes how a positive outlook can greatly affect one's state of mind and physical health. It states that a cheerful appearance has the ability to bring happiness to the heart, and receiving good news can even improve one's physical well-being.

Tohru's ability to find the good in even the most difficult situations and to extend love and forgiveness to others is a reminder of the power of a positive outlook on life. Her character exemplifies important Christian values such as gratitude, forgiveness, and love. She reminds us to be thankful for all that we have, even in the face of adversity.

The character of Tohru extending forgiveness and love to those who have wronged her is a reflection of the Christian message of redemption and the transformative power of love. Her story is a reminder that, even in the midst of pain and suffering, there is always hope for a better tomorrow. Tohru's unwavering faith in the goodness of people and the power of love can inspire us all to approach life with a more positive outlook, trusting that even in the darkest of times, there is always a reason to hope and find joy.

"My happiness comes from the kindness of those around me." - Tohru Honda

January 17

I can do all things through him who strengthens me.
Philippians 4:13

Caped Baldy

(One-Punch Man)

Saitama, the protagonist of One Punch Man, is a character who demonstrates remarkable physical strength and power. He is able to defeat his enemies with just one punch, which often leaves him feeling unfulfilled and bored. However, despite his incredible abilities, Saitama maintains a humble and down-to-earth attitude, never seeking fame or recognition for his actions.

The character of Saitama can be related to the message found in Philippians 4:13, which states that we can do all things through Christ who strengthens us. While Saitama's strength comes from his physical abilities, this verse reminds us that our strength comes from our faith in God. It is through God's strength and power that we can accomplish anything that we set our minds to.

Saitama's strength and power are not just physical, but also mental and emotional. Despite his overwhelming strength, he maintains a humble and grounded attitude, always seeking to help those in need and never seeking glory for himself. These attributes of humility and selflessness are important for us as followers of Christ.

In spite of being the most powerful hero, Saitama never stops training and striving to become even stronger. This emphasizes the importance of working towards our goals, even with the strength that God provides. Saitama's character reminds us that true strength is not just about physical abilities, but also about having a humble and selfless attitude, persevering through challenges, and having faith in God. We need to cultivate these qualities in our own lives and rely on God's strength to accomplish all that we set our minds to.

"If you really want to become strong, stop caring about what others think about you. Living your life has nothing to do with what others think." - Saitama

January 18

To do righteousness and justice is more acceptable to the Lord than sacrifice. Proverbs 21:3

Sorcerer Gentleman

(Dr. Stone)

Senku, the main character in Dr. Stone, is a scientific genius who uses his knowledge and expertise to rebuild civilization after a mysterious event turns all of humanity to stone. Throughout the series, Senku demonstrates a strong sense of morality and a desire to help others through his inventions and discoveries.

Proverbs 21:3 emphasizes the importance of living a life that reflects God's values and principles, rather than simply going through religious rituals or making offerings. It highlights the idea that true righteousness comes from doing what is right and just, even in the face of difficult challenges and obstacles.

Senku uses his scientific knowledge and abilities to benefit others and improve society. He is driven by a desire to help others and make the world a better place, rather than seeking personal gain or recognition. His actions demonstrate a commitment to doing what is right and just, even in the face of difficult challenges and obstacles. He finds innovative solutions to complex problems by using scientific principles and creative thinking, rather than resorting to violence or force. Senku prioritizes doing what is right and just, even if it means taking a more challenging or unconventional approach.

Our aim should be to lead a life that mirrors the values and principles of God, and give importance to doing what is right and fair, even in the midst of difficulties and challenges. We can use our own unique talents and abilities to benefit others and improve society, just as Senku does in the anime. We should also remember that true righteousness comes not from religious rituals or offerings, but from living a life that reflects God's values and principles.

"A man who praises a man to his face is full of ulterior motives." - Senku Ishigami

January 19

For I know the plans I have for you, declares the Lord, plans for welfare and not for evil, to give you a future and a hope. Jeremiah 29:11

Fire Soldier

(Fire Force)

Shinra Kusakabe, the protagonist in Fire Force, is a firefighter who possesses the unique ability to control flames and move at incredibly fast speeds. He works alongside other members of the Fire Force to extinguish Infernals, humans who have turned into mindless, fiery creatures due to spontaneous human combustion.

The well-known verse of Jeremiah 29:11 conveys God's promise to bless His people, affirming His desire to bring them prosperity, protect them from harm, and provide them with hope and a promising future. The verse emphasizes that God has a unique plan for each person's life, and we can have faith in Him to lead us towards fulfilling that plan.

Despite facing numerous challenges and obstacles in his role as a Fire Force member, Shinra personifies hope, committed to his duty and driven by a desire to help others. He uses his abilities to protect others from danger and to bring peace to the chaotic world of Fire Force. His actions demonstrate a trust in God's plan and a willingness to use his gifts for the betterment of society.

We can learn from Shinra's example and strive to use our own gifts and abilities to serve others and fulfil God's plan for our lives. We can trust in God's guidance and wisdom, even in the face of difficult circumstances and challenges. Like Shinra, we can give others hope and make a positive impact in the world around us. We can also find hope and encouragement in the word of God, knowing that He has a plan for our lives that is ultimately for our good and His glory.

"I will get back up as often as it takes, and each time, I won't be beaten." - Shinra Kusakabe

January 20

Likewise, you who are younger, be subject to the elders. Clothe yourselves, all of you, with humility toward one another, for God opposes the proud but gives grace to the humble. 1 Peter 5:5

White T-Poison

(Mob Psycho 100)

Shigeo Kageyama, also known as Mob, is the main character in the anime Mob Psycho 100. He possesses extraordinary psychic abilities, but despite his incredible power, he remains humble and gentle. Mob uses his gifts to help others and to bring peace to his community, showing a deep sense of compassion and empathy towards others. He also demonstrates a willingness to submit to the guidance and advice of his mentor, Arataka Reigen, who serves as a father figure to him.

Believers are urged in 1 Peter 5:5 to clothe themselves with humility towards one another, recognizing that God opposes the proud but shows favour to the humble. Mob exemplifies this kind of humility, recognizing that his powers do not make him superior to others and using them in service to others rather than for his own benefit.

Shigeo recognizes that his power does not make him invincible or above others, but rather that he has a responsibility to use his abilities for good and to serve others. He also demonstrates respect for his mentor and the elders in his life, recognizing the value of their wisdom and guidance.

We can learn from Shigeo's example and strive to cultivate a spirit of humility and submission in our own lives. We can also seek guidance and wisdom from elders, recognizing the value of their insights and perspectives. By embracing humility and submission, we can grow in our relationship with God and become more like Christ.

"Everyone lacks something. People making up for other's deficiencies is what makes this world go around."
- Shigeo Kageyama

January 21

For if anyone thinks he is something, when he is nothing, he deceives himself. Galatians 6:3

Living Legend

(Sword Art Online)

The character Akihiko Kayaba, who goes by the alias Heathcliff in Sword Art Online, is known for his hypocritical behaviour throughout the series. His hypocrisy can be seen as a manifestation of his own self-deception. Heathcliff presents himself as a strong and righteous leader within the virtual world of Sword Art Online. However, in reality, he is a manipulative and power-hungry individual who uses his position for personal gain.

Galatians 6:3 warns against self-deception and arrogance, highlighting that when someone thinks they are superior to others or above the law, they are deceiving themselves. It is essential to recognize our limitations and not think of ourselves more highly than we ought to. When we become prideful and arrogant, we deceive ourselves and can cause harm to those around us.

In the show, Heathcliff is portrayed as someone who believes that his position as a leader gives him the right to do as he pleases and make decisions for others, regardless of the consequences. His hypocrisy and arrogance caused harm to those around him, leading to conflict and ultimately resulting in his downfall. This serves as a reminder for us to be vigilant in examining our own lives and motives, recognizing the potential harm that can arise from pride and arrogance.

As humans, we are all flawed and imperfect, and recognizing this is essential to our growth and development as individuals. We can prevent the same fate as Heathcliff by acknowledging our own limitations and making a conscious effort to understand and empathize with others.

"A person is very strong when he seeks to protect something." - Heathcliff

January 22

But love your enemies, and do good, and lend, expecting nothing in return, and your reward will be great, and you will be sons of the Most High, for he is kind to the ungrateful and the evil. Luke 6:35

Detective Weretiger

(Bungou Stray Dogs)

Atsushi Nakajima, the main character in the anime series Bungou Stray Dogs, is known for his kind and compassionate nature, even towards his enemies. Despite facing numerous challenges and obstacles in his life, Atsushi consistently displays a willingness to help others and a desire to make a positive difference in the world.

This kindness and compassion can be related to Luke 6:35, which encourages people to love and do good to their enemies, even when it may seem difficult or undeserved. We are called to follow the example of Jesus Christ, who demonstrated love and compassion for all people, regardless of their background or circumstances.

Atsushi demonstrates his kindness by showing empathy and understanding towards those who are marginalized or mistreated, such as the characters Kyouka and Akutagawa. Rather than viewing them as enemies or adversaries, Atsushi shows them empathy and understanding, seeking to understand their struggles and help them overcome their challenges. This selfless behaviour is a powerful example of how we can strive to embody the teachings of Jesus Christ in our own lives.

The character of Atsushi Nakajima in the anime serves as a reminder of the significance of kindness, empathy, and selflessness in our lives. By following his example, we can work to make a positive difference in the world and demonstrate the love and compassion of God to all those around us.

"People need to be told they're worthy of being alive by someone else or they can't go on." - Atsushi Nakajima

January 23

This is my commandment, that you love one another as I have loved you. John 15:12

Self-proclaimed Villainess

(My Next Life as a Villainess)

Katrina Claes, from the anime My Next Life as a Villainess, is initially portrayed as self-centred and privileged. However, as the story progresses, we witness a transformation in her character as she makes a conscious effort to build genuine connections with her classmates, whom she previously viewed as enemies, by showing them love and care.

This transformation can be related to the biblical verse in John 15:12, where Jesus commands his disciples to love one another as he has loved them. Katrina begins to demonstrate this kind of love towards others, even those who previously mistreated her or whom she had seen as rivals. Her selflessness in sacrificing her own reputation to help a friend reflects the kind of love that Jesus showed to his disciples, which values the needs of others above one's own.

Despite being reincarnated as the antagonist in a game, Katrina chooses to live a life filled with kindness, compassion, and love towards those around her. Katrina's transformation serves as a reminder that it is never too late to change one's ways and strive to love others as Jesus did. Her example encourages us to be intentional about our actions and to show love and kindness to those around us, regardless of their status or background. Her transformation from a self-centred villain to a kind and loving person reminds us of the transformative power of God's love in our lives.

As we reflect on Katrina Claes' character and her transformation, we can also examine our own lives and how we treat those around us. Are we quick to judge and hold grudges, or are we willing to extend kindness and compassion even to those who may not seem to deserve it? By following Katrina's example, we can learn to live a life of love and service, reflecting the love of Jesus Christ to the world around us.

"We all have things we handle well and things we don't." - Katarina Claes

January 24

As in water face reflects face, so the heart of man reflects the man. Proverbs 27:19

Robot Hero

(Astro Boy)

Astro Boy is one of the most iconic and instantly recognizable characters in anime, known for his bravery, kindness, and compassion. As a robot created to replace a scientist's deceased son, he is endowed with superhuman abilities and a heart that is filled with love and empathy for all living beings.

Proverbs 27:19 means that a person's true character is reflected in their actions and behaviour. Astro Boy's willingness to help those in need, fight against injustice, and protect the innocent is an embodiment of the message of the Gospel. As Jesus Christ demonstrated his love for us, we are called to love our neighbours as ourselves and to be a light in the world, bringing hope and joy to those around us.

Astro Boy's actions reflect the purity of his heart. He is always ready to help those in need, even if it means putting himself in danger. Astro Boy's abilities are not used for his own gain, but rather to help those in need and to fight against injustice. This reminds us that as human beings; we too have unique gifts and talents that can be used to make a positive impact on the world. Astro Boy's character also teaches us about the value of life, regardless of its form. As a robot, he represents a being created by human hands, yet he possesses a heart and soul, just like any other living being. This reminds us that all life is precious in God's eyes, and we must respect and care for all living creatures, as they are part of God's creation.

The life of Astro Boy reflects the goodness of his heart, his willingness to help others, and his respect for all forms of life. As children of God, we can be inspired to live our lives with these same values in mind, striving to make a positive impact on the world and to show love and compassion to all living beings.

"This is it. This is what I was created for. This is my destiny." - Astro Boy

January 25

Better is the sight of the eyes than the wandering of the appetite: this also is vanity and a striving after wind.
Ecclesiastes 6:9

God's Tongue

(Food Wars!)

Erina Nakiri, a character from the anime series Food Wars, is renowned for her exceptional culinary skills and refined taste buds. She hails from a wealthy family and has access to the best ingredients and equipment. However, despite this, she is never satisfied with her accomplishments and continually seeks to improve and perfect her craft.

The message of Ecclesiastes 6:9 emphasizes the importance of finding fulfilment and happiness in what we currently possess, instead of relentlessly chasing after our desires and yearning for more. The relentless pursuit of culinary perfection by Erina is akin to the wandering of the appetite mentioned in the verse, and her inability to find satisfaction in her accomplishments is a form of "vanity and a striving after wind." Despite having the best of everything, Erina is still not content and always looks for something more.

As the series progresses, however, Erina learns to appreciate the value of collaboration and the joy of cooking for others. She discovers that true culinary excellence is not just about creating the perfect dish but also about sharing it with others and bringing joy to their lives. In this way, Erina's character undergoes a transformation from a perfectionist who is never satisfied to someone who finds contentment and fulfilment in sharing her gifts with others.

The transformation of Erina Nakiri in Food Wars serves as a reminder of the importance of humility, gratitude, and a willingness to learn and grow. By adopting these principles, we can cultivate a sense of peace and contentment in our lives and find joy in the simple pleasures that God has given us.

"I feel that those who recognize one right way will never go beyond and reach truly amazing things." - Soma Yukihira

January 26

Fear not, for I am with you; be not dismayed, for I am your God; I will strengthen you, I will help you, I will uphold you with my righteous right hand. Isaiah 41:10

Anti-Magic Wielder

(Black Clover)

Asta, the main protagonist in Black Clover, faces numerous obstacles and setbacks on his journey to become the Wizard King. Despite being born without magical abilities in a world where magic is everything, Asta remains determined and motivated to achieve his dream through hard work, perseverance, and sheer willpower.

The motivation that drives Asta can be compared to the promise of God's strength and support mentioned in Isaiah 41:10. This verse speaks of God's promise to be with his people, to give them strength and support when they face challenges and obstacles in their lives. It reminds us that we are not alone and that God will always be there to uphold us with his righteous right hand, just as Asta is upheld by his friends and his unshakeable determination.

Despite facing insurmountable odds and numerous rejections, Asta continues to press on and fight for his dream, knowing that he is not alone in his journey. He finds strength in his friendships, his love for magic, and his unwavering belief in his abilities. The unwavering determination and refusal of Asta to give up in the face of adversity is a reminder of the power of resilience and perseverance.

The character of Asta emphasizes the importance of never giving up on one's dreams, no matter how daunting they may seem. His unyielding spirit and dedication to his goals inspire others to pursue their own passions and aspirations, even in the face of obstacles. Asta serves as a powerful reminder of the potential within all of us to overcome challenges, pursue our dreams, and achieve greatness through hard work, determination, and faith.

"As you live you lose reasons and hope. But as you keep on going, you pick up new reasons and hope." - Asta Staria

January 27

Peace, I leave with you; my peace I give to you. Not as the world gives do I give to you. Let not your hearts be troubled, neither let them be afraid. John 14:27

Palmtop Tiger

(Toradora!)

Taiga Aisaka from Toradora is a young woman who experiences emotional pain and turmoil due to her difficult family life and struggles with expressing her true feelings. She often feels alone and isolated, leading her to put up a tough exterior and push others away.

The verse John 14:27 speaks of the peace that Jesus gives to his followers, a peace that is different from what the world offers. This verse can be related to Taiga's situation, as she is constantly troubled by her inner turmoil and struggles to find peace in her relationships and life. However, just as Jesus promises peace to his followers, Taiga also finds peace and comfort in her relationships with her friends and loved ones, especially with Ryuuji.

Like Taiga, we can sometimes carry our own pain and struggles and put-up walls to protect ourselves from being hurt. But Jesus promises to give us a peace that is not of this world, a peace that can calm our troubled hearts and bring us comfort in times of fear and distress. As Taiga learns to trust and open up to those around her, she begins to experience a sense of peace and comfort in her relationships.

Through Ryuuji's love and support, Taiga learns to open up and express her true feelings, leading to a greater sense of peace and happiness in her life. The journey of Taiga reminds us of the importance of trusting in God's promises and relying on His peace, rather than relying on our own strength or the things of this world. Her story serves as a reminder to us all to let go of our fears and doubts and trust in God's promise of peace, even in the midst of our struggles and pain.

"It's not about being right or being wrong. There are more important things than that. That's why apologies and forgiveness become necessary." - Taiga Aisaka

January 28

Do not be anxious about anything, but in everything by prayer and supplication with thanksgiving let your requests be made known to God. And the peace of God, which surpasses all understanding, will guard your hearts and your minds in Christ Jesus. Philippians 4:6-7

Psychic Four Eyes

(The Disastrous Life of Saiki K.)

Saiki Kusuo, the protagonist of The Disastrous Life of Saiki K., possesses extraordinary psychic powers that he uses to navigate his daily life. However, despite his incredible abilities, Saiki often finds himself in situations that require patience and endurance.

Philippians 4:6-7 encourages us not to be anxious about anything, but rather to pray and present our requests to God with thanksgiving. This promise also guarantees that the peace of God, which is beyond human understanding, will protect our hearts and minds in Christ Jesus. By praying and presenting our requests to God with thanksgiving, we can experience the peace of God that transcends all understanding. This peace will guard our hearts and minds in Christ Jesus and give us the strength to endure through any situation.

Saiki's patience can be related to this verse, as he demonstrates the ability to remain calm and collected even in stressful and challenging situations. Instead of becoming anxious or worried in the face of challenges, he remains calm and trusts in his abilities and those of his friends to overcome obstacles in his life.

Through the example of Saiki, we are reminded of the importance of trusting in our own abilities and the support of those around us, as well as trusting in God's plan for our lives. By having patience and remaining calm, we can overcome any challenge and experience the peace that comes from knowing God's love and faithfulness.

"No matter how big an accident is, it's triggered by a minor thing, so a minor change can avoid it entirely."
- Saiki Kusuo

January 29

Blessed is the man who remains steadfast under trial, for when he has stood the test he will receive the crown of life, which God has promised to those who love him. James 1:12

Strongest Sorcerer

(Jujutsu Kaisen)

Gojo Satoru, from Jujutsu Kaisen, is a character who exemplifies perseverance and strength in the face of adversity. He is often called upon to protect his fellow jujutsu sorcerers and fight against evil curses that threaten humanity. Despite facing many challenges and setbacks, he remains committed to his mission and always finds a way to overcome even the most difficult obstacles.

The message of James 1:12 is to urge believers to remain steadfast in their faith even when faced with difficult circumstances or peer pressure and to trust in God's promise of eternal life. As Christians, we are not only called to emulate this same spirit of perseverance and faith in God but also to stand up against evil and be a light in the darkness.

In Jujutsu Kaisen, Gojo Satoru also faces peer pressure from other jujutsu sorcerers who may not always agree with his methods or decisions. However, Gojo remains steadfast in his commitment to protect others and uphold his duties as a jujutsu sorcerer, even when it means going against the wishes of his peers. He demonstrates the importance of staying true to one's values and beliefs, even when it may be difficult or unpopular.

In the face of peer pressure, it can be tempting to compromise one's principles to fit in or avoid conflict. However, those who persevere under trial and stand firm in their faith will be blessed and rewarded. Gojo Satoru embodies the ideas of perseverance, courage, and selflessness in the face of danger and adversity. Like him, we might face difficult trials and hardships in our lives, but we must trust in God's promise of eternal life and stay steadfast in our commitment to serve Him.

"When granted everything, you can't do anything."
- Satoru Gojo

January 30

Being strengthened with all power, according to his glorious might, for all endurance and patience with joy;
Colossians 1:11

Symbol of Peace

(My Hero Academia)

All Might from My Hero Academia is a symbol of hope, strength, and inspiration for many viewers. His character embodies the idea of being a true hero, selflessly risking his own life to protect others and fight against evil. He serves as a reminder of the power of determination, courage, and perseverance in the face of adversity.

In Colossians 1:11, the apostle Paul prays for the Colossian Christians, asking that God may strengthen them with all power, according to His glorious might, so that they may have endurance, patience, and joy. This verse highlights the importance of relying on God's power and strength to endure in difficult times.

Throughout the series, All Might faces many challenges, both physical and emotional. He suffers from a debilitating injury caused by All for One that limits his strength and ability to fight, but he continues to push forward, determined to be a hero for as long as he can. He also grapples with the weight of his legacy and the responsibility that comes with being a symbol of hope for so many people. Despite his immense strength and power, All Might never looks down on others or belittles them. Instead, he seeks to lift others up and inspire them to be their best selves.

Even after losing his physical strength, All Might remained committed to his mission and continued to inspire others to be heroes in their own right. In our faith journeys, we may face challenges and obstacles that seem insurmountable, but All Might's example encourages us to keep going and to rely on our faith and the strength of God to carry us through difficult times.

"When there's nothing to be gained, rising to the challenge at those times...is surely the mark...of a true hero!!!"
- All Might

January 31

When pride comes, then comes disgrace, but with the humble is wisdom. Proverbs 11:2

Point Guard

(Kuroko's Basketball)

Seijūrō Akashi from Kuroko's Basketball is known for his incredible skills as a basketball player and his intense focus and determination on the court. He often exhibits a sense of pride and superiority over his opponents, stemming from his belief in his own abilities and the effectiveness of his team's tactics. However, his arrogance can sometimes lead him to make reckless decisions and to underestimate his opponents.

The message of Proverbs 11:2 highlights the dangers of pride and the importance of humility in obtaining wisdom. It is a reminder that when we become too self-centred and proud, we may lose sight of our true goals and make mistakes that lead to our downfall. Despite Akashi's exceptional talent and leadership abilities, his pride and arrogance ultimately lead to his team's downfall in the Winter Cup finals. He learns the hard way that humility and respect for one's opponents are just as important as skill and strategy in achieving success.

As viewers, we can relate to Seijūrō Akashi's character and examine our own hearts for signs of pride. Like him, we may have areas of expertise or natural talents that we are tempted to rely on too heavily, leading us to neglect the contributions of others or even actively hinder their success. However, by practicing humility, we gain wisdom and insight that can help us navigate difficult situations and build stronger relationships with those around us.

In Akashi's character, we can see the importance of balancing our desire for success and excellence with humility, kindness, and a commitment to serving others. Therefore, we must guard against the dangers of pride and cultivate a spirit of humility and respect towards others, recognizing that all good things come from God and that we are not self-sufficient. Only then can we obtain true wisdom and achieve lasting success.

"I don't allow people who go against me to look down upon me." - Seijūrō Akashi

February 1

The Spirit of the Lord God is upon me, because the Lord has anointed me to bring good news to the poor; he has sent me to bind up the broken hearted, to proclaim liberty to the captives, and the opening of the prison to those who are bound; Isaiah 61:1

Full Score Trio

(The Promised Neverland)

Emma, Norman, and Ray are the three main protagonists of the anime series The Promised Neverland who led the other children in their escape from the orphanage where they were being raised to be harvested for their brains by demons. This trio demonstrate their heroic qualities throughout the series as they outsmart the demons, protect the other children, and lead them to freedom

Isaiah 61:1 is a strong testament that speaks of the anointed one, chosen by the Lord, who is tasked to bring glad tidings to the destitute, heal the wounded hearts, and announce liberty to those in captivity, along with freedom from the darkness that surrounds them. It highlights the importance of bringing hope, healing, and liberation to those who are in need.

The characters of Emma, Norman, and Ray demonstrate the qualities of compassion, courage, and perseverance as they work to free themselves and the other children from captivity. Their actions bring hope to the other children and serve as an example of the power of love and selflessness in the face of adversity.

The children serve as role models for us as they put the well-being of others before their own, displayed bravery when faced with danger, persisted in their pursuit of freedom despite setbacks, showed compassion towards those in need, and represented hope in the face of darkness. As believers in Christ, we can learn from their examples and strive to embody these qualities to spread love and hope to those around us.

"We're a family that grew up together. Even if that person gets in the way, betrays us, or says I'm naive, I want to believe in that person!" - Emma

February 2

And walk in love, as Christ loved us and gave himself up for us, a fragrant offering and sacrifice to God. Ephesians 5:2

Revolutionary Assassin

(Akame Ga Kill!)

Tatsumi, the protagonist of the anime Akame ga Kill, is portrayed as a courageous and selfless fighter who is always willing to put himself in harm's way to protect others. His actions often demonstrate his willingness to sacrifice his own well-being for the greater good. Throughout the series, Tatsumi consistently demonstrates his bravery and commitment to fighting for justice, even in the face of seemingly insurmountable odds.

In Ephesians 5:2, Paul speaks of the sacrificial love that Jesus demonstrated through his death on the cross and encourages us to imitate that love by putting the needs of others before our own. Tatsumi's willingness to put his own life on the line for the sake of his friends and fellow citizens is a testament to his selflessness and courage. His actions reflect the kind of love that Christ demonstrated on the cross by giving up His own life for the sake of humanity.

Through the character of Tatsumi in Akame Ga Kill, we are reminded to sacrifice our own desires and comforts for the sake of others, putting their needs before our own. It also reminds us that courage and selflessness are essential qualities for anyone seeking to make a positive impact in the world, and that it is often through our struggles and hardships that we are able to grow and become stronger.

Tatsumi provides a compelling example of the kind of person we can aspire to be: someone who is brave, selfless, and committed to making the world a better place. His story encourages us to reflect on our own values and beliefs, and to think about how we can use our own strengths and abilities to create positive change in the world.

"The reason doesn't matter. As long as a tiny bit of hope exists, that's all that matters." - Tatsumi

February 3

I praise you, for I am fearfully and wonderfully made. Wonderful are your works; my soul knows it very well.
Psalm 139:14

Projectile Hero

(The Rising of The Shield Hero)

At the beginning of The Rising of the Shield Hero anime series, Rishia Ivyred is portrayed as a timid and insecure person who lacks confidence in herself and her abilities. She is often bullied and mistreated by others, which only reinforces her negative self-image. However, as she begins to interact with the protagonist Naofumi and his allies, she gradually gains more self-esteem and courage and eventually becomes a valuable member of the team.

The verse Psalm 139:14 reminds us that each person is a unique and valuable creation of God, with inherent worth and dignity. No matter what others may say or do to us, we can find comfort and strength in the knowledge that we are loved and valued by our Creator. Rishia's journey can be seen as a reflection of this truth - as she learns to embrace herself and her abilities, she discovers her own worth and value as a person.

As Rishia discovers her own worth and talents, she becomes more confident in herself and her abilities. She learns to stand up for herself and others, and to use her skills to contribute to the greater good. In a similar way, we too can find greater self-esteem and purpose when we recognize the gifts that God has given us and use them to serve others and make a positive impact in the world.

The story of Rishia Ivyred serves as a reminder of our inherent worth and value as creations of God, as well as the hope and forgiveness that we can find in God's love. Her journey towards self-confidence and acceptance can inspire us to seek growth and healing in our own lives, trusting in God's guidance and grace.

"Don't try to carry all the burdens yourself. We can all think together about what to do. We're all comrades now!"
- Rishia Ivyred

February 4

Do not be deceived: God is not mocked, for whatever one sows, that will he also reap. Galatians 6:7

Hawk of Darkness

(Berserk)

Griffith from the anime Berserk is a complex and tragic character who elicits a range of emotions and reflections from viewers and readers. On the one hand, his charisma, ambition, and skill make him an impressive and compelling figure. On the other hand, his actions throughout the story reveal a dark and dangerous side, leading to tragic consequences for himself and those around him.

The message of Galatians 6:7 reminds us that we cannot escape the consequences of our actions. It is a call to avoid giving in to the temptations of sinful behaviour and instead, to pursue a life characterized by righteousness and moral uprightness. It reminds us to be vigilant in making choices that align with our moral compass, and to avoid actions that may compromise our values.

Throughout the story, Griffith commits various sins, including betrayal, murder, and sacrilege. He is willing to do whatever it takes to achieve his goals, even if it means sacrificing his own comrades or desecrating holy places. However, as the story progresses, the consequences of his actions catch up with him, leading to his downfall and the destruction of those around him.

Griffith can serve as a compelling example of the dangers of sin, unchecked ambition, the importance of relationships and trust, and the possibility of redemption and forgiveness. His tragic character serves as a warning against the perils of pride and the importance of humility and self-awareness.

"A friend would not just follow another's dream… a friend would find his own reason to live." - Griffith

February 5

Rejoice always, pray without ceasing, give thanks in all circumstances; for this is the will of God in Christ Jesus for you. 1 Thessalonians 5:16-18

Black Lady

(Sailor Moon)

Chibiusa Tsukino is the daughter of the series protagonist Sailor Moon. She comes from the future and travels back in time to seek help in saving her kingdom. She faces many trials and obstacles, including being kidnapped and brainwashed by the series' villains, the Black Moon Clan. Despite this, Chibiusa remains optimistic and determined, never losing hope in her mission to save her family and kingdom.

The scripture passage 1 Thessalonians 5:16-18 encourages us to pray without ceasing and maintain a perspective of gratitude and trust in God, no matter what happens in our lives. It calls us to cultivate a habit of thankfulness, recognizing that God is at work in all things and that His plans are good and perfect.

Despite facing numerous challenges, Chibiusa maintains a grateful and optimistic attitude. She is thankful for the love and support of her family and friends, and she always tries to see the good in people and situations. Her thankfulness also manifests in her compassion and empathy towards others. Chibiusa is quick to offer encouragement and support to her friends, and she shows kindness and understanding towards her enemies. This attitude of gratitude and compassion reflects the love and grace of Christ.

Chibiusa serves as a reminder that having a heart filled with gratitude not only pleases God but also has the power to bring joy and positivity into our own lives and the lives of those around us. We can strive to follow her example by cultivating a spirit of thankfulness, practicing gratitude in prayer, and seeking to spread love and kindness to others.

"The mirror always shows the truth. But the heart of the viewer distorts it." - Chibiusa Tsukino

February 6

Therefore welcome one another as Christ has welcomed you, for the glory of God. Romans 15:7

Golden Child

(Naruto)

Gaara of the Sand from the anime Naruto is initially portrayed as a cold, emotionless character who views others as tools to be used for his own gain. However, as the series progresses, we see that this behaviour was the result of a traumatic childhood and a deep sense of loneliness and isolation. Eventually, he becomes the Kazekage of the Hidden Sand Village and works to create a better life for his people.

The Bible teaches in Romans 15:7 that God accepts all people, regardless of their past mistakes, failures, or shortcomings. This acceptance is not based on anything that a person can do or achieve, but rather on the unconditional love and grace of God. Therefore, we are called to accept others in the same way that God accepts us.

Naruto is one of the few characters who understands Gaara's pain and reaches out to him. Through his friendship and kindness, Naruto helps Gaara learn to open up and trust others. Through this, Gaara is able to overcome his inner demons and connect with others on a deeper level. This reflects the Christian value that acceptance has the power to heal and transform lives, bringing people closer to God and to each other.

The story of Gaara can serve as a reminder of the importance of acceptance in our lives and in our relationships with others. We are called to follow the example of Christ by accepting and loving others unconditionally, just as God has accepted and loved us. Gaara's acceptance is a powerful message that shows that no one is beyond redemption and that everyone deserves a chance to be understood and accepted.

"To escape the road of solitude, you have to work hard. You have to forge a new path with your own power."
- Gaara

February 7

Be angry and do not sin; do not let the sun go down on your anger, and give no opportunity to the devil.
Ephesians 4:26-27

Suicidal Blockhead

(Attack on Titan)

Eren Yaeger from Attack on Titan is a complex character who experiences a wide range of emotions, including anger. He lives in a world where humanity is constantly under attack from Titans, and he witnesses the death of his mother as a child, which fuels his desire for revenge against the Titans. At times, Eren struggles to control his anger and lets it consume him, causing him to act recklessly and sometimes harm others.

In relation to Ephesians 4:26-27, the journey of Eren shows the importance of controlling one's anger and not letting it consume them. It also shows the danger of holding onto anger and letting it fester, as it can lead to harmful actions and negative consequences. Instead, the passage encourages us to deal with our anger in a constructive way and not let it give the devil a foothold in our lives.

Furthermore, as we see in Eren's character arc, it's possible to channel our anger towards productive goals, rather than letting it consume us and lead us towards destructive actions. For example, we can use our anger to fight against injustice and work towards creating a better world for all people.

The journey of Eren in Attack on Titan serves as a reminder of the importance of controlling our anger and channelling it towards positive goals, rather than letting it control us and lead us towards harmful actions. It also reminds us that anger is a powerful emotion that can be both destructive and productive. It's important to learn to control our anger and channel it towards positive goals, rather than letting it control us and lead us towards harmful actions.

"You'll never know if you're not the one who's continuing to take that path... Unless you keep moving forward." - Eren Yeager

February 8

Do not judge by appearances, but judge with right judgment. John 7:24

Boar Head

(Demon Slayer)

Inosuke Hashibira from Demon Slayer is a character who often rushes into situations without considering the consequences of his actions. He is quick to judge others based on their appearance or abilities, and his impulsive nature sometimes leads him into dangerous situations. However, as he grows and learns throughout the series, he comes to understand the importance of looking beyond appearances and understanding others on a deeper level.

In John 7:24, Jesus urges his listeners not to judge based on appearances but to exercise righteous judgment. This means making judgments based on truth and fairness, rather than superficial factors like appearance or social status. As Inosuke grows and learns to work with his fellow Demon Slayers, he comes to understand the importance of looking beyond appearances and making judgments based on righteousness and truth.

Inosuke's journey also teaches us the importance of humility and recognizing our own limitations. This demon slayer often overestimates his abilities and rushes into situations without considering the consequences, leading to negative outcomes. However, as he grows and learns from his mistakes, he becomes humbler and more willing to learn from others. This growth can be seen as a reflection of the Christian value of humility and recognizing that we are all imperfect and in need of growth and learning.

The character of Inosuke from Demon Slayer can serve as a reminder of the importance of exercising righteous judgment and the value of humility. By looking beyond appearances and seeking righteousness and truth, we can make informed and fair judgments that benefit both ourselves and those around us.

"Don't cry, even if you have regrets! No matter how pathetic or humiliated you feel, you still have to go on living!" - Inosuke Hashibira

February 9

Do nothing from selfish ambition or conceit, but in humility count others more significant than yourselves. Let each of you look not only to his own interests, but also to the interests of others. Philippians 2:3,4

Arrancar of Espada

(Bleach)

Grimmjow Jaegerjaquez is a character from the anime Bleach known for his fierce and aggressive personality. He is often seen as selfish and unconcerned with the needs or feelings of others, willing to go to extreme lengths to achieve his goals. However, as the series progresses, we see glimpses of a softer side to Grimmjow as he shows moments of loyalty and compassion towards those he cares about.

Philippians 2:3-4 urges us to have an attitude of humility and to consider others as more important than ourselves. This means putting the needs and desires of others before our own and treating others with kindness and respect. Grimmjow initially puts his own desires and goals above the needs of others, but as he begins to develop relationships with others, we see him start to show glimpses of humility and consideration towards them.

Grimmjow's growth shows the importance of striving towards a humbler and more considerate attitude. He also reminds us of the dangers of selfishness and pride, which can lead us to harm others and damage our relationships with them. Instead, we should approach others with humility and a willingness to serve them, rather than seeking to elevate ourselves above them.

The journey of Grimmjow towards growth and development can inspire us to adopt a mindset of empathy and humility when interacting with others, rather than allowing selfishness and pride to guide our actions.

"Do you need any other reason to fight? Come on. The one who remains standing will return alive. That's all it comes down to!" - Grimmjow Jaegerjaquez

February 10

No temptation has overtaken you that is not common to man. God is faithful, and he will not let you be tempted beyond your ability, but with the temptation he will also provide the way of escape, that you may be able to endure it. 1 Corinthians 10:13

Jet-Black Hero

(My Hero Academia)

Fumikage Tokoyami is a character from the anime My Hero Academia who possesses the quirk Dark Shadow, which allows him to control a shadow-like creature that resides within him. Despite his formidable abilities, Fumikage faces many challenges and struggles throughout the series. He often feels insecure and uncertain about his own abilities, and he is plagued by self-doubt and fear of failure.

The verse 1 Corinthians 10:13 reminds us that God is faithful and won't let us be tempted beyond our ability to resist. This verse teaches us that even when we face challenges and struggles, we can find comfort in the knowledge that God is with us and will provide a way out of our difficulties.

Fumikage's character teaches us the importance of perseverance and determination. Despite his fears and doubts, he never gives up and continues to work hard to overcome his challenges. This determination reminds us of perseverance in the face of adversity, trusting that God will provide a way through even the toughest of trials. The struggles which Fumikage face also teaches us the importance of seeking support from others. Similarly, we are called to support and uplift one another in times of need.

The story of Fumikage in My Hero Academia reminds us of the importance of perseverance, seeking support from others, and trusting in God's faithfulness even in the midst of trials and struggles. As we face our own challenges and obstacles, we can find comfort in the knowledge that God is with us and will provide a way out of our difficulties.

"No matter what the environment, we must choose wisely."
- Fumikage Tokoyami

February 11

And return to the Lord your God, you and your children, and obey his voice in all that I command you today, with all your heart and with all your soul. Deuteronomy 30:2

Strong-Willed Rider

(One-Punch Man)

In the One-Punch Man anime, Mumen Rider is a hero who is not particularly powerful or skilled, but he is deeply committed to his duty of protecting others and upholding justice. He rides a bicycle to get to his assignments and protect his city. Despite his lack of significant physical strength or special abilities, he is deeply committed to his role as a hero and always strives to do what is right, even if it means risking his own life.

The verse from Deuteronomy 30:2 serves as a call to action, challenging us to examine our hearts and lives and to make changes where necessary. It reminds us that true repentance involves more than just feeling sorry for our mistakes. It requires a complete turning away from sin and a wholehearted commitment to follow God's ways. When we make this commitment, God promises to have compassion on us and to restore us.

Mumen Rider is committed to doing what is right and just, even in the face of overwhelming odds or criticism from others. His commitment is rooted in his desire to help others and to uphold the values of justice and righteousness. Mumen Rider's willingness to put himself in danger for the sake of others is an act of compassion, reflecting the kind of love and concern that God has for His people. Like him, we are called to put the needs of others before our own and to use our gifts and talents to help those who are in need.

The commitment which Mumen Rider shows in protecting others and upholding justice can serve as a powerful reminder of the importance of commitment, compassion, and obedience to God's commands. We are called to serve others with humility and love, just as Mumen Rider serves his community with courage and devotion.

"It's not about winning. It's about taking a stand!"
- Mumen Rider

February 12

Bear one another's burdens, and so fulfil the law of Christ.
Galatians 6:2

Strongest Chivalric Order

(Seven Deadly Sins)

The group known as the Seven Deadly Sins from the anime of the same name is made up of seven powerful and skilled knights who were once accused of betraying the kingdom. Despite this, they are still committed to protecting the kingdom and its people, and they work together to defeat powerful enemies and protect the innocent. Each member of the group has their own unique strengths and weaknesses, but they rely on each other to overcome any obstacle.

Galatians 6:2 is a powerful reminder of our responsibility to care for and support one another in the body of Christ. It calls us to be compassionate, kind, and loving towards our brothers and sisters in Christ, and to be willing to lend a helping hand when needed. By carrying each other's burdens, we fulfil the law of Christ and show the world the love and compassion of our Lord and Saviour.

In many ways, the Seven Deadly Sins order led by Meliodas embodies this message as they carry each other's burdens, both in battle and in their personal lives. They support each other emotionally, physically, and spiritually, and they are always there for each other when someone needs help.

As the Seven Deadly Sins rely on each other to fulfil their mission, we are called to rely on each other as members of the body of Christ. We are all called to carry each other's burdens and support one another in love, just as the Seven Deadly Sins do. This kind of love and support is what allows us to grow stronger together and overcome any obstacle. Therefore, let us strive to show compassion and kindness to those around us and rely on each other's strengths and weaknesses as we work together to fulfil God's mission for our lives.

"Everyone has to die someday. But what they believed in will never fade away as long as someone protects it."
- Meliodas

February 13

Therefore, my beloved brothers, be steadfast, immovable, always abounding in the work of the Lord, knowing that in the Lord your labour is not in vain. 1 Corinthians 15:58

Girl of Steel

(Jujutsu Kaisen)

Nobara Kugisaki, a character from the anime Jujutsu Kaisen, displays remarkable courage in her battles against evil spirits, despite the odds stacked against her. She is a strong-willed and confident character who is not afraid to take risks or face danger, and she always puts the safety of others before her own. Her courage and determination are an inspiration to those who watch her story unfold.

The verse 1 Corinthians 15:58 reminds us of the importance of standing firm in our faith and being steadfast in our efforts to serve the Lord. It encourages us to be strong and immovable in our faith, knowing that our work for the Lord is not in vain. This verse also speaks to the idea that our actions and choices matter, and that we should not be discouraged by setbacks or difficulties, but rather persevere in our efforts to serve God.

Nobara is rooted in her unwavering commitment to her mission and to protecting others. She does not give up in the face of danger or adversity, but instead rises to the challenge and fights with all her might. Her courage is an embodiment of the idea that our actions and choices matter, and that we should not be discouraged by setbacks or difficulties, but rather persevere in our efforts to protect others and do what is right. She is willing to take risks and put herself in harm's way for the sake of others, just as Jesus did for us on the cross.

Just as Nobara's work as a Jujutsu Sorcerer has eternal significance, our work in serving God and others also has eternal significance and reward. Let us, therefore, be steadfast and immovable, always giving ourselves fully to the work of the Lord, standing firm in our faith, and not giving up in the face of difficulty or opposition.

"I can. It means being true to myself after all." - Nobara Kugisaki

February 14

A false balance is an abomination to the Lord, but a just weight is his delight. Proverbs 11:1

Chimer a Ant King

(Hunter x Hunter)

In the anime Hunter x Hunter, Meruem, the king of the Chimera Ants, faces a pivotal decision when he begins to question the violent and destructive nature of his race. Despite his upbringing as a ruthless and merciless ruler, Meruem begins to show compassion towards humans and starts to consider a different path for his people. This change of heart leads him to make a difficult decision to put an end to the conflict between his army and humanity.

Proverbs 11:1 speaks to the importance of honesty and integrity in our actions and decisions. It means that the Lord detests dishonesty and unfairness, but delights in justice and integrity. This verse reminds us that our actions should be guided by a sense of fairness and honesty, and that we should strive to make just decisions in all areas of our lives.

Meruem's decision to seek a peaceful resolution to the conflict between his race and humanity reflects the idea of seeking justice and fairness in our dealings with others. He recognizes that the actions of his people have been unjust and seeks to make things right. In doing so, he shows a true sense of morality and fairness that is in line with God's desire for justice and righteousness. Meruem's decision to seek a peaceful resolution to the conflict with humanity can be seen as an embodiment of the idea of seeking justice and fairness in our dealings with others.

As followers of Christ, we are called to live with integrity, honesty, and justice in all areas of our lives. Let us, therefore, strive to make just decisions in our own lives and to always put the needs of others before our own desires, just as Meruem did.

"Fear and desire hold the power to disrupt one's rhythm. Desire clouds one's vision, while fear stills one's step."
- Meruem

February 15

And he died for all, that those who live might no longer live for themselves but for him who for their sake died and was raised. 2 Corinthians 5:15

Valhalla Poindexter

(Tokyo Revengers)

Keisuke Baji is an important character from Tokyo Revengers who plays a significant role in the story. He is a former member of the Tokyo Manji gang and one of the founding members of the Toman gang. Baji is a strong-willed and charismatic leader who inspires his followers to achieve great things. He is willing to put his own safety and well-being on the line to protect those he cares about and to fight for what he believes is right.

Paul's statement in 2 Corinthians 5:15 emphasizes that Christ's death on the cross was for the purpose of enabling those who live to no longer live for themselves, but rather to live for the One who died and was raised again for their sake. This emphasizes the sacrifice that Jesus made for us on the cross and the call to live for Him rather than for ourselves.

Keisuke Baji's actions and motivations are aligned with the idea of living for something greater than oneself. He is willing to put himself in harm's way to protect his friends and achieve his goals. His leadership inspires his followers to do the same. Just as Jesus gave His life for us, Baji is willing to make sacrifices for the sake of others. He lives not for his own benefit but for the benefit of his friends and his gang. In doing so, he shows a selflessness and devotion similar to Jesus Christ, who gave His own life for the sake of others.

Baji's devotion to his friends is an inspiration to us all, as it reminds us of the importance of sacrificing our own desires and needs for the sake of others. We are called to live not for ourselves but for Jesus and to follow His example of selfless love and sacrifice. Let us, therefore, be willing to make sacrifices for the sake of others and to live for something greater than ourselves, just as Baji did for his gang.

"Didn't I tell you this over and over? Don't trust anybody but your friends." - Keisuke Baji

February 16

Behold, how good and pleasant it is when brothers dwell in unity! Psalm 133:1

Saiyan Prince Family

(Dragon Ball)

In Dragon Ball, Vegeta's family exemplifies the importance of unity. Despite their differences and individual personalities, they collaborate to protect each other and achieve common goals. While Vegeta started as an antagonist who was keen on destroying the earth, he eventually became a devoted husband to Bulma and a loving father to his children, Trunks and Bulla. His family became his source of strength and motivation, driving him to become a better person.

Psalm 133:1 reminds us of the significance of unity among believers. When we come together in love and harmony, we can accomplish great things for God's kingdom. We can support and encourage each other, and our relationships can be a source of joy and blessings. Vegeta realizes that his family brings him joy and purpose in life, and that there is strength in unity.

The unity within Vegeta's family serves as an example of the blessings that can arise from being in harmony with one another. Despite their differences and individual strengths, they are a close-knit group that supports and cares for each other. Their unity allows them to face difficult challenges together and emerge stronger as a family.

Just as Vegeta's family stands as an example of how unity can bring blessings and strength, we are called to live in unity with our families and loved ones. By working together and supporting each other, we can experience the blessings and joy that come from being part of a united family. Let us therefore seek to cultivate unity among our own families and in our communities of faith.

"Spend most of your life ruled by another, watch your race dwindle to a handful, and then tell me what has more meaning than your own strength." - Vegeta

February 17

Have I not commanded you? Be strong and courageous. Do not be frightened, and do not be dismayed, for the Lord your God is with you wherever you go. Joshua 1:9

Légumes Koro-pok-guru

(Food Wars!)

Megumi Tadokoro is a character from Food Wars! who struggles with fear and anxiety in the competitive culinary world. She often doubts her own abilities and is afraid of failure. However, she also possesses a strong determination and a desire to improve her skills. Despite her fear, she continues to push forward and work hard to achieve her goals.

In Joshua 1:9, God encourages Joshua to be strong and courageous and not to be afraid or discouraged, for the Lord is with him wherever he goes. Megumi's fear and self-doubt are common experiences for many people, especially when facing new challenges and opportunities. But just as God commands Joshua to be strong and courageous, we too can find courage and confidence in God's presence and promises. When we trust in God, we can overcome our fears and doubts and pursue our goals with boldness and courage.

As Megumi faces culinary challenges and competitions, she learns to overcome her fear and self-doubt by relying on her skills and the encouragement of her friends. We too can find encouragement and support from our friends, family, and community of faith, as well as through prayer and reading the Bible. We can also trust in God's promises of love, guidance, and strength to help us overcome our fears and doubts and pursue our goals with confidence.

As believers in Christ, we need not be fearful or disheartened because God will provide us with the courage and strength, we need to overcome any obstacles. Like Megumi, we can rely on our own inner strength as well as the support of those around us to face our fears and strive for excellence.

"Repeating trial and error and failing many times... it's that process which makes the dishes shine." - Soma Yukihira

February 18

Blessed are the merciful, for they shall receive mercy.
Matthew 5:7

Mage Titania

(Fairy Tail)

In the anime series Fairy Tail, Erza Scarlet is a character who has faced numerous hardships and traumas throughout her life, including being enslaved as a child soldier. Despite her past, Erza learns to forgive those who have wronged her and seeks to show kindness and compassion to others. She becomes a strong and compassionate member of the Fairy Tail guild, inspiring those around her with her courage and forgiveness.

In Matthew 5:7, Jesus teaches us that blessed are the merciful, for they shall obtain mercy. Forgiveness is a vital aspect of the Christian faith, as it is through God's mercy and forgiveness that we are saved. Erza Scralet's forgiveness of those who have wronged her is a reflection of God's love and grace towards us. When we forgive others, we show them the same mercy and compassion that God has shown us. Forgiveness also brings freedom from bitterness and resentment, allowing us to move forward in our lives with renewed purpose and hope.

In her journey towards forgiveness, Erza learns that it is not easy to let go of hurt and pain. However, she also learns that forgiveness is not about excusing the wrong that has been done, but rather about freeing oneself from the burden of anger and bitterness. It takes great strength and courage to forgive those who have wronged us, but it is through the power of God's grace and love that we can find the strength to do so.

When we choose to forgive others, we reflect the mercy that God has shown us. As we follow Erza Scarlet's example of forgiveness, we become more like Christ and experience the blessings of living a merciful and compassionate life.

"A strong person is not the one who doesn't cry. A strong person is the one who cries and sheds tears for a moment, then gets up and fights again." - Erza Scarlet

February 19

Therefore encourage one another and build one another up, just as you are doing. 1 Thessalonians 5:11

Karasuno's Volleyball Duo

(Haikyu!!)

In the Haikyu anime, Hinata and Kageyama start off as rivals who eventually become teammates on their high school volleyball team. Despite their initial differences and conflicts, they develop a strong bond of friendship and trust through their shared love of volleyball and their mutual desire to win. They learn to communicate and work together as a team, with Hinata's speed and agility complementing Kageyama's skill and precision as a setter.

1 Thessalonians 5:11 teaches us to encourage and build up one another, and we are called to love and support one another, even in the midst of our differences and disagreements. Hinata and Kageyama's friendship is a great example of how teammates can support and encourage each other to be their best selves. They learn to put their differences aside and work together towards a common goal, and their trust and respect for each other grows as a result.

At times, building up others may require humility, patience, and perseverance. Hinata and Kageyama's friendship is not without its challenges, as they must learn to navigate their differences and work together as a team. Likewise, in our own friendships, we may encounter conflicts and challenges. However, by following the example of Hinata and Kageyama and seeking to encourage and build up one another, we can overcome these challenges and grow stronger together.

Hinata and Kageyama's friendship in the Haikyu anime reflects the biblical teachings of encouraging and building up one another, as well as the importance of communication and teamwork in achieving success. As we strive to follow Christ, we must also seek to support and encourage our fellow believers and work together towards a common goal.

"You don't win alone. That's just how it is." - Tobio Kageyama

February 20

Like new-born infants, long for the pure spiritual milk, that by it you may grow up into salvation. 1 Peter 2:2

Avaricious Homunculus

(Fullmetal Alchemist: Brotherhood)

In Fullmetal Alchemist: Brotherhood, Greed is one of the seven Homunculi created through alchemy. Greed embodies the sin of avarice, symbolizing an insatiable desire for material possessions and power. He is driven by his selfish nature and seeks immortality and ultimate control over everything. However, as the story progresses, we witness a remarkable evolution in Greed's character.

In 1 Peter 2:2, believers are encouraged to approach their spiritual journey with the innocence and hunger of new-born babies. The verse highlights the importance of craving pure spiritual milk, symbolizing the nourishment and sustenance found in God's teachings and wisdom. It reminds us to prioritize our spiritual growth and to seek the nourishment that comes from aligning our desires with God's will.

Through his interactions with the Elric brothers and their allies, Greed begins to question his own desires and the emptiness of his pursuit for immortality and control. He starts to develop a sense of camaraderie, loyalty, and even compassion towards those he once saw as mere tools for his ambitions. This growth leads him to make selfless choices and even sacrifice himself for the greater good.

Just as Greed evolves from self-centred desires to developing loyalty and a willingness to sacrifice, we too can experience transformation by aligning our desires with God's purposes. This transformation can lead us to a greater sense of purpose and fulfilment in our relationship with God.

"You humans think greed is just for money and power! But everyone wants something they don't have." - Greed

February 21

May the God of hope fill you with all joy and peace in believing, so that by the power of the Holy Spirit you may abound in hope. Romans 15:13

Free-spirit Violinist

(Your Lie in April)

Kaori Miyazono from Your Lie in April is a passionate violinist who brings a newfound sense of joy and vibrancy into the life of the main character, Kōsei Arima. Despite her own struggles and health issues, Kaori radiates an infectious happiness through her music and vibrant personality. She inspires those around her to embrace life's beauty and pursue their passions wholeheartedly.

Romans 15:13 reminds believers of the abundant joy and hope that come from placing their trust in God. It emphasizes that true happiness is rooted in a relationship with God and the assurance of His promises. Kaori's ability to find joy despite her circumstances reflects the transcendent nature of God's joy and peace that surpass worldly understanding. Her passion for music and zest for life can be seen as an expression of the overflowing hope that comes from trusting in God's plan.

Kaori's impact on the main character, Kōsei, and those around her reflects the transformative power of spreading hope and joy. Her unwavering spirit and contagious happiness demonstrate the possibility of bringing God's love and light into the lives of others. She becomes a vessel through which others experience joy and find solace in their own struggles.

By seeking our ultimate happiness in God, we can experience a joy that transcends circumstances and become vessels of God's love and joy in the world. Like Kaori, we too can share the happiness we have experienced through God's love with others, spreading hope and inspiring them to pursue their passions and embrace the beauty of life.

"Maybe there's only a dark road up ahead. But you still have to believe and keep going. Believe that the stars will light your path, even a little bit." - Kaori Miyazono

February 22

Commit your work to the Lord, and your plans will be established. Proverbs 16:3

Aspiring Artist

(Blue Period)

Yatora Yaguchi's story in the Blue Period anime revolves around his passion for art and his desire to become a successful artist. He faces numerous challenges and uncertainties along the way but consistently demonstrates a deep commitment to his work. Yatora pours his heart and soul into his art, constantly striving to improve his skills and understanding of the craft.

Proverbs 16:3 encapsulates a profound truth about our relationship with God and the way we approach our work and aspirations. To commit our work to the Lord means to surrender our efforts, ambitions, and desires to Him. It involves recognizing that God is the ultimate source of wisdom, guidance, and purpose in our lives. When we acknowledge God's sovereignty and align our work with His will, we invite Him to be the guiding force behind our endeavours.

Yatora embodies the idea of committing his work to the Lord. While Yatora's artistry may not have explicit religious connotations, his dedication and determination reflect a level of devotion to his craft. He recognizes the significance of his talent and the responsibility he has been given to steward it well. Through his perseverance and dedication, he gains recognition and opportunities to showcase his art. His commitment to his craft aligns with the biblical principle of entrusting our endeavours to God, believing that He will guide and establish our plans according to His divine purpose.

The journey of Yatora Yaguchi serves as a reminder that when we commit our work to the Lord, He can establish our plans and use our talents for His glory. By committing our work, talents, and aspirations to the Lord, we invite His presence and guidance into every aspect of our lives. Through this commitment, we can find purpose, fulfilment, and the establishment of our plans in alignment with God's perfect will.

"Maybe I'm not talented, but I'm risking everything for now." - Yatora Yaguchi

February 23

Little children, let us not love in word or talk but in deed and in truth. 1 John 3:18

Billionaire Adventurer

(KonoSuba)

In the anime Konosuba, Satou Kazuma is known for his blunt honesty and straightforward nature. While this often leads to comedic situations, it also reveals a sense of authenticity and transparency in his character. He doesn't hesitate to speak his mind or confront uncomfortable truths, even if it means exposing his own weaknesses or vulnerabilities.

The verse 1 John 3:18 encourages believers to demonstrate their love not merely through empty words or superficial expressions, but through genuine actions and sincere honesty. It also emphasizes the importance of aligning our words with our deeds and living out our faith with integrity. Honesty is not only about avoiding lies, but also about embracing transparency and truthfulness in our thoughts, words, and actions. By embodying the honesty depicted by Satou Kazuma, we have the opportunity to build trust, foster genuine relationships, and reflect the character of Christ to those around us.

Satou Kazuma fearlessly expresses his opinions and confronts uncomfortable truths, even if it means revealing his own weaknesses and vulnerabilities. His authenticity and honesty are evident in both his words and actions, making him relatable and refreshing. His example encourages us to examine our motives and ensure that our words and actions align with truth and love. It challenges us to embrace transparency and authenticity, living out our faith through tangible acts of kindness, compassion, and sincerity.

The honesty of Satou Kazuma serves as a reminder for us to embody the principles of genuine honesty in our own lives. We are called to love others not just with words, but through our actions and truth. By doing so, we can foster genuine connections, build trust, and reflect the love of Christ in our daily interactions.

"Any gullible fool who gets tricked has only himself to blame." - Satou Kazuma

February 24

Who through him are believers in God, who raised him from the dead and gave him glory, so that your faith and hope are in God. 1 Peter 1:21

Zero Gravity

(My Hero Academia)

Ochaco Uraraka, a character from My Hero Academia, embodies a strong sense of hope throughout the series. She is determined and resilient, always striving to become a hero and make a positive impact on the world around her. Despite the challenges she faces, Ochaco maintains a hopeful outlook and believes in her own potential to create a better future.

1 Peter 1:21 reminds believers that our faith and hope are anchored in God's power and the resurrection of Jesus Christ. It emphasizes the transformative nature of our faith, which gives us a living hope that transcends worldly circumstances. Ochaco Uraraka's character reflects the importance of placing our hope in something greater than ourselves. By trusting in God's plan and relying on His strength, we can navigate through difficult times with resilience and maintain a hopeful outlook.

Ochaco's hope is not merely grounded in her own abilities or circumstances, but in her belief in herself and the potential for growth and change. She looks beyond the present challenges and focuses on her goals, aspiring to become a hero who can make a positive impact on the lives of others. Ochaco's hope is rooted in her determination, her belief in the goodness of humanity, and her desire to contribute to a better future.

The unwavering hope of Ochaco Uraraka is an inspiration for us to cultivate a similar mindset. By anchoring our hope in God, we can find the strength and courage to persevere in the face of adversity. We can hold onto the belief that our actions, fuelled by hope and guided by faith, have the power to bring positive change to the world around us.

"Everyone is giving all they can, which only makes it fair that I do the same." - Ochaco Uraraka

February 25

Humble yourselves before the Lord, and he will exalt you.
James 4:10

Leidenschaftlich's Soldier Maiden

(Violet Evergarden)

Violet Evergarden undergoes a journey of growth and humility throughout the anime series. Initially portrayed as emotionally detached and unfamiliar with human emotions, she gradually learns the value of empathy and understanding as she works as an Auto Memory Doll, writing letters on behalf of others. Her experiences with different clients and their heartfelt stories shape her character, leading her on a path of humility and self-discovery.

James 4:10 teaches believers about the importance of humility before God, recognizing our own limitations and submitting ourselves to His will. It reminds us that true greatness comes from acknowledging our dependence on God and seeking His guidance in all aspects of our lives. Violet Evergarden's character arc reflects this principle of humility as she learns to let go of her pride and opens herself to the experiences and emotions of others.

Violet's transformation is evident in her journey from a stoic and mechanical individual to someone who is more compassionate and understanding. Her humility is demonstrated through her willingness to learn, adapt, and grow, as well as her ability to empathize with the struggles and emotions of others. She also recognizes her own shortcomings and takes responsibility for her actions, seeking to make amends. Through her journey, she learns the importance of seeking forgiveness and extending grace to others, reflecting the humility we are called to embrace as believers.

The transformation of Violet Evergarden serves as a powerful reminder of the importance of humility in our own lives. Her journey highlights the transformative power of humility, enabling us to connect with others on a deeper level and reflect the love and grace of God in our interactions.

"Sometimes we create our own heartbreaks through expectations." - Violet Evergarden

February 26

Beware of practicing your righteousness before other people in order to be seen by them, for then you will have no reward from your Father who is in heaven.
Matthew 6:1

Archangel of Stigma

(Seven Deadly Sins)

Ludociel, a character from the Seven Deadly Sins anime, exhibits hypocrisy throughout his story arc. He presents himself as a righteous and noble figure, fighting for justice and claiming to embody virtue. However, his actions often contradict his professed ideals, revealing hidden hypocrisy within his character.

Matthew 6:1 addresses the issue of hypocrisy and warns believers against performing acts of righteousness solely for the purpose of receiving recognition and praise from others. It encourages followers of Christ to practice their faith genuinely, seeking to please God rather than seeking approval from people. It cautions against the danger of seeking self-glorification and recognition, as these can lead to hypocrisy and a distorted representation of one's faith.

Ludociel's hypocrisy is evident in his tendency to prioritize personal agendas and the pursuit of power over the well-being and genuine justice he claims to uphold. He frequently manipulates others and uses his position and authority for his own ambitions, disregarding the true principles of righteousness and fairness. This misalignment between his words and actions exposes the hypocrisy within his character.

The portrayal of Ludociel's hypocrisy in the Seven Deadly Sins anime serves as a cautionary tale, prompting us to reflect on our own attitudes and actions. It reminds us to align our behaviour with our professed beliefs, striving for sincerity, humility, and integrity in all aspects of our lives. By seeking God's approval rather than the applause of others, we can avoid the pitfalls of hypocrisy and live out our faith authentically.

"It's troublesome if the villain doesn't show their evil. Villains are necessary to make knights into heroes."
- Helbram

February 27

But I say to you who hear, love your enemies, do good to those who hate you, bless those who curse you, pray for those who abuse you. Luke 6:27-28

Dimensional Traveller

(Tokyo Revengers)

Hanagaki Takemichi, a character from the Tokyo Revengers anime, embodies kindness throughout the series. Despite facing numerous challenges and hardships, Takemichi consistently displays compassion and empathy towards others, even in the face of adversity. His commitment to kindness is seen in his efforts to protect and support his friends, as well as his determination to prevent tragedy and create a better future. Takemichi's genuine care for others extends beyond personal gain, reflecting a selfless and compassionate nature.

The verses in Luke 6:27-28 presents Jesus' teachings on kindness and love towards enemies. It encourages believers to extend kindness, mercy, and forgiveness to those who may mistreat or oppose them. These verses emphasize the transformative power of kindness, as it can break cycles of hostility and promote healing and reconciliation.

Takemichi exemplifies this message through his interactions with various characters in the anime. He consistently shows kindness towards both friends and enemies, seeking to understand their perspectives and find peaceful resolutions. This kindness highlights the transformative power of love in changing hearts and fostering positive change. Just as his acts of kindness inspire others to reconsider their actions and motivations, our kindness has the potential to touch lives, promote healing, and lead others to experience God's love and grace.

The portrayal of kindness by Hanagaki Takemichi reminds us of the importance of extending love, compassion, and forgiveness to all, regardless of how they treat us. Through our acts of kindness, we can contribute to breaking cycles of hostility, promoting reconciliation, and sharing the transformative power of God's love with others.

"In the past and the present, I have to change, or nothing else will." - Hanagaki Takemichi

February 28

With all humility and gentleness, with patience, bearing with one another in love, eager to maintain the unity of the Spirit in the bond of peace. Ephesians 4:2-3

Ice Princess

(Kaguya-Sama: Love is War)

Kaguya Shinomiya, a character from the anime Kaguya-Sama: Love Is War, exemplifies the virtue of love throughout the series. Despite her initially competitive and prideful nature, Kaguya's character undergoes development, and she learns to express love and compassion towards others genuinely. Her journey showcases the transformative power of love and its ability to transcend barriers and bring people closer together.

In Ephesians 4:2-3, we see the significance of love in the lives of believers. It encourages believers to cultivate qualities such as humility, gentleness, and patience, and to bear with one another in love. These verses highlight the importance of fostering unity, peace, and understanding in relationships, promoting a spirit of harmony and reconciliation.

Initially, Kaguya views love as a strategic game, attempting to outwit her romantic interest, Miyuki Shirogane. However, she later realizes that true love goes beyond competition and manipulation. Kaguya's growth is marked by her increasing gentleness and understanding towards others, as she learns to genuinely care for their well-being and happiness. She encounters various obstacles and misunderstandings in her relationships, but she learns to persevere and work through them with grace and empathy.

Just as Kaguya experiences transformation and learns to love with humility, gentleness, and patience, we too are called to express love in our interactions with others. By reflecting the love of God through our actions and relationships, we can create a positive impact on the world, promoting unity, reconciliation, and the flourishing of genuine love.

"The merit of your courage comes from the intensity of your fear. That's what true strength is!" - Kaguya Shinomiya

February 29

The Lord will keep you from all evil; he will keep your life. The Lord will keep your going out and your coming in from this time forth and forevermore. Psalm 121:7,8

White Ghost

(Kekkai Sensen)

In Kekkai Sensen, Mary Macbeth faces various challenges and dangers as a member of Libra, an organization tasked with maintaining peace in the chaotic city of Hellsalem's Lot. She encounters dangerous supernatural beings, engages in intense battles, and confronts personal struggles. However, despite the difficulties she faces, Mary relies on her faith and inner strength to persevere.

The verses Psalm 121:7-8 remind us that God is our protector and guardian. They assure us that the Lord watches over our lives, our comings, and our goings. In Mary's story, we witness her journey of growth and development, where she learns to make difficult decisions, discerning the difference between right and wrong, and remains faithful to her mission. In our lives, we can find solace in knowing that God is attentive to every aspect of our existence.

Mary's character inspires us to seek God's guidance and protection in our daily lives. We can cultivate a deep relationship with Him through prayer, studying His Word, and relying on the power of the Holy Spirit. Just as Mary relies on her fellow members of Libra, we can also find strength and encouragement through the community of believers. Together, we can face the spiritual battles and challenges of life, knowing that God is watching over us.

Just as God watches over Mary's coming and going, He also watches over our lives, providing comfort, strength, and guidance through our own challenges and trials. By placing our trust in Him, we can navigate the complexities of life with confidence, knowing that we are under His watchful care both now and forevermore.

"Even now, twenty centuries after the death of Christ, the world is a long way from peace." - Mary Macbeth

March 1

She considers a field and buys it; with the fruit of her hands, she plants a vineyard. Proverbs 31:16

Anime Producer

(Keep Your Hands Off Eizouken!)

Sayaka Kanamori is a character from Keep Your Hands Off Eizouken who is portrayed as someone who is very pragmatic and focused on the financial aspects of their animation projects. She is often seen negotiating prices, seeking ways to reduce costs, and keeping a watchful eye on the budget. Her practical approach often clashes with the more creative and idealistic approach of her fellow club members, Asakusa and Mizusaki.

Proverbs 31:16 is part of a larger passage that describes the qualities of an excellent wife and portrays her as a woman who is wise and industrious. In particular, it highlights the woman's ability to make sound business decisions and invest her resources wisely. This verse encourages us to be diligent and strategic in managing our resources and to use our earnings wisely to build a secure and prosperous future.

Kanamori's approach to budgeting and financial management can be seen as a reflection of this biblical principle. She is not wasteful with the resources she has been given but rather seeks to use them in the most efficient and effective way possible. However, it's important to remember that material possessions should never become our ultimate focus or source of security. Our ultimate security is found in our relationship with God. We are called to trust in God and not in our possessions or financial status.

Kanamori's financial management reminds us of the importance of being good stewards of the resources that we have been given. While it's okay to be practical and pragmatic in our approach to finances, we must never lose sight of our ultimate source of security and trust, which is in God.

"We need to make a big impact with the least effort possible." - Sayaka Kanamori

March 2

She dresses herself with strength and makes her arms strong. Proverbs 31:17

Demon President

(Maid Sama!)

Misaki Ayuzawa is a strong-willed and hardworking character in the anime Maid Sama who works diligently to support her family and create a better environment for her school. She is known for her strong-willed personality and her dedication to her studies and her responsibilities as the student council president.

The verse Proverbs 31:17 speaks to the idea of working with strength and determination in all aspects of our lives, including our daily responsibilities and tasks. Misaki's commitment to her work as a maid and as a student council president demonstrates her determination and strength in achieving her goals. Additionally, the verse implies that physical strength is required to perform tasks with vigour, but it also suggests that inner strength and determination are just as important. Misaki's strength of character and her unwavering dedication to her work and her family illustrate this idea.

As Christians, we are called to use our talents and abilities to serve and glorify God. Like the woman described in Proverbs 31, we should approach our work with diligence and determination, giving our best effort in all that we do. Misaki's commitment to her work as a maid and as a student council president demonstrates the kind of attitude and work ethic that is pleasing to God.

Misaki's motivation and determination can serve as an example for us to follow in our own lives. However, we should always remember that our ultimate motivation and strength come from our relationship with God. By relying on Him and seeking to serve Him in all that we do, we can work with the same kind of determination and vigour as Misaki, ultimately bringing glory and honour to God in our work.

"Don't ever lie, even if it's about your feelings." - Misaki Ayuzawa

March 3

Not only that, but we rejoice in our sufferings, knowing that suffering produces endurance, and endurance produces character, and character produces hope.
Romans 5:3-4

Crazy Explosion Girl

(KonoSuba)

The character Megumin from the anime KonoSuba is known for her explosive magic. Despite the physical strain and limitations imposed by that magic, she persists in using her abilities. This perseverance in the face of pain shows her commitment and dedication to her craft. Megumin's pain serves as a catalyst for her determination and resilience, deepening her resolve to continue practicing and refining her magic, even at a cost.

The verses in Romans 5:3-4 encourages believers to find value in their sufferings, as they can lead to personal growth and the development of hope. The verse calls for rejoicing in our sufferings, not in the pain itself, but in the opportunity for growth and perseverance that suffering presents. It emphasizes that suffering produces perseverance, and we are called to endure through difficult times, knowing that our perseverance builds character and strengthens our faith.

The pain Megumin faces comes from her devotion to her explosive magic. Her pain and perseverance shape her character, making her a more resilient and determined individual. We witness her unwavering hope and belief in her abilities, even when facing challenges. Her character can motivate us to pursue our goals with unwavering dedication, while also reminding us to consider the costs and sacrifices associated with our choices.

Megumin's perseverance in the midst of pain exemplifies the importance of enduring hardships, allowing our character to develop and leading to a deepened sense of hope. As Christians, we can draw inspiration from her unwavering hope and apply it to our own lives, knowing that our suffering can ultimately lead to a stronger and more hopeful outlook.

"When man stares into the abyss, the abyss stares back." - Megumin

March 4

And let us not grow weary of doing good, for in due season we will reap, if we do not give up. Galatians 6:9

Grill Master

(Dragon Ball)

Piccolo, a prominent character from the Dragon Ball series, is often depicted as patient and steadfast, especially in his role as a mentor and protector of Gohan. He faces numerous obstacles along the way but never loses sight of his goal. His patient approach allows Gohan to develop and grow into a strong and capable individual.

Galatians 6:9 encourages us not to grow weary or give up in doing good. It reminds us that our efforts to follow Christ, serve others, and live according to God's principles may encounter challenges and setbacks. However, by remaining patient and persistent, we can trust that God will bring forth a harvest of blessings in His perfect timing.

Piccolo's patience shows us that true growth often requires time and perseverance. It is in the waiting and enduring that our character is refined, and our faith is strengthened. Just as Piccolo's patient guidance influences Gohan's transformation, our patient pursuit of righteousness and obedience to God's Word can have a transformative impact on ourselves and those around us. Piccolo's commitment to Gohan's well-being, even in the face of personal challenges, demonstrates selflessness and a willingness to invest in another person's growth. We are called to love others sacrificially, exhibiting patience and compassion as we support and encourage them on their own journeys.

We are reminded by the patience of Piccolo of the importance of persisting in our efforts to do good and make a positive impact, even when faced with challenges. Just as his patience brings about positive change in Gohan's life, our patience can lead to the fulfilment of God's purposes and blessings in our own lives.

"We can't just give up just because things aren't going the way we want them." - Piccolo

March 5

My son, if sinners entice you, do not consent. Proverbs 1:10

Silver Ranked Adventurer

(Goblin Slayer)

The anime Goblin Slayer features a character named Goblin Slayer who is often pressured by his peers to abandon his single-minded focus on goblin hunting and to pursue other quests. Despite this pressure, Goblin Slayer remains steadfast in his mission and continues to devote himself to protecting the innocent from goblin attacks.

One Bible verse that speaks to this issue of peer pressure is Proverbs 1:10, which warns against following the crowd into sinful behaviour and encourages us to be wise and discerning, seeking guidance from God. This verse reminds us that peer pressure can often lead us astray from our values and morals. It encourages us to resist the temptation to go along with the crowd and to stand firm in our beliefs, even when it is difficult to do so.

Goblin Slayer is often tempted to abandon his mission and pursue other quests that may be more socially acceptable or lucrative. However, he remains true to his values and to the people he has pledged to protect. Goblin Slayer's unwavering commitment to his mission inspires and encourages others to join him in his cause. His commitment to his mission, despite pressure from his peers, serves as an example of the importance of standing firm in our beliefs, even when it may be unpopular or difficult.

The experience of Goblin Slayer with peer pressure reminds us of the importance of standing firm in our convictions and avoiding the temptation to follow the crowd. We should not be swayed by the opinions of others but should instead hold fast to what we know to be true and right. We are called to resist peer pressure and to follow the path that God has set for us, even if it is challenging or unpopular. We must seek wisdom and guidance from God and allow our faith to guide our decisions and actions.

"A good goblin? I guess there might be one if you looked really hard." - Goblin Slayer

March 6

Finally, be strong in the Lord and in the strength of his might. Ephesians 6:10

Ghost of Uchiha

(Naruto)

Madara, the once legendary leader of the Uchiha clan, is a primary antagonist in the Naruto series known for his incredible power, ambition, and desire for control. He seeks to establish a world ruled by his own vision, and his actions are often driven by a thirst for power and dominance. He possesses immense strength and abilities that set him apart from others.

Ephesians 6:10 reminds us to be strong in the Lord and in His mighty power. This verse directs our attention away from placing excessive trust in our own strength or abilities and instead encourages us to find our true source of strength in God. We can draw inspiration from this verse to approach the challenges and trials of life with confidence, knowing that we can rely on God's strength and guidance.

Madara's power, on the other hand, is largely self-driven and self-focused. He relies solely on his own abilities and desires to exert control and dominance over others. This portrayal serves as a cautionary tale, reminding us of the dangers of pride and the misuse of power. As Christians, we are called to use our power and influence for the greater good, in alignment with God's will, rather than for selfish gain or the oppression of others.

The reflection on Madara's power prompts us to examine our own lives and how we wield the power we possess, whether it be physical, intellectual, or spiritual. It challenges us to evaluate whether we are aligning our power with God's purpose and seeking His guidance in its application. When we recognize that our power comes from God, we can humbly submit it to His will and use it to bring about positive change, justice, and compassion in the world.

"What good is power if you are unable to stand up for those who you love? The purpose of power should be to help you protect your loved ones. If not, then that power is futile." - Madara Uchiha

March 7

And we know that for those who love God all things work together for good, for those who are called according to his purpose. Romans 8:28

Black Prince

(Code Geass)

Lelouch's character in Code Geass is defined by his intellectual brilliance and strategic genius, which often leads to a sense of pride and self-reliance. He believes that he alone possesses the ability to change the world and shape its destiny. However, Lelouch's pride ultimately becomes his downfall as his ambition and desire for power blind him to the potential consequences of his actions. He becomes consumed by his thirst for control, losing sight of the bigger picture and neglecting the well-being of those around him.

The verse Romans 8:28 emphasizes the belief that God is actively involved in the lives of those who love Him and have a relationship with Him. It assures believers that no matter the circumstances they face, God is able to work everything for their ultimate good. This includes both favourable and challenging situations because God has the power to bring about positive outcomes, growth, and blessings even in the midst of trials.

Through humbling his heart and recognizing his own weaknesses, Lelouch begins to grasp the limitations of his own power and the need for a higher authority. By acknowledging our dependence on God and humbling ourselves before Him, we can experience His guiding hand and participate in His divine purposes.

As Lelouch humbles himself and acknowledges his own weaknesses, he confronts the consequences of his actions and ultimately finds a path towards reconciliation and sacrifice. Similarly, when we acknowledge our dependence on God and humble ourselves before Him, we can experience His guiding hand and participate in His divine purposes.

"You will never be able to love anybody else until you love yourself." - Lelouch Lamperouge

March 8

Behold, this is our God; we have waited for him, that he might save us. This is the Lord; we have waited for him; let us be glad and rejoice in his salvation. Isaiah 25:9

Unit Captain

(Attack on Titan)

In the Attack on Titan series, Hannes serves as a member of the Garrison and initially appears as a cowardly soldier who failed to save Eren's mother from a Titan attack in the show's opening episodes. However, as the story progresses, Hannes confronts his fears and chooses to protect Eren and Mikasa, the two main protagonists. Despite his previous failures, he finds the courage to fight against a powerful Titan and ultimately sacrifices himself to save them.

The verse from Isaiah 25:9 resonates with Hannes' character transformation. It expresses the joy and gratitude of a people who have placed their trust in God and experienced His saving grace. In a similar vein, Hannes' sacrifice and redemption reflect the transformative power of salvation, as he evolves from a fearful and regretful individual to a hero who brings hope and protection to others.

Though Hannes was initially characterized by fear and regret, he eventually finds the courage to confront his past failures. His sacrificial act mirrors the concept of salvation, as he offers himself as a shield and deliverer for those he cares about. Hannes' sacrifice also brings a sense of hope and renewed purpose to Eren and Mikasa, who find solace in his act of selflessness. He becomes a symbol of redemption, demonstrating that even in the face of past mistakes, one can find redemption and become a source of hope and salvation for others.

Just as Hannes' sacrificial act brought deliverance and hope, the ultimate saviour, Jesus Christ, offers salvation to all who trust in Him. Through His sacrifice on the cross, Jesus redeemed us from sin and death, providing a way to eternal life and restoration. Let us hold onto hope, trusting in God's faithfulness and His promise of ultimate redemption.

"This world is cruel, and it's also very beautiful." - Mikasa Ackerman

March 9

I have been crucified with Christ. It is no longer I who live, but Christ who lives in me. And the life I now live in the flesh I live by faith in the Son of God, who loved me and gave himself for me. Galatians 2:20

Fire Fist

(One Piece)

Portgas D. Ace, a central character in the anime and manga series One Piece, serves as the adopted older brother of Monkey D. Luffy, the protagonist. Their strong bond exemplifies the power of familial love and the importance of unwavering support, even in the face of adversity. In Ace's final moments, he willingly sacrifices himself to protect Luffy, embodying the sacrificial love that Christ demonstrated on the cross.

Galatians 2:20 emphasizes that through faith in Christ, believers experience a spiritual union with Him. Ace's sacrifice reflects a profound unity between his actions and the principles he stood for. By surrendering his life, Ace exemplifies dying to oneself and allowing Christ's love and purpose to manifest through him. As followers of Christ, we are called to die to our own desires and allow Christ to live in and through us, positively impacting others.

As the son of the Pirate King, Ace carries the weight of his past and the sins associated with his lineage. However, in his act of self-sacrifice, he seeks redemption and aims to protect and save others. Ace's sacrifice inspires transformative growth in Luffy and his crew. Similarly, we are called to live by the example of Christ's sacrificial love, allowing it to ignite transformation within ourselves and positively influence the lives of those around us.

The sacrifice of Portgas D. Ace from One Piece aligns with Christian principles of selflessness, redemption, forgiveness, and spiritual union with Christ. Ace's selfless act serves as a poignant reminder of the transformative power of Christ's love and inspires us to emulate His example in our own lives.

"We have to live a life of no regrets." - Portgas D. Ace

March 10

Trust in the Lord with all your heart, and do not lean on your own understanding. In all your ways acknowledge him, and he will make straight your paths. Proverbs 3:5-6

Flame Hashirama

(Demon Slayer)

In Demon Slayer anime, Kyojuro Rengoku is depicted as a skilled swordsman who exudes remarkable self-esteem and confidence in his abilities as a Demon Slayer, even when confronted with daunting challenges. Rengoku is portrayed as a passionate and enthusiastic character who consistently strives to protect humanity from the threat of demons.

Proverbs 3:5-6 encourages us to wholeheartedly place our trust in the Lord, acknowledging that His wisdom surpasses our own understanding. While Rengoku's self-esteem is rooted in his trust in his own skills, as Christians, we are called to place our ultimate trust in God, recognizing Him as the source of our strength and guidance.

The self-esteem and reliance that Rengoku demonstrates in his own abilities can be seen as a reflection of his commitment to his training and his desire to safeguard humanity from demons. While it is important for us to have confidence in our skills and abilities, we must always remember to place our ultimate trust in God, acknowledging His wisdom and guidance that exceed our limited understanding.

Rengoku acknowledges the significance of hard work, training, and self-improvement. He continually strives to become a better Demon Slayer each day, constantly pushing himself to enhance his skills. His self-esteem and confidence serve as an example of how trusting in God can strengthen our own sense of self-worth and courage. By placing our faith in God, we can face our challenges with confidence and find the strength to overcome them.

"If you are feeling disheartened, that you are somehow not enough, set your heart ablaze. Dry your eyes and look ahead. You may feel like you are digging your heels in, but the flow of time waits for no one. It won't patiently stand by as you grieve." - Kyojuro Rengoku

March 11

Woe to those who call evil good and good evil, who put darkness for light and light for darkness, who put bitter for sweet and sweet for bitter! Isaiah 5:20

Sewing-Life Alchemist

(Fullmetal Alchemist: Brotherhood)

Shou Tucker from Fullmetal Alchemist: Brotherhood is a character known for his unethical experiments involving alchemy and the transmutation of living beings, including his own daughter and their dog. Shou Tucker's sin lies in his complete disregard for the sanctity of life, perverting what is right and wrong and blurring the lines between good and evil. His actions are driven by his ambition and desire to maintain his State Alchemist status.

Isaiah 5:20 warns us to uphold and promote moral values based on God's truth. We are called to discern between good and evil according to His standards. Shou Tucker's sin demonstrates the tragic consequences of tampering with the natural order and the ripple effect it has on the lives of others. It highlights the dangers of playing God, seeking to control and manipulate aspects of creation beyond our rightful authority.

As believers, we must uphold righteousness and truth, discerning between good and evil based on God's revealed will. We should resist redefining morality according to our desires or societal norms, seeking wisdom and guidance from God's Word. By aligning ourselves with His divine standards and values, we can honour the sanctity of life and exercise moral discernment.

Shou Tucker's sin prompts us to reflect on the importance of respecting the sanctity of life, honouring the inherent dignity of all human beings, and exercising moral discernment. It reminds us that perverting good and evil has severe consequences, and true wisdom lies in following God's righteous path rather than succumbing to sinful desires.

"Stand up and walk. Keep moving forward. You've got two good legs. So, get up and use them. You're strong enough to make your own path." - Edward Elric

March 12

When I was a child, I spoke like a child, I thought like a child, I reasoned like a child. When I became a man, I gave up childish ways. 1 Corinthians 13:11

Blue Bolt of Konoha

(Boruto)

Boruto Uzumaki is the son of Naruto Uzumaki and the protagonist of the anime series Boruto. He is part of the new generation of shinobi who goes on various adventures and missions with his friends and teammates. At the beginning of the series, Boruto exhibits more immature and selfish behaviour, similar to how a child thinks and acts. However, as he faces various challenges and learns from his experiences, he gradually matures and gains a deeper understanding of the world around him.

The apostle Paul speaks in 1 Corinthians 13:11 about the process of maturing and leaving behind childish ways. As Christians, we are called to leave behind our childish ways and embrace a mature perspective. Gratitude enables us to shift our focus from ourselves to God and others. It helps us recognize and appreciate the countless blessings we receive daily, fostering humility and contentment.

The journey of Boruto can remind us of the transformative power of thankfulness in our own lives. Just as he comes to understand the role of his loved ones and mentors in his growth, we acknowledge God's hand in our own lives. Our gratitude becomes a reflection of our faith, recognizing that God is the ultimate source of all that is good.

As Boruto grows and matures, he learns to appreciate the blessings, support, and lessons in his life. Similarly, we are encouraged to cultivate a grateful heart, recognizing the transformative power of thankfulness and acknowledging God's abundant grace and provision in our lives.

"Forget who hurt you yesterday. But don't forget those who love you every day." - Boruto Uzumaki

March 13

If we confess our sins, he is faithful and just to forgive us our sins and to cleanse us from all unrighteousness. 1 John 1:9

Blue Flame

(My Hero Academia)

Dabi, also known as Toya Todoroki, is the eldest son of Endeavor in My Hero Academia. His story highlights the devastating consequences of a fractured parent-child relationship. Endeavor's rejection and neglect of Dabi caused deep emotional wounds that drove him towards darkness and villainy. Dabi yearned for his father's love and acceptance, but instead, he faced disappointment and abandonment.

In 1 John 1:9, we find solace and hope for the brokenness Dabi experienced. It reminds us that God, our Heavenly Father, offers forgiveness and purification to those who humbly confess their sins. Even when earthly parents fail us, God's love is unconditional, and His acceptance is unwavering.

Toya Todoroki longed for his father's love and acceptance, and when he faced rejection, he turned towards darkness. Just like Dabi, we all have moments when we make mistakes or go down the wrong path. However, we must remember that God's forgiveness is available to all who seek it. It is through confessing our sins, acknowledging our faults, and turning to God that we find His loving acceptance and forgiveness.

Dabi's story highlights the importance of acceptance and forgiveness not only from God but also from others. As followers of Christ, we are called to extend forgiveness and acceptance to those who have hurt us, just as we have been forgiven by God. It challenges us to see beyond someone's past actions and believe in their potential for change and redemption. We should let go of grudges, resentments, and the weight of past mistakes. Instead, we can embrace the healing and restoration that comes from God's acceptance and forgiveness.

"To be an overachiever, you have to be an over-believer."
- Dabi

March 14

Know this, my beloved brothers: let every person be quick to hear, slow to speak, slow to anger; for the anger of man does not produce the righteousness of God. James 1:19-20

Black Swordsman

(Berserk)

Guts, a wandering swordsman from Berserk, is driven by an intense desire for revenge against his former best friend, Griffith, who betrayed him and made dark sacrifices for power. He carries the heavy burden of his past, haunted by memories and detached from those around him. Despite his isolation, Guts shows unwavering loyalty to his friends, willing to protect them at any cost. His journey is one of self-discovery and redemption as he searches for a purpose beyond vengeance.

In light of James 1:19-20, we are urged to approach anger in a different manner. We are called to listen attentively and speak with caution, emphasizing understanding and effective communication. The verse also reminds us that human anger does not align with the righteousness desired by God. Guts' anger often leads him down a path of violence and suffering, distancing him from righteousness and peace.

Guts' anger serves as a warning about the dangers of unchecked anger, as it can result in harmful actions and consequences. It reminds us that uncontrolled anger can hinder our relationship with God and others. Instead, we are encouraged to channel our anger in constructive ways, seeking understanding, forgiveness, and reconciliation.

The story of Guts in Berserk serves as a powerful reminder of the transformative power of God's love and the importance of seeking righteousness in all aspects of our lives, including how we respond to anger. It calls us to embody the grace and forgiveness exemplified by Christ, even in the face of pain and injustice.

"Even if we painstakingly piece together something lost, it doesn't mean things will ever go back to how they were."
- Guts

March 15

Do not let your adorning be external - the braiding of hair and the putting on of gold jewellery, or the clothing you wear - but let your adorning be the hidden person of the heart with the imperishable beauty of a gentle and quiet spirit, which in God's sight is very precious. 1 Peter 3:3-4

Androgynous Student

(Ouran High School Host Club)

Haruhi Fujioka from Ouran High School is known for her unique appearance and her role as the commoner among the wealthy students at Ouran Academy. Her simple style and lack of adornment contrast with the glamorous and extravagant outfits of her peers. Haruhi, despite her simple and androgynous appearance, possesses a kind heart, intelligence, and empathy. She teaches us that true worth and beauty come from within.

1 Peter 3:3-4 emphasizes the importance of inner beauty over outward adornment. This verse encourages us to prioritize inner qualities, such as a gentle and quiet spirit, which are precious in God's sight. Haruhi doesn't focus on extravagant hairstyles, jewellery, or fashionable attire. Instead, she values simplicity and lets her character shine through.

Haruhi serves as a reminder that true beauty is found in the content of one's character rather than external appearance. Her humble and unassuming appearance reflects a gentle and quiet spirit. She doesn't seek attention or try to impress others with her outward appearance but demonstrates the beauty of her heart through her kindness, intelligence, and empathy.

Haruhi Fujioka's appearance in Ouran High School exemplifies the idea that true beauty lies in the hidden person of the heart, characterized by a gentle and quiet spirit. Haruhi's simple and unadorned style teaches us to value inner qualities above external appearances, as they hold greater significance in the sight of God.

"Besides, it doesn't really matter, does it? Why should I care about appearances and labels anyway. It's what's on the inside that counts." - Haruhi Fujioka

March 16

Iron sharpens iron, and one man sharpens another.
Proverbs 27:17

King of the Court

(Haikyu!!)

Tobio Kageyama is initially known as an arrogant and controlling volleyball player in the Haikyu!! anime, earning the nickname as king of the court. However, Kageyama gradually learns to value and respect his teammates, realizing that true success is achieved through cooperation and considering the needs and interests of others, rather than solely focusing on his own ambitions.

The verse Proverbs 27:17 reminds us that just as iron sharpens iron, we can impact and refine each other through our interactions and relationships. We are called to be both recipients and agents of sharpening, receiving guidance, wisdom, and support from others who help us grow spiritually. Additionally, we are called to be instruments of God's grace in the lives of others, encouraging and challenging them to become more like Christ.

Kageyama's attitude reflects the value of teamwork and collaboration. He recognizes that the collective effort and the influence of teammates and mentors play a vital role in his personal growth and development. His attitude serves as a reminder that we have a responsibility to positively influence and sharpen one another through our words, actions, and example.

The character development of Kageyama showcases the transformation that occurs when we let go of selfish ambitions and ego, prioritizing the growth and success of the team. We are called to humbly serve others, valuing their needs and interests above our own. By actively engaging in sharpening one another, we contribute to the formation of a vibrant and impactful community that radiates Christ, where individuals are continually transformed and empowered to live out their faith.

"The last ones standing are the victors. Only the strongest. If you want to be the last one standing become strong." - Tobio Kageyama

March 17

Casting all your anxieties on him, because he cares for you. 1 Peter 5:7

Human Demon Swoner

(Mairimashita! Iruma-kun)

In the anime series Mairimashita! Iruma-kun, the protagonist Iruma Suzuki finds himself in an unexpected and challenging circumstance when he is unwittingly enrolled in a demon school. This new situation brings about anxiety, fear, and uncertainty in his life. Despite being initially overwhelmed and out of his comfort zone, Iruma maintains a positive and optimistic attitude.

The verse from 1 Peter reminds us that we can find solace in God during times of anxiety and uncertainty. It encourages us to cast all our worries and burdens onto Him, knowing that He cares for us deeply. We are also called to lean on our faith community and seek support from fellow believers. By sharing our burdens with others and seeking their prayers and encouragement, we find comfort and reassurance.

Iruma's experience resonates with many of us who have faced overwhelming situations that cause anxiety and stress. In his journey, he discovers the importance of relying on others for help and support. He builds relationships with friends who become his source of strength and encouragement. Through their assistance and care, he finds the strength and courage to face the challenges before him.

The circumstance of Iruma Suzuki serves as a reminder that even in the midst of unfamiliar and challenging situations, we can find solace and peace by entrusting our anxieties to God. Just as Iruma finds support in his friends, we can find support in our faith community, knowing that God cares deeply for each one of us. By placing our trust in Him and casting our burdens upon Him, we can experience His love, comfort, and guidance in navigating through life's difficulties.

"Anyone can say they care. But watch their actions, not their words." - Iruma Suzuki

March 18

Let all that you do be done in love. 1 Corinthians 16:14

Orphan 63194

(The Promised Neverland)

Emma from the anime series The Promised Neverland displays a remarkable commitment to the well-being and safety of her fellow orphans. Despite the harrowing circumstances they face in the orphanage, she consistently demonstrates love, compassion, and selflessness in her actions. Emma's actions are driven by a deep sense of care and a desire to protect the children from being devoured by the Demons.

The verse 1 Corinthians 16:14 reminds us that love should be the driving force behind all that we do. It should permeate every aspect of our lives, guiding our thoughts, words, and actions. Emma's commitment to her friends exemplifies this principle, as she puts their needs above her own and seeks to protect them from harm. Her unwavering love and dedication motivate her to make difficult choices and face immense challenges.

Emma's commitment also reminds us that true love involves self-sacrifice. She puts the needs and well-being of others before her own, willing to face danger and make difficult choices for the sake of those she cares about. This mirrors the sacrificial love of Jesus Christ, who laid down His life for the salvation of humanity. It calls us to emulate His example by sacrificially loving and serving others.

By relating Emma's commitment in the Promised neverland, we are reminded of the transformative power of love. It motivates us to go the extra mile, make sacrifices, and act in ways that positively impact the lives of others. Just as Emma's commitment brings hope and protection to her friends, our commitment to love can bring healing, reconciliation, and positive change to the world around us.

"If there isn't one, then let's make a place for humans to live outside. Let's change the world." - Emma

March 19

Two are better than one, because they have a good reward for their toil. For if they fall, one will lift up his fellow. But woe to him who is alone when he falls and has not another to lift him up! Ecclesiastes 4:9-10

Wings of Freedom

(Attack on Titan)

In Attack on Titan, the Survey Corps represents a community of soldiers who devote themselves to protecting humanity from the threat of the Titans. They exemplify sacrificial love and unity, which are central to the teachings of Christ. Just as Jesus called his followers to love one another and lay down their lives for their friends, the members of the Survey Corps display a selfless commitment to their comrades.

Ecclesiastes 4:9-10 reminds us that having a partner or companion enhances our efforts and offers support when we stumble. The Survey Corps relies on each other's unique strengths and abilities, recognizing that their collective labor yields a greater impact. This mirrors the biblical principle of unity in the body of Christ, where individuals come together to serve a common purpose, lifting each other up and making a significant impact for God's kingdom.

The determination of the Survey Corps to help their fallen comrades aligns with the biblical call to extend compassion and aid to those in need. Their willingness to sacrifice for the greater good echoes the example set by Jesus, who laid down his life for all humanity. This resonates with the core message of Christianity – that love, selflessness, and support for one another are fundamental to our faith and the building of a strong community.

The selfless love, unity, and unwavering commitment within the Survey Corps serve as a powerful example for believers, urging us to embrace community, uplift one another, and fulfil our purpose while bringing glory to God.

"Whether you trust in your own strength or trust in the choices made by reliable comrades, no one knows what the outcome will be." - Levi Ackerman

March 20

For God gave us a spirit not of fear but of power and love and self-control. 2 Timothy 1:7

Captain of Scraps Disposal

(Seven Deadly Sins)

Hawks, the talking pig in The Seven Deadly Sins, is known for his loud personality. Despite being intimidated at times, he has shown courage in dangerous situations. His loyalty to Meliodas is unwavering, and his flying ability and keen senses make him a valuable asset to the group. Hawks' bravery and loyalty have endeared him to fans of the series.

In 2 Timothy 1:7, we are reminded that God has not given us a spirit of fear but has equipped us with a spirit of power, love, and self-discipline. This verse encourages believers to embrace the strength and courage that comes from God's presence within us. Despite facing overwhelming odds and daunting challenges, Hawks displays unwavering bravery. His courage is not rooted solely in his own abilities but in the power that God provides.

Hawks' fights for justice and the protection of others, demonstrating selfless and sacrificial love. This echoes the greatest commandment given by Jesus to love God and love our neighbours as ourselves. Furthermore, Hawks exemplifies self-discipline in his approach to his mission. He remains focused, strategic, and in control of his emotions and impulses. This aligns with the call for believers to exercise self-discipline, ensuring that our actions are guided by the wisdom and discernment provided by the Holy Spirit.

Reflecting on Hawks' courage in The Seven Deadly Sins anime, we are reminded that true courage is not found in our own strength but in our reliance on God. It is a courage rooted in love and self-discipline, seeking to bring honour and glory to God in all that we do. We can draw inspiration from Hawks' example, remembering that our strength and courage come from God, enabling us to face challenges with boldness, love, and self-discipline.

"A person who knows he's weak but still faces a strong opponent is the bravest of them all." - Meliodas

March 21

For what will it profit a man if he gains the whole world and forfeits his soul? Or what shall a man give in return for his soul? Matthew 16:26

Magus Killer

(Fate/Zero)

In the Fate/Zero anime, Kiritsugu Emiya is a skilled mage and a master in the Holy Grail War, a battle royale where mages summon heroic spirits to compete for a wish-granting artifact. His decision-making is driven by his desire to create a world free from suffering and conflict. He believes that he must make tough choices and sacrifice individual lives for the greater good. His actions reflect a utilitarian approach, where the end justifies the means.

Matthew 16:26 reminds believers that worldly achievements and material gain are ultimately insignificant if they come at the expense of one's soul. It serves as a call to prioritize spiritual well-being, moral integrity, and love for one's fellow human beings. Jesus taught that gaining the whole world but losing one's soul is a tragic exchange, as true fulfilment and eternal life are found in a relationship with God and living according to His commands.

Kiritsugu's relentless pursuit of his ideals often comes at a great personal cost. By sacrificing his humanity and disregarding the value of individual lives, he risks losing his own soul and moral integrity. His decisions, although made with good intentions, lead him down a path where he loses sight of his own humanity and becomes consumed by his mission.

The decisions made by Kiritsugu Emiya illustrate the dangers of a utilitarian mindset that seeks to justify unethical means for the sake of a perceived greater good. They challenge us to wrestle with the tension between pursuing justice and upholding moral values, encouraging them to seek alternative paths that align with the teachings of Christ. These teachings emphasize the value of every human life and the transformative power of selfless love.

"As long as people don't repent and don't regard it as the most evil taboo, then hell will endlessly reappear in the world." - Kiritsugu Emiya

March 22

As soon as he had finished speaking to Saul, the soul of Jonathan was knit to the soul of David, and Jonathan loved him as his own soul. 1 Samuel 18:1

Thunderbolt Hunter

(Hunter x Hunter)

Killua Zoldyck is a main character in the Hunter x Hunter anime who demonstrates unwavering trust and loyalty towards his best friend, Gon Freecss. Despite being raised in a cold and ruthless environment as a member of an assassin family, Killua forms a deep bond with Gon and commits himself to protect and support him throughout their journey. He places great faith in their friendship, finding strength and guidance in it.

In 1 Samuel 18:1, we witness the profound friendship between Jonathan and David. Their connection goes beyond mere companionship as they become "one in spirit," displaying a love that is selfless and sacrificial. This level of devotion reflects the love that Christ calls His followers to exhibit towards one another.

Both the story of Jonathan and David and Killua's devotion in Hunter x Hunter teach us about the transformative power of selfless love and friendship. They inspire us to seek and nurture relationships characterized by genuine care, loyalty, and sacrificial love. Killua's devotion serves as a reminder for us to be selfless, supportive, and loyal in our friendships, putting the needs of others above our own and being willing to make sacrifices for the sake of our friends, just as Christ did for us.

The devotion displayed by Killua and the friendship of Jonathan and David encourage us to strive for deeper and more meaningful relationships, reflecting the love and selflessness of our Saviour. They remind us that through friendships, we have the opportunity to demonstrate Christ's love and serve as agents of His grace and compassion in the lives of others.

"If I ignore a friend, I have the ability to help, wouldn't I be betraying him?" - Killua Zoldyck

March 23

Do not be overcome by evil, but overcome evil with good.
Romans 12:21

Kamado Family

(Demon Slayer)

In the world of Demon Slayer, the Kamado family faces immense challenges and encounters evil in the form of demons. Despite the darkness and tragedy, they experience, they embody resilience, compassion, and a determination to protect others. Tanjiro Kamado, in particular, demonstrates unwavering love and a commitment to overcoming evil.

Romans 12:21 teaches believers not to be overwhelmed by evil but to conquer it with good. It reminds us that responding to evil with acts of kindness, forgiveness, and righteousness has the power to overcome darkness and bring about positive change. The Kamado family's story reflects the Christian call to resist being overcome by evil influences and to respond with love and goodness. We are called to follow the example of Christ, who conquered evil through His sacrificial love on the cross.

The dedication of the Kamado family in protecting humanity and their unwavering pursuit of justice reflects the transformative power of love and its impact on overcoming darkness. They challenge us to examine our own lives and consider how we can respond to evil with acts of goodness, compassion, and righteousness. It reminds us that even in the face of adversity, we have the ability to make a positive difference by choosing love over hatred, forgiveness over vengeance, and selflessness over selfishness.

The Kamado family encourages us to live out our faith by actively opposing evil and working towards the restoration and redemption of those affected by it. By aligning ourselves with Scripture and following the example of Christ, we can overcome evil with good and bring about the transformative power of God's love in our lives and in the lives of those around us.

"No matter how many people you may lose, you have no choice but to go on living. No matter how devastating the blows might be." - Tanjiro Kamado

March 24

When I am afraid, I put my trust in you. Psalm 56:3

World's Champion

(Dragon Ball)

Hercule, also known as Mr. Satan, is a character from Dragon Ball who often displays exaggerated bravado and seeks validation from others. Despite his outward confidence, his actions reveal a deep insecurity and fear. This highlights the human tendency to rely on our own strength and understanding, which proves inadequate in the face of fear.

Psalm 56:3 directs us to place our trust in God when fear arises within us. It acknowledges fear as a natural response but redirects our focus to the One who is greater and more powerful. It reminds us that we are not alone in our fears and anxieties but have a loving and faithful God who is with us. Hercule's fear serves as a reminder that relying solely on ourselves can hinder our ability to live with confidence and peace. By trusting in God, we find comfort in His presence and assurance that He is greater than any fear we encounter. Through faith, we can approach our fears with courage, knowing that God's strength and guidance will sustain us.

In our own lives, the fear of Hercule prompts us to examine our reliance on external validation and the limitations of our own strength. It challenges us to place our trust in God, who is faithful and capable of providing the peace and courage we need. By surrendering our fears to Him, we can experience His transformative power, finding strength and confidence to face life's challenges.

Ultimately, the fear of Hercule and the call to trust in God remind us of the importance of seeking refuge in Him. As we anchor ourselves in His presence and trust in His sovereignty, we can overcome fear and live with boldness, knowing that He is with us and will guide us through every situation.

"Sometimes, we have to look beyond what we want and do what's best." - Piccolo

March 25

For if you forgive others their trespasses, your heavenly Father will also forgive you, but if you do not forgive others their trespasses, neither will your Father forgive your trespasses. Matthew 6:14-15

Petting Hero Anima

(My Hero Academia)

Koji Koda from My Hero Academia is a character who possesses a unique ability to communicate with animals. He demonstrates a compassionate and gentle nature, often using his power to understand and care for animals in need. Koji's journey includes moments of forgiveness, both towards himself and others, as he learns to overcome past mistakes and embrace a more empathetic outlook.

Matthew 6:14-15 emphasizes the importance of forgiveness and its connection to our own experience of God's forgiveness. By forgiving others, we align ourselves with the heart of God and demonstrate our understanding of the forgiveness we have received through Christ. Just as Koji learns to forgive others, we are reminded that our own forgiveness from God is contingent upon our willingness to extend forgiveness to those who have wronged us.

Forgiveness is a powerful act that breaks the cycle of hurt and resentment, offering an opportunity for reconciliation and restoration. It aligns us with the heart of God, who forgives us of our own sins and calls us to extend that same forgiveness to others.

Koji's journey of forgiveness challenges us to examine our own hearts and confront any areas of unforgiveness within us. It encourages us to extend forgiveness to those who have wronged us, knowing that in doing so, we participate in God's redemptive work and foster a culture of reconciliation and healing. By choosing to forgive others, we demonstrate our understanding of the depth of God's forgiveness towards us and actively participate in His transformative work in our lives and in the world around us.

"That's right, my heart should always be Plus Ultra!"
- Koji Koda

March 26

A friend loves at all times, and a brother is born for adversity. Proverbs 17:17

Mage Exceed Duo

(Fairy Tail)

Natsu and Happy, beloved characters from the anime Fairy Tail, share a friendship filled with warmth, loyalty, and adventure. Together, they experience excitement, laughter, and sorrow, creating lasting memories and deepening their bond. They bring out the best in each other, inspiring courage and strength, reminding us of the joy and enrichment that genuine friendship brings.

The verse Proverbs 17:17 highlights the importance of friendship during adversity. Natsu and Happy uplift and encourage each other when faced with difficulties. They offer a helping hand, a listening ear, and unwavering support, demonstrating the strength and comfort that true friendship provides during challenging times.

The friendship of Natsu and Happy reminds us that true friendship transcends differences and backgrounds. Despite being a human and an Exceed (a cat-like creature), they embrace and celebrate their unique qualities, recognizing that their differences only enhance their bond. In a world often divided by prejudice and judgment, their friendship encourages us to look beyond appearances and appreciate the diversity that friendships can bring.

Natsu and Happy's friendship serves as a model of love, loyalty, and adventure. They remind us of the profound impact friendship can have, shaping us into better individuals and offering unwavering support and companionship. Their friendship encourages us to cherish and nurture our own friendships, to be loyal and dependable friends, and to seek joy and shared experiences with those we hold dear.

"Maybe we can't help feeling scared alone! But we're all right here, together! We've got our friends close by! Now there's nothing to fear, because we are not alone!" - Natsu Dragneel

March 27

Remember not the former things, nor consider the things of old. Behold, I am doing a new thing; now it springs forth, do you not perceive it? I will make a way in the wilderness and rivers in the desert. Isaiah 43:18-19

Devil Child

(One Piece)

Nico Robin is a complex and intriguing character from the anime and manga series One Piece. As an archaeologist with a tragic past, she initially appears as a reserved and enigmatic individual. However, as the story unfolds, we witness her growth and transformation. Through her journey with her newfound friends, she learns to let go of her past, embrace new opportunities, and forge a brighter future.

Isaiah 43:18-19 encourages individuals to let go of their former circumstances and focus on the new things that God is doing. It emphasizes that God can bring about remarkable changes and make a way even in the most challenging and desolate situations. This verse resonates with Nico Robin's growth as she leaves behind the wilderness of her past and discovers a path of hope, companionship, and personal growth.

Nico Robin's growth also serves as a reminder that our past does not define us. Through God's grace, we can overcome our past mistakes, find healing, and embrace a new identity. We are called to perceive and embrace the new things that God is doing in our lives, trusting that He will lead us on a path of purpose and fulfilment.

The story of Nico Robin showcases the transformative power of embracing new beginnings and finding purpose beyond one's past. By relating her growth, we are reminded of God's ability to bring about positive change and provide a way forward, even in the midst of difficult circumstances. It encourages us to let go of past burdens, trust in God's leading, and embrace the new opportunities and possibilities that lie ahead.

"When you have a hard time, just laugh!" - Nico Robin

March 28

You make known to me the path of life; in your presence there is fullness of joy; at your right hand are pleasures forevermore. Psalm 16:11

Sukuna's Vessel

(Jujutsu Kaisen)

In Jujutsu Kaisen, Yuji Itadori experiences genuine happiness despite the challenges and dangers he faces as a Jujutsu sorcerer. He finds joy in his relationships with his friends and his dedication to protecting others. Despite the surrounding darkness and hardships, Yuji's happiness shines through as he embraces his purpose and uses his abilities to bring hope and safety to those in need.

The verse Psalm 16:11 reminds us that in God's presence, there is abundant joy and eternal pleasures. It highlights that true happiness is not found in temporary worldly pursuits but in a deep relationship with God. This resonates with Yuji, as his happiness is not rooted in personal gain or fleeting pleasures but in living a life dedicated to righteousness and protecting those in need.

Yuji's happiness reflects the joy that comes from aligning one's life with God's will. As he embraces his responsibilities as a Jujutsu sorcerer and selflessly fights against evil, he exemplifies the teachings of Jesus to love and serve others. His happiness is not rooted in personal gain or fleeting pleasures, but in living a life dedicated to righteousness and protecting those in need. We are called to selflessly love and serve others, finding happiness in making a positive impact on the world around us.

By relating Yuji's happiness, we are reminded that lasting joy comes from living a life aligned with God's purpose, finding fulfilment in His presence, and using our abilities to make a positive impact in the world. It encourages us to seek true happiness by walking in righteousness and finding joy in serving others.

"Smart people usually don't brag about being smart." - Yuji Itadori

March 29

In all toil there is profit, but mere talk tends only to poverty. Proverbs 14:23

Demon Lord

(The Devil is a Part-Timer!)

Sadao Maou from The Devil is a Part-Timer is the Devil himself who finds himself in the human world, working tirelessly at a fast-food restaurant to make a living. Despite his powerful background, he embraces the value of hard work and dedicates himself to his job. He understands that it is through his diligent efforts that he can achieve success and provide for himself.

Proverbs 14:23 emphasizes the importance and rewards of hard work. It contrasts hard work, which brings profit and positive outcomes, with mere talk or idleness, which leads only to poverty or lack. This verse resonates with Sadao Maou's character, as he consistently demonstrates the determination and work ethic necessary to thrive in his new environment.

Sadao Maou's commitment to hard work reflects the biblical principle of diligence and the importance of taking action. His example encourages us to approach our work as an opportunity to glorify God. It reminds us that our efforts and industriousness can lead to favourable outcomes and prosperity. By diligently and wholeheartedly engaging in our tasks, we demonstrate our faithfulness and commitment to the calling that God has placed upon us. Whether in our jobs, studies, or daily responsibilities, we are called to work as if we are working for the Lord Himself.

The hard work of Sadao Maou from The Devil is a Part-Timer provides a Christian reflection on the importance of diligence, responsibility, and the pursuit of excellence in all aspects of life. It encourages us to embrace our work as a means to honour God and serve others, while cautioning us against idleness and empty talk. Through our dedicated efforts, we can bring glory to God and experience the abundant blessings that come from faithful labor.

"Careless is the greatest enemy." - Sadao Maou

March 30

The integrity of the upright guides them, but the crookedness of the treacherous destroys them. Proverbs 11:3

Hina Doll Craftsman

(My Dress-Up Darling)

Wakana from My Dress-Up Darling consistently demonstrates integrity and honesty in his actions and interactions. As a skilled cosplayer, he upholds the principles of authenticity and truthfulness in his craft. He takes pride in his work and refuses to compromise his artistic vision through dishonesty or deceit. Wakana's commitment to honesty guides him and shapes his character, leading him on a path of personal growth and building strong relationships.

The verse Proverbs 11:3 teaches us that integrity serves as a guiding principle for the upright. We are called to embrace honesty as a foundational principle in our lives. Our integrity should be a reflection of the character of God, who is the ultimate standard of truth and righteousness. Wakana's commitment to truthfulness not only earns him the trust and respect of others but also allows him to form genuine connections and deep friendships.

Wakana's commitment to honesty reminds us that true success and fulfilment come from living with integrity. While dishonesty may offer short-term gains, it eventually leads to destruction. On the other hand, choosing honesty and integrity aligns us with God's will and ensures a solid foundation for our lives.

By relating Wakana's honesty, we are encouraged to embrace integrity as a guiding principle in our lives. It reminds us of the importance of being honest in our words and actions, both in our relationships with others and in our commitment to living out our faith. Through our dedication to honesty and integrity, we can navigate life with wisdom and experience the blessings that come from walking in alignment with God's truth.

"We can't see what they are feeling inside, but everyone has a lot going on." - Wakana Gojo

March 31

Why are you cast down, O my soul, and why are you in turmoil within me? Hope in God; for I shall again praise him, my salvation and my God. Psalm 42:11

Substitute Soul Reaper

(Bleach)

Ichigo Kurosaki from Bleach is a character who consistently brings hope to those around him, even in the face of adversity. As a Soul Reaper with incredible powers, he protects both the living and the spirit world from dangerous threats. Despite facing overwhelming challenges and confronting his own fears and limitations, he remains steadfast in his determination. In the midst of darkness and despair, Ichiro's hope shines as a beacon of light, inspiring those around him and offering a glimmer of possibility and redemption.

Psalm 42:11 reminds us to examine the reasons behind our downcast souls and disturbed spirits. It prompts us to reorient our focus and place our hope in God, recognizing Him as our Saviour and the ultimate source of comfort and restoration. Ichigo's embodiment of hope reflects the essence of this verse, as he continuously seeks strength and guidance from a higher power, acknowledging the limitations of his own strength.

Ichigo's journey resonates with our own human experiences, as we often find ourselves grappling with difficulties and uncertainties. His unwavering hope reminds us that, in the face of adversity, we can find solace and renewal by anchoring our hope in God. Our hope should not be based solely on external circumstances but on a deeper, eternal foundation.

By reflecting on Ichigo's embodiment of hope in the anime, we are encouraged to examine the state of our own souls and find renewed hope in God. Just like Ichigo, we too can be vessels of hope to those around us by pointing them towards the ultimate source of hope and restoration. May we put our trust in God, praising Him even in the midst of challenges, knowing that our hope is secure in Him.

"We can't waste time worrying about the what ifs." - Ichigo Kurosaki

April 1

Whoever exalts himself will be humbled, and whoever humbles himself will be exalted. Matthew 23:12

Sage of the West

(Fullmetal Alchemist: Brotherhood)

Van Hohenheim is a complex character from Fullmetal Alchemist: Brotherhood who reflects the transformative power of humility. Despite being an immortal being with immense knowledge and alchemical abilities, he never seeks personal glory or dominance over others. Instead, he recognizes the consequences of his past actions and takes responsibility for them. He carries the weight of his mistakes, showing deep remorse and a desire for redemption.

The verse Matthew 23:12 teaches that those who promote themselves will be brought low, while those who humble themselves will be lifted up. Van Hohenheim through his humility serves as an example of how selflessness and acknowledging one's faults can lead to personal growth and the opportunity for redemption. His humility ultimately brings him exaltation in the form of reconciliation, forgiveness, and a chance to rebuild what was broken.

By humbling himself, Van Hohenheim becomes a catalyst for positive change. He actively seeks to make amends, seeking forgiveness and working towards restoring what he has destroyed. His actions demonstrate the Christian principle of valuing others above oneself, as he consistently prioritizes the well-being and happiness of others.

Van Hohenheim's journey reminds us of the transformative power of humility in our own lives. It encourages us to reflect on our own actions, acknowledge our mistakes, and seek reconciliation with God and others. By humbling ourselves, we can experience the grace and restoration that comes from surrendering our pride and embracing a life of humility, ultimately finding exaltation in the eyes of God.

"We live for the bonds we form with friends and family members. That's who we humans are." - Van Hohenheim

April 2

Woe to you, scribes and Pharisees, hypocrites! For you are like whitewashed tombs, which outwardly appear beautiful, but within are full of dead people's bones and all uncleanness. Matthew 23:27

Fleet Admiral

(One Piece)

Akainu, also known as Sakazuki, is a high-ranking Marine Admiral and a major antagonist in One Piece. He is portrayed as a ruthless individual who prioritizes absolute justice and the eradication of pirates above all else. He firmly believes in the Marine's duty to maintain order and eliminate any threats to society. However, his methods often involve excessive violence and cruelty, leading some to view him as a symbol of hypocrisy.

Matthew 23:27 warns against the danger of being like whitewashed tombs, appearing righteous on the outside but being filled with spiritual decay within. It reminds us that God sees beyond outward appearances and looks into our hearts. It encourages us to cultivate a deep, authentic relationship with God, allowing His transforming grace to cleanse us from within and empower us to live lives of integrity and genuine love.

Akainu's hypocrisy reminds us of the importance of integrity and authenticity in our own lives as followers of Christ. True Christian discipleship requires us to align our actions with our beliefs and cultivate genuine love and compassion for others. Just as Akainu's actions contradicted his supposed commitment to justice, we should examine our own lives to ensure that our words and deeds align with the teachings of Christ.

The portrayal of Akainu can spark discussions about the complexities of justice and the need for humility and self-reflection in the pursuit of righteousness. It highlights the importance of examining our own motives and actions, ensuring that they align with the teachings of Christ, which emphasize love, forgiveness, and genuine concern for the well-being of others.

"Justice is absolute! No forgiveness for those who oppose it!" - Akainu

April 3

Love one another with brotherly affection. Outdo one another in showing honour. Romans 12:10

Selfless Genius

(Rascal Does Not Dream of Bunny Girl Senpai)

Sakuta Azusagawa, the protagonist of the anime series Rascal Does Not Dream of Bunny Girl Senpai, demonstrates genuine care and concern for others, always willing to lend a helping hand or offer emotional support. Whether he is comforting Mai Sakurajima during her personal struggles or being there for his sister Kaede, Sakuta's actions reflect a deep sense of love and compassion.

The verse Romans 12:10 encourages believers to love one another with familial affection, treating fellow believers as brothers and sisters. Additionally, it urges believers to outdo one another in showing honour. Sakuta's kindness aligns with this call, as he consistently displays empathy, understanding, and respect towards others, going above and beyond to honour and uplift them. His willingness to sacrifice his own time and desires to support and uplift those around him showcases a selfless and sacrificial love.

Sakuta's character exemplifies a love rooted in brotherly affection, emphasizing the importance of treating fellow believers as family and fostering unity within the Christian community.

Through the kindness of Sakuta, we are reminded of the transformative power of love and compassion. As we strive to love one another with brotherly affection and surpass one another in showing honour, we reflect the love of Christ and create a community where individuals feel valued, supported, and uplifted. Sakuta's character serves as a reminder to actively cultivate kindness and extend the love of Christ to those around us.

"No matter who you were before, how you look right now is who you are." - Sakuta Azusagawa

April 4

There is no fear in love, but perfect love casts out fear. For fear has to do with punishment, and whoever fears has not been perfected in love. 1 John 4:18

Witch Queen

(Fire Force)

Maki Oze, a fire soldier and former military member from Fire Force, exemplifies love characterized by fearlessness, selflessness, and compassion. She fearlessly puts herself in harm's way to protect her comrades and those in need, demonstrating a deep care and concern for their well-being. Her love is not driven by self-preservation or the fear of punishment but rooted in a perfect love that emanates from within her.

1 John 4:18 reminds us that perfect love eliminates fear. Maki's love for others reflects this principle, as she embraces a love that surpasses fear. It enables her to face dangerous situations without hesitation and provide comfort and protection to those around her. Her unwavering love drives out fear, creating an atmosphere of safety and security.

As followers of Christ, we are called to embrace and cultivate this perfect love. When we allow the love of Christ to dwell in us and flow through us, it casts out fear and empowers us to love others genuinely and selflessly. It challenges us to transcend our own fears and insecurities, placing our trust in God's love and extending that love to those around us.

Maki's character serves as a reminder of the transformative power of perfect love in our lives. It prompts us to examine our own motives and actions, ensuring that our love is rooted in Christ and free from fear. When we embody perfect love, we create an environment where others can experience the unconditional love of God and find refuge from their own fears and struggles. By surrendering our fears and allowing God's love to permeate our hearts, we become vessels of His love, bringing hope, healing, and comfort to those we encounter.

"If you pray with all your heart, you can find comfort, and people have been saved by it." - Iris

April 5

But he said to me, "My grace is sufficient for you, for my power is made perfect in weakness." Therefore, I will boast all the more gladly of my weaknesses, so that the power of Christ may rest upon me. 2 Corinthians 12:9

Clan Killer

(Naruto)

In the anime series Naruto, Itachi belongs to the Uchiha clan, a group of powerful ninjas known for their Sharingan eye technique. Itachi's life is filled with challenges, sacrifices, and inner turmoil. He carries the burden of a dark secret and is faced with difficult choices for the sake of his village and loved ones. Despite the heavy burdens he bears, Itachi draws strength and comfort from his unwavering faith, particularly in his love for his brother Sasuke.

The verse 2 Corinthians 12:9 serves as a reminder that God's grace is more than sufficient, and His power is made perfect in our weaknesses. Itachi's journey is characterized by moments of vulnerability, doubt, and personal limitations. Nevertheless, he embraces his sickness and weaknesses, driven by his love for Sasuke.

Itachi's character exemplifies the transformative power of surrendering to God's grace and finding strength in our weaknesses. Through his life, we are encouraged to accept our own vulnerabilities and limitations, recognizing that God's grace is more than enough to sustain us. By embracing our weaknesses and boasting in them, we open ourselves to experiencing the power of Christ resting upon us. Itachi's story serves as a reminder that it is in our moments of weakness and our reliance on God's grace that His power is most evident.

Similar to how Itachi drew strength from his faith and love for his brother, we can also discover comfort and empowerment in the assurance that God's grace is more than enough for us. By acknowledging our weaknesses and depending on His strength, we can overcome challenges and accomplish great things for His glory.

"It is foolish to fear what we have yet to see and know." - Itachi Uchiha

April 6

For the love of money is a root of all kinds of evils. It is through this craving that some have wandered away from the faith and pierced themselves with many pangs. 1 Timothy 6:10

Travelling Merchant

(Spice & Wolf)

Kraft Lawrence from the Spice & Wolf anime is often portrayed as a materialistic individual, driven by his desire for wealth and success. He engages in trade and seeks profit, placing significant emphasis on material possessions and financial gain. His outlook on life revolves around the acquisition of wealth and the pursuit of a comfortable lifestyle.

This portrayal of Kraft Lawrence resonates with the message of 1 Timothy 6:10, which reminds us of the dangers associated with the love of money and material possessions. It warns that the love of money is a root of all kinds of evil and can lead us astray from our faith. It emphasizes that it is not money itself that is inherently evil, but rather the love and attachment we have towards it.

Kraft Lawrence's materialistic tendencies serve as a cautionary tale for us to examine our own hearts and attitudes towards wealth. We must evaluate our own desires and motivations, ensuring that we do not become consumed by the pursuit of worldly gain. Instead, we should seek to cultivate a balanced perspective, recognizing that true fulfilment and contentment come from our relationship with God and the pursuit of His kingdom.

The materialism depicted in Kraft Lawrence's character teaches us to examine our own lives and re-evaluate our priorities. It is a call to pursue a life marked by simplicity, gratitude, and a deep trust in God's provision. We must recognize that true wealth lies in the treasures of heaven and in serving others. By shifting our perspective from materialism to eternal values, we can find contentment, peace, and a deeper connection with God.

"We humans can indeed lose again something we've lost already." - Kraft Lawrence

April 7

For even the Son of Man came not to be served but to serve, and to give his life as a ransom for many. Mark 10:45

Take-Over Sorceress

(Fairy Tail)

Mirajane Strauss is a former S-Class mage of the Fairy Tail Guild and a member of the Strauss family, renowned for their exceptional magical abilities. Initially portrayed as a fearsome and formidable mage, her motivation and character undergo significant development throughout the series. She possesses a profound love for her friends and guild members, making their protection and support her primary motivation. Mirajane is known for her compassionate nature and willingness to go to great lengths to ensure their well-being.

The servant leadership of Mirajane reflects the Christian virtue exemplified in Mark 10:45, where Jesus declares His purpose to serve rather than be served, offering His life as a ransom for many. Similarly, Mirajane exhibits a deep desire to serve and safeguard her friends and guild members in Fairy Tail. Consistently prioritizing their needs above her own, she willingly makes personal sacrifices to ensure their well-being.

Mirajane is recognized for her impressive transformation magic, which allows her to change her appearance and abilities at will. However, she consciously utilizes her powers for good and strives to inspire hope in others. Despite facing her own struggles, Mirajane remains a steadfast pillar of support for her friends, offering wise words and encouragement.

The motivation shown by Mirajane showcases the transformative power of love. Just as Jesus' love led Him to sacrifice His life, Mirajane's love for her friends drives her to make selfless sacrifices. She serves as a reminder of the importance of embodying these virtues in our own lives, following the example of Jesus, who came not to be served but to serve.

"We are all different from each other and that's what makes us all special." - Mirajane Strauss

April 8

The Lord is near to the broken hearted and saves the crushed in spirit. Psalm 34:18

Insecure Casanova

(Fruits Basket)

Yuki Sohma, a popular high school student, hides his family issues and struggles with imposter syndrome. Tohru Honda, a kind and compassionate girl, offers her support and helps him confront his inner demons. Yuki feels trapped by his controlling and abusive mother but finds the courage to break free with Tohru's unconditional love. Together, they grow stronger, facing their fears and learning the importance of true friendship. Yuki discovers the power of love and acceptance, finding peace and embracing his true self.

Psalm 34:18 reminds us of God's closeness to the broken hearted and His ability to save those who are crushed in spirit. It speaks of His compassionate presence in the midst of pain, offering solace and hope to those who are hurting. Yuki's experiences reflect the reality that God is near, even in our darkest moments.

Yuki's pain resonates with the pain many individuals face in their lives. We all encounter moments of suffering, whether from past traumas, broken relationships, or internal struggles. Just as Yuki finds healing through the love and support of others, we too can find healing through the transformative power of God's love and the healing presence of Christ. It is through our pain that we can experience growth, develop empathy for others, and ultimately find restoration and renewal.

Through Yuki's character, we are reminded of the transformative power of God's presence and His ability to bring light into the darkest places of our lives. As we trust in Him, we can find comfort, strength, and hope, knowing that He is near to mend our brokenness and save our crushed spirits.

"It's okay to feel weak sometimes. It's okay to be afraid. The important thing is that we face our fears. That's... that's what makes us strong." - Yuki Sohma

April 9

Wait for the Lord; be strong, and let your heart take courage; wait for the Lord! Psalm 27:14

Phantom Sixth Player

(Kuroko's Basketball)

In the basketball anime, Kuroko encounters numerous challenges and setbacks on his basketball journey. Despite being overshadowed by more prominent teammates and facing formidable opponents, he exhibits remarkable patience and perseverance. He understands the importance of waiting for the right moment and trusting in the process.

Psalm 27:14 encourages us to wait for the Lord, be strong, and take courage in our hearts. It reminds us that patience is not passive waiting but an active expression of trust and faith. Kuroko's patience reflects his unwavering belief in his abilities and his commitment to improving his skills over time.

In a world that often prioritizes instant gratification and quick results, Kuroko's patience reminds us of the value of waiting for the Lord. It encourages us to trust in God's timing and have confidence in His plans for our lives. Just as Kuroko's patience led him to overcome obstacles and achieve success on the basketball court, our patience can lead to spiritual growth and blessings in our own lives. Through patience, we develop endurance, character, and a deeper reliance on God. It is during times of waiting that our faith is refined and our trust in God's goodness is strengthened.

By waiting on God with a strong and courageous heart, we align ourselves with His perfect will and experience the fulfilment of His promises. Just as Kuroko's patience led to triumph, our patience in God's timing will lead us to experience His faithfulness and the manifestation of His plans for our lives.

"If we give our best in something we love, we'll enjoy the victories from the bottom of our hearts." - Tetsuya Kuroko

April 10

The fear of man lays a snare, but whoever trusts in the LORD is safe. Proverbs 29:25

Commander Eyebrow

(Attack on Titan)

Erwin Smith, the commander of the Scout Regiment in the anime Attack on Titan, exhibits remarkable composure and resolve under pressure, even in the face of imminent danger. He consistently demonstrates a steadfast determination and refuses to yield to the pressures imposed by others, despite facing opposition and criticism. Erwin remains focused on his goals and the greater mission, often making tough decisions that go against popular opinion.

The verse Proverbs 29:25 warns us about the dangers of seeking the approval and acceptance of others, as it can ensnare us in fear and lead us to compromise our values. Erwin's unwavering trust in his convictions and his commitment to the greater good highlight the importance of placing our trust in the Lord rather than relying on people's opinions.

Peer pressure is a common challenge that many individuals face, often feeling compelled to conform to societal expectations and the desires of others. However, Erwin's character serves as a reminder of the perils of being driven by the fear of man. He resists the temptation to seek validation and acceptance from his peers, understanding that true security lies in trusting in the Lord. Erwin's ability to handle peer pressure inspires us to stand firm in our convictions, even when faced with opposition or criticism.

In a world that often prioritizes conformity and seeks the approval of others, we can draw inspiration from Erwin's resilience. By trusting in the Lord, we can overcome the fear of man and remain steadfast in our commitment to God's truth and righteousness. Through prayer, seeking God's wisdom, and relying on His strength, we can find the courage to stand firm in our faith, even in challenging circumstances or amidst societal pressures.

"If you begin to regret, you'll dull your future decisions and let others make your choices for you." - Erwin Smith

April 11

Then I heard what seemed to be the voice of a great multitude, like the roar of many waters and like the sound of mighty peals of thunder, crying out, "Hallelujah! For the Lord our God the Almighty reigns." Revelation 19:6

Omni King

(Dragon Ball)

Zeno, the Omni-King in Dragon Ball, is the most powerful character in the series, capable of destroying anything from individuals to entire universes. Despite his innocent appearance, he commands fear and respect from even the Gods of Destruction. He displays wisdom and occasionally shows fondness for Goku. Zeno's power, coupled with his unpredictable nature, makes him a formidable and influential figure in the Dragon Ball universe.

Revelation 19:6 reminds us of God's absolute sovereignty and unmatched power, emphasizing the worship and praise given to God as the one who reigns over all creation. This collective declaration of praise signifies the recognition of God's authority and power. Similarly, Zeno's power in the Dragon Ball series is portrayed as all-encompassing and supreme, making him the ruler of all universes.

While Zeno's power is supreme within the Dragon Ball universe, it is important to differentiate it from God's power. Zeno's power is a creation of human imagination, while God's power is an eternal, divine reality. Reflecting on Zeno's power serves as a reminder of the limitations of human imagination and the vastness of God's true power. It encourages us to turn our hearts towards the Almighty, giving Him the worship and honour, He deserves as the one true God who reigns over all things.

Though the power of Zeno in Dragon Ball is fictional, it can remind us of the awe-inspiring nature of God's power. This reflection prompts us to acknowledge God's authority and sovereignty, offering Him the worship and praise that He alone deserves.

"You'll laugh at your fears when you find out who you are." - Piccolo

April 12

Pride goes before destruction, and a haughty spirit before a fall. Proverbs 16:18

Captur ing God

(The World Only God Knows)

Keima Katsuragi, the protagonist of The World Only God Knows, is a socially awkward teenager who becomes a self-appointed god of dating simulators. His expertise in dating sims allows him to capture the hearts of female characters with unparalleled skill. He applies this knowledge to the real world, leading to amusing situations. Keima's unique character and obsession with dating sims make him a captivating and entertaining presence in the anime.

However, just as the verse Proverbs 16:18 warns, Keima's haughty spirit ultimately leads to his own downfall. His arrogance blinds him to the importance of true human connection and empathy, causing him to treat relationships as conquests and neglect the emotions of others. As a result, he faces challenges and learns that his prideful approach to love is flawed.

Keima's story serves as a reminder to examine our own hearts and motives, seeking to rid ourselves of pride and embrace humility. Elevating ourselves above others and relying solely on our abilities can damage the relationships we seek to nurture. We are called to humble ourselves before God, recognizing our need for His guidance and grace in all aspects of our lives. Through humility, we open ourselves to God's transformative work, enabling us to build meaningful relationships founded on care and selflessness.

Reflecting on Keima's journey encourages us to strive for relationships that honour God and reflect His love for us, avoiding the destructive consequences of pride. By acknowledging God's sovereignty and our own limitations, we can cultivate humility and foster healthier connections with others.

"If everyone were perfect, there would be no need to look out for others. Sympathy or love is needed because people are imperfect. A perfect human cannot love anyone." - Keima Katsuragi

April 13

Blessed are the peacemakers, for they shall be called sons of God. Matthew 5:9

Warrior Prince

(Princess Mononoke)

In Princess Mononoke, Ashitaka acts as a bridge between conflicting parties, seeking peace and reconciliation. His selflessness and compassionate actions mirror the teachings of Jesus Christ. Throughout the film, Ashitaka demonstrates a deep commitment to peace, seeking to understand both sides of the conflict and empathizing with the struggles and motivations of humans and the spirits of the forest. Rather than choosing a side, he actively works to bridge the gap between them.

Similar to the promise in Matthew 5:9, Ashitaka's role as a peacemaker earns him the respect and admiration of both humans and spirits. His selfless acts of compassion and willingness to sacrifice for the greater good inspire others to pursue peace as well. His portrayal as a saviour emphasizes the importance of peace-making and the blessings that come from fostering harmony and reconciliation.

Like Ashitaka, Jesus came to reconcile humanity with God and with one another, teaching love, forgiveness, and compassion as a means to restore broken relationships. Ashitaka's willingness to sacrifice himself for the greater good echoes Christ's ultimate sacrifice on the cross. His determination to find a solution that benefits both sides demonstrate the importance of seeking common ground and understanding in conflicts.

Prince Ashitaka can thus be seen as a reflection of Christ's teachings on peace, reconciliation, and sacrificial love. His efforts to mediate and find common ground illustrate the values of love, understanding, and compassion that Christ exemplified, reminding us of the value of striving for harmony in our relationships and the world around us.

"Life is suffering. It is hard. The world is cursed, but still, you find reasons to keep living." - Lady Eboshi

April 14

For one will scarcely die for a righteous person though perhaps for a good person one would dare even to die but God shows his love for us in that while we were still sinners, Christ died for us. Romans 5:7-8

Miasma of the Void

(JoJo's Bizarre Adventure)

Vanilla Ice's sacrifice in JoJo's Bizarre Adventure, although driven by his loyalty to the villainous Dio Brando, showcases a willingness to lay down his life for his master. While his actions are misguided, they reflect the idea that people can be moved to extraordinary acts of self-sacrifice for those they deeply care about, regardless of the recipient's moral standing.

In a similar way, Romans 5:7-8 reminds us that it is rare for someone to die for a righteous person, but for a good person, someone might dare to make such a sacrifice. The verse goes on to explain that God's love surpasses human understanding, as demonstrated by the fact that while we were still sinners, Christ died for us. This highlights the immeasurable love and grace of God, who offered His Son as a sacrifice to reconcile humanity to Himself, even in our sinful state.

When contemplating Vanilla Ice's sacrifice, it serves as a reminder of the capacity within humans to display sacrificial love, albeit sometimes in flawed or distorted ways. It underscores the importance of discerning and directing our loyalty and self-sacrifice toward worthy causes, aligning them with God's perfect love and truth.

While Vanilla Ice's sacrifice may not possess the redemptive power and divine significance of Christ's sacrifice, it prompts us to reflect on the transformative power of sacrificial love and the depth of God's love demonstrated through Christ's sacrifice for humanity on the cross. This reminds us to strive for a deeper understanding and expression of sacrificial love, guided by God's perfect example.

"What is "Courage"? Courage is owning your fear!"
- Will Anthonio Zepelli

April 15

For we are his workmanship, created in Christ Jesus for good works, which God prepared beforehand, that we should walk in them. Ephesians 2:10

Bodybuilding Gorilla

(Fire Force)

Captain Akitaru Ōbi is a character in Fire Force who lacks any ignition abilities. Despite this, he has accomplished many great things, including leading Company 8 in their fight against Infernals and the White-Clad. Akitaru is a paternal figure who cares deeply for his fellow soldiers and is willing to put his life on the line to protect them. He is courageous, creative, and confident in his abilities without being arrogant. His unwavering dedication to his team and his belief in their cause make him a standout character in the anime.

The verse Ephesians 2:10 reminds us that as believers, we are God's handiwork. This verse emphasizes that we have been uniquely created in Christ Jesus for a purpose. It highlights that God has already prepared good works for us to do, indicating that each of us has a specific role to fulfil in His plan.

Akitaru Ōbi recognizes his inherent value and purpose. His confidence stems from understanding that he is part of God's design and has a vital role to play in the larger scheme of things. His leadership and contributions are not based on external factors but on the understanding that he has been intricately crafted by God for a specific mission.

By relating Akitaru's self-esteem, we are reminded of our own worth and purpose. Just as he embraces his role as captain and fulfils his duties with confidence, we too can find assurance in knowing that we are God's handiwork and have been entrusted with specific good works to accomplish. We need to embrace our unique identities, exercise our gifts and talents, and fulfil the purposes that God has prepared for us.

"Having a sense of fear allows you to make cool-headed decisions. Just… don't chicken out because of it."
- Akitaru Ōbi

April 16

For the wages of sin is death, but the free gift of God is eternal life in Christ Jesus our Lord. Romans 6:23

Ultimate Fashionista

(Danganronpa)

Junko Enoshima, a character from the Danganronpa series, embodies the essence of sin and its consequences. She is manipulative, deceitful, and revels in chaos and despair. Her actions throughout the story lead to suffering, despair, and even death for those involved. She revels in chaos and despair, orchestrating events that lead to suffering and death. Her actions can be seen as representative of sin and the destructive consequences it can have in people's lives.

In Romans 6:23, the verse highlights the fundamental principle that sin has grave consequences, ultimately leading to death. The verse also presents the counterpoint that God offers a way out of this cycle of sin and death. It highlights the gift of eternal life through Jesus Christ. This gift represents God's love, mercy, and grace, offering forgiveness and redemption for those who turn away from sin and embrace a relationship with Christ.

Junko Enoshima's sins are reflected in the choices she makes and the harm she inflicts upon others. Her manipulative tactics, lies, and manipulation of despair sow destruction and suffering, both physically and emotionally. Her actions also disregard the inherent worth and dignity of others, leading to their suffering and death.

The sin of Junko Enoshima, as portrayed in Danganronpa, can serve as a powerful reminder of the reality and consequences of sin. It calls us to examine our own lives, turn away from sin, and embrace the gift of eternal life offered through Jesus Christ. Through God's grace and forgiveness, we can find redemption, healing, and a renewed purpose in aligning our lives with His loving and righteous ways.

"We've always been filled with despair, so when we do something, we go all the way and live without regret!"
- Junko Enoshima

April 17

This is the day that the Lord has made; let us rejoice and be glad in it. Psalm 118:24

Unpopular Girl

(WataMote)

In the anime series, Tomoko Kuroki grapples with social anxiety and feelings of isolation. Despite her struggles, she occasionally experiences moments of thankfulness and joy, even if they are unconventional or may seem insignificant to others. Through these glimpses of gratitude, she reminds us that thankfulness can be found in the simplest of things, in the ordinary moments of life.

Psalm 118:24 reminds us that each day is a gift from God, and we are called to find reasons to rejoice and be thankful, regardless of our circumstances. It invites us to recognize that each day is a gift from God, and within it, there are opportunities for joy and reasons to be thankful. It prompts us to shift our focus from what may be lacking to what we can appreciate in the day that the Lord has made.

Tomoko's character encourages us to shift our perspective and embrace each day as an opportunity to find reasons for gratitude. While her expressions of thankfulness may not align with societal norms, they reflect a desire to appreciate the present and recognize the goodness that can be found in even the smallest details of life. Tomoko's character serves as a reminder that thankfulness is not limited to perfect situations or ideal conditions. Instead, it calls us to seek gratitude in the midst of our own struggles, challenges, and imperfections.

Through Tomoko's character, we are reminded that true gratitude goes beyond external circumstances and societal expectations. It invites us to embrace the present, finding reasons to rejoice and be glad in even the simplest aspects of life. Ultimately, it is a call to cultivate a grateful heart that acknowledges God's faithfulness, regardless of our circumstances.

"I read in some book that sad and painful things are the spices of an enjoyable life." - Tomoko Kuroki

April 18

There is neither Jew nor Greek, there is neither slave nor free, there is no male and female, for you are all one in Christ Jesus. Galatians 3:28

Konoha's Green Beast

(Naruto)

Might Guy, a character from the Naruto series, exemplifies acceptance and inclusion. Despite his eccentricities and unique approach to life, he embraces others and treats them with kindness and respect. He values teamwork, loyalty, and wholeheartedly supports his comrades. His acceptance of others is not based on their strengths or abilities, but on their inherent worth as individuals.

Galatians 3:28 emphasizes the unity we have in Christ, transcending social, cultural, and gender differences. It reminds us that in God's eyes, there is no hierarchy or favouritism based on external distinctions. This verse challenges us to look beyond surface-level differences and embrace one another as equals, recognizing the inherent worth and value that each person possesses as a beloved child of God.

The character of Might Guy teaches us that acceptance is not contingent on outward appearance or achievements. Instead, it is rooted in recognizing the intrinsic worth and dignity that each person possesses as a creation of God. By accepting others in this way, we create a space where people feel valued, heard, and included, fostering unity and harmony.

Might Guy's acceptance remind us of our responsibility to break down barriers and cultivate a culture of acceptance and love. It calls us to examine our hearts, confront biases and prejudices, and embrace others fully. By doing so, we embody the unity and acceptance that Christ calls us to, creating a community where everyone can flourish and experience the love of God.

"It's not always possible to do what we want to do, but it's important to believe in something before you actually do it." - Might Guy

April 19

Whoever is slow to anger has great understanding, but he who has a hasty temper exalts folly. Proverbs 14:29

Orange Cat

(Fruits Basket)

Kyo Sohma is one of the main characters in the anime series Fruits Basket. He is a member of the Sohma family, which is cursed to turn into animals of the Chinese zodiac. At the beginning of the series, he is short-tempered, aggressive, and hot-headed. However, after meeting Tohru, he grows into a calmer, gentler, and more emotionally mature person. Kyo is violent, self-sacrificing, and defensive, but he cares deeply for the people he loves.

The verse Proverbs 14:29 provides valuable wisdom, stating that those who are slow to anger possess great understanding, while those who have a hasty temper elevate folly. It teaches us that true understanding lies in the ability to restrain our anger, seeking reconciliation rather than perpetuating conflict. It also reminds us that our words and actions should reflect the love and grace of God, even when we feel provoked or wronged.

Kyo's character exhibits a hasty temper that often leads to destructive consequences. His anger, driven by feelings of frustration, isolation, and a sense of being misunderstood, frequently manifests as impulsive behaviour and strained relationships. As Christians, we are called to imitate Christ in all aspects of our lives, including how we manage our emotions.

In contemplating Kyo's anger, we are challenged to examine our own responses to anger and strive for growth. It reminds us that the transformation of our hearts and minds requires us to surrender our emotions to God and allow His wisdom to shape our thoughts and actions. By cultivating understanding, patience, and self-control, we can navigate anger in a way that reflects God's character and contributes to the restoration and healing of our relationships.

"Maybe I'm not perfect. Maybe I have a long way to go. But someday, I'll be able to stand and walk on my own. Without hurting anyone and without being a burden." - Kyo Sohma

April 20

For he grew up before him like a young plant, and like a root out of dry ground; he had no form or majesty that we should look at him, and no beauty that we should desire him. He was despised and rejected by men, a man of sorrows and acquainted with grief; and as one from whom men hide their faces he was despised, and we esteemed him not. Isaiah 53:2-3

King of Knights

(Fate/Zero)

In the Fate/Zero series, Saber is depicted as a strong and noble knight with a regal appearance. While Saber may appear powerful and imposing on the surface, her true character and inner struggles are revealed throughout the series. She carries the weight of her responsibilities and has a deep desire to protect others, even at great personal cost.

Isaiah 53:2-3 speaks of someone who lacks outward beauty or attractiveness and is despised and rejected by others. This passage points to Jesus Christ, who came as the suffering servant, bearing the weight of our sins and experiencing rejection from the world. Despite Saber's visually striking appearance, she carries a burden of responsibility and faces numerous challenges. Her character embodies aspects of humility, honour, and self-sacrifice.

Saber's unwavering commitment to her ideals and her willingness to bear the burdens placed upon her can serve as a reminder to us of the sacrificial love and servant-heartedness that Christ exemplified. We can learn from her determination, strength, and selflessness, and strive to imitate these qualities in our own lives as we follow the example of Christ.

The reflection on Saber's appearance can encourage us to look beyond external appearances and recognize the inner qualities that define a person's true worth. It reminds us to seek the character traits that align with the teachings of Christ and to cultivate a heart that is willing to serve and make sacrifices for the greater good.

"If you do evil out of a hatred for evil, that rage and hate will merely birth new conflict." - Saber

April 21

Even though I walk through the valley of the shadow of death, I will fear no evil, for you are with me; your rod and your staff, they comfort me. Psalm 23:4

Goofiest Joestar

(JoJo's Bizarre Adventure)

Joseph Joestar is the grandson of Jonathan Joestar, and he possesses a strong-willed, confident, and loud-mouthed personality. His character embodies resilience and courage in the face of danger and adversity. He confronts various challenges and battles throughout his journey, often finding himself in perilous situations. Despite the daunting circumstances, Joseph remains steadfast and determined, refusing to be overcome by fear or evil.

The verse Psalm 23:4 speaks of walking through the darkest valley without fear because God is with us. In a similar way, Joseph's resilience and refusal to succumb to evil can remind us of the constant presence of God in our lives. As believers in Christ, we can find comfort in knowing that God walks alongside us, providing guidance, protection, and strength during times of adversity.

The psalmist finds solace in the rod and staff of God, which symbolize His guidance and care. Joseph, too, relies on the support and encouragement of his friends and loved ones throughout his journey. This highlights the significance of Christian fellowship and community, where we can lean on one another, offer support, and uplift each other in times of difficulty.

The attitude of Joseph Joestar in JoJo's Bizarre Adventure aligns with the themes of trust, courage, and reliance on God's presence. We can draw inspiration from Joseph's character to embrace our God-given abilities, trust in His constant presence, and find strength and comfort through Christian community as we navigate the challenges and valleys of life.

"A true gentleman needs to be brave enough to go into a fight he knows he'll lose." - Joseph Joestar.

April 22

Be sober-minded; be watchful. Your adversary the devil prowls around like a roaring lion, seeking someone to devour. 1 Peter 5:8

Lower Rank One

(Demon Slayer)

Enmu from Demon Slayer represents an enemy who prowls around like a roaring lion, seeking to devour and harm. Similarly, the verse warns believers to be alert and of sober mind, acknowledging the presence of the devil and his deceptive tactics. It reminds us that as Christians, we are engaged in a spiritual battle against the forces of evil.

1 Peter 5:8 urges us to remain vigilant, maintaining a sober mind and being aware of the enemy's presence. Enmu's tactics of manipulation and exploiting vulnerabilities can serve as a reminder of the devil's schemes in our own lives. The devil seeks to deceive, tempt, and lead us away from God's path.

Enmu's ability to create illusions and mislead his victims draws parallels to the devil's role as the father of lies. This reminds us of the importance of discernment and spiritual discernment. We are called to test every spirit and cling to the truth found in God's Word, knowing that the devil's deceptions can lead us astray. Moreover, just as how the characters in Demon Slayer must actively confront and resist the threats of demons, we are called to stand firm against the devil. We are to equip ourselves with the armour of God, rooted in prayer and grounded in the truth of God's Word.

The circumstance of Enmu from Demon Slayer can serve as a reflection of the spiritual battle believers face. It reminds us to be alert, discerning, and steadfast in resisting the devil's temptations and deceptions. Through prayer, reliance on God's Word, and the guidance of the Holy Spirit, we can navigate the challenges of spiritual warfare and remain faithful to our calling in Christ.

"A human's driving force is the heart, the spirit!" - Enmu

April 23

I press on toward the goal for the prize of the upward call of God in Christ Jesus. Philippians 3:14

Turbo Hero

(My Hero Academia)

The commitment of Tenya Iida from My Hero Academia can be seen in his unwavering determination and relentless pursuit of becoming a hero. Despite facing countless challenges and setbacks, he remains steadfast in his pursuit, never losing sight of his goal. His unwavering determination reflects the perseverance and resilience that Christians are called to exhibit in their own lives.

In Philippians 3:14, the apostle Paul urges believers to continue striving towards the goal and the prize that comes with God's upward call in Christ Jesus. This verse speaks of persevering commitment to the purpose and calling that God has placed upon our lives. Like Tenya Iida, we are called to press on in our faith journey, striving to become more Christ-like and fulfil the calling that God has placed upon us.

Furthermore, Tenya Iida's commitment serves as a reminder that our ultimate goal is not merely earthly achievements or recognition, but the upward call of God in Christ Jesus. Our ultimate prize is found in our relationship with Him and the eternal life that awaits us. We are encouraged to maintain focused commitment to pursuing godliness, fulfilling our calling, and ultimately seeking the prize of eternal life with God.

Tenya Iida's commitment in My Hero Academia inspires us to press on in our faith, remain steadfast in our pursuit of godliness, and focus on the upward call of God in Christ Jesus. Just as Tenya Iida strives to become a hero, we are called to live out our faith with unwavering commitment, knowing that our ultimate prize is found in our relationship with God.

"I'm a novice. I can't measure up to their standards! Be that as it may... I have to stand up!" - Tenya Iida

April 24

He has told you, O man, what is good; and what does the Lord require of you but to do justice, and to love kindness, and to walk humbly with your God? Micah 6:8

Non-Governmental Organization

(Hunter x Hunter)

In Hunter x Hunter, the Hunter Association is a governing group responsible for training and enlisting Hunters and handling sensitive cases. They strive to maintain balance in the world, protect the innocent, and bring wrongdoers to justice. The hunters dedicate themselves to upholding righteousness and ensuring that justice is served, reflecting God's desire for His people to actively pursue justice in their actions.

Micah 6:8 is a powerful verse that calls us to reflect on our relationship with God and how we live out our faith. This verse serves as a guiding principle for our Christian walk, reminding us of the qualities and attitudes that God desires from His people. It reminds us to be actively engaged in pursuing justice, extending mercy, and cultivating a humble and intimate relationship with our Creator.

The Hunter Association values compassion and mercy. The hunters exemplify the importance of showing kindness, compassion, and forgiveness, reflecting God's own merciful nature. Despite their exceptional abilities and accomplishments, hunters understand the vastness of the world and their own limitations. By recognizing their reliance on their own abilities and seeking guidance from a higher power, the hunters exhibit a humble posture in their pursuits.

The values and actions of the Hunter Association in Hunter x Hunter serve as a reminder that as Christians, we are called to actively engage in the world, standing up for what is right, showing mercy, and humbly relying on God's guidance and strength. By doing so, we can make a positive impact on the world and bring glory to God's name.

"Enjoy the little detours to the fullest. Because that's where you'll find the things more important than what you want." - Ging Freecss

April 25

The Lord is my light and my salvation; whom shall, I fear? The Lord is the stronghold[a] of my life; of whom shall I be afraid? Psalm 27:1

Sea Urchin Head

(Jujutsu Kaisen)

In the world of Jujutsu Kaisen, Megumi Fushiguro exhibits tremendous bravery as he confronts formidable adversaries and puts his life on the line to protect others. While he does not see himself as a hero, his courage in dire situations proves otherwise. His character development throughout the series is notable as he learns to trust himself and his abilities more. Despite his strength, Megumi struggles with the weight of responsibility that comes with being a sorcerer.

The verse Psalm 27:1 reminds us that our courage stems from our faith and trust in God. We can find our ultimate courage in the Lord. He is our light, illuminating our path and giving us the confidence to face the challenges before us. He is our salvation, delivering us from fear and empowering us to overcome any obstacle. He is the stronghold of our lives, providing a secure refuge and a firm foundation even in the midst of uncertainty.

Megumi's courage serves as an inspiration for believers to rely on God's presence and promises when facing adversity. It demonstrates that true courage comes not from our own strength alone but from our relationship with God. By trusting in His guidance and protection, we can confront the trials and tribulations of life with boldness and assurance.

The courage displayed by Megumi reminds us that our faith should not be a passive belief but an active pursuit. It requires stepping out of our comfort zones, standing up for what is right, and protecting those in need, just as Megumi does in his role as a jujutsu sorcerer. Through our courageous actions, we can be a reflection of God's love, grace, and strength in a world that desperately needs it.

"It's not about whether I can, I have to do it!" - Megumi Fushiguro

April 26

For what does it profit a man to gain the whole world and forfeit his soul? Mark 8:36

Fuhrer King

(Fullmetal Alchemist: Brotherhood)

Bradley's character in the Fullmetal Alchemist: Brotherhood anime embodies the pursuit of worldly power and control. He seeks to gain the whole world, amassing political dominance and authority over the nation of Amestris. He is driven by ambition and a desire to secure his own interests at any cost. However, as the story unfolds, it becomes evident that his choices come at a great spiritual and moral expense.

Mark 8:36 reminds us that the accumulation of wealth, power, and worldly achievements ultimately holds no eternal value if it comes at the expense of our spiritual well-being. As followers of Christ, we are called to prioritize the state of our souls over earthly pursuits. This verse challenges us to consider the true worth of our actions and the alignment of our choices with God's will. The path to genuine contentment lies not in gaining the whole world but in faithfully following Christ and seeking the transformation of our hearts.

While Bradley may achieve temporary success and wield immense power, he forfeits his soul in the process and becomes entangled in the web of the Homunculi's dark plans, losing his humanity and compromising his moral integrity. This prompts us to reflect on our own lives and the temptations we face in the pursuit of success and influence. It reminds us that true fulfilment is found in a relationship with God and in living according to His principles of love, justice, and compassion.

By examining the consequences of Bradley's decisions through the lens of Mark 8:36, we are reminded to seek a balanced perspective on power, success, and the temporal nature of worldly achievements. It encourages us to prioritize the eternal well-being of our souls and to cultivate virtues such as humility, selflessness, and integrity in all that we do.

"The life of each human is worth one life, that's it. Nothing more, nothing less." - Bradley

April 27

Love bears all things, believes all things, hopes all things, endures all things. 1 Corinthians 13:7

Backout Queen

(Death Note)

Misa's character in Death Note exhibits a deep and unwavering love for Light Yagami. She bears the weight of their relationship, enduring the challenges and sacrifices that come with it. Despite Light's questionable actions and manipulations, Misa wholeheartedly believes in him and holds onto hope for a positive outcome. Her devotion leads her to endure emotional turmoil, physical dangers, and personal losses.

The verse in 1 Corinthians 13:7 highlights the power and extent of love when directed in a virtuous manner. It reminds us that true love is patient, persevering, and willing to face challenges without giving up. In a broader Christian context, this verse serves as a reminder of the kind of love God calls us to express towards others. It encourages us to bear the burdens of those we love, believe in their potential, hold onto hope even in difficult circumstances, and endure trials and tribulations together.

It is crucial to note that Misa's devotion is not necessarily rooted in a healthy or virtuous foundation. Her love for Light is obsessive and unbalanced, leading her to make questionable choices and compromises. Therefore, it's important to differentiate between selfless love and love that is based on obsession or idolatry. The ultimate example of perfect love is found in God Himself, who bears, believes, hopes, and endures all things for the sake of His children.

While Misa's character may not exemplify an ideal form of love, her devotion prompts us to reflect on the qualities of love demonstrated by Jesus Christ. It encourages us to seek a love that is rooted in God's truth and guided by His principles, leading us to build healthy, selfless, and enduring relationships that honour and reflect His love in the world.

"To defeat evil there must be sacrifices." - Misa Amane

April 28

Be not quick in your spirit to become angry, for anger lodges in the heart of fools. Ecclesiastes 7:9

Sharingan Clan

(Naruto)

The Uchiha family in Naruto depicts the destructive consequences of unresolved anger and the pursuit of revenge. Itachi Uchiha, driven by a desire to protect his loved ones, makes the difficult choice to wipe out his entire clan, leaving only his younger brother, Sasuke, alive. This act of extreme anger and violence sets Sasuke on a path of darkness and vengeance.

Ecclesiastes 7:9 advises against being quickly provoked in one's spirit, recognizing that anger often resides in the realm of foolishness. We are called to seek wisdom and self-control, allowing the Holy Spirit to guide our emotions and actions. We are also reminded that anger resides in the lap of fools. As believers, we are called to lay aside our anger and seek God's wisdom, which includes extending forgiveness and grace to others. The Uchiha family's journey illustrates the destructive nature of anger but also highlights the potential for transformation and redemption through forgiveness and reconciliation.

The Christian faith emphasizes the transformative power of forgiveness and reconciliation. Despite the Uchiha family's tragic history, the narrative offers moments of redemption and healing. Sasuke, burdened by anger and hatred for much of the series, eventually confronts the truth about his brother's sacrifice and is moved by Itachi's love for him. This realization leads Sasuke to re-evaluate his path and seek forgiveness and reconciliation.

Ultimately, reflecting on the Uchiha family's story in the Naruto anime encourages us to examine our own hearts, address our anger in healthy ways, and strive for wisdom, forgiveness, and reconciliation in our relationships.

"No matter how powerful you become, don't try to shoulder everything alone. If you do, you will surely fail."
- Itachi Uchiha

April 29

For I, the Lord your God, hold your right hand; it is I who say to you, "Fear not, I am the one who helps you." Isaiah 41:13

Lion Sin of Pride

(Seven Deadly Sins)

The fear experienced by Escanor from the Seven Deadly Sins anime arises from the immense power he possesses and his struggle to control it. Despite his extraordinary abilities, he fears the potential harm he could inflict on his friends and loved ones. This fear can be relatable to our own lives, as we often grapple with fears and anxieties that stem from our unique strengths and challenges.

In Isaiah 41:13, God assures His people that He is their God who takes hold of their right hand. This imagery conveys a sense of intimacy and guidance. God not only acknowledges our fears but also offers His help and reassurance, urging us not to fear. It serves as a reminder that we have companionship in our struggles. God's presence and support are always available to us. The verse also encourages us to trust in His guidance and assistance, even when we feel overwhelmed by our own strengths or challenged by our circumstances. It reminds us that God's presence is with us, providing comfort and strength in moments of fear.

Escanor begins to find strength and courage by forming deep connections with his companions, who offer their support and acceptance. In a similar way, we can draw strength from our relationships with others and from the knowledge that God is there to take hold of our hand. We are called to bring our fears and anxieties to God, knowing that He will help us.

Through the fear experienced by Escanor, we are reminded to lean on God's support and the support of others. We can find solace in knowing that God is intimately aware of our fears and is ready to guide us through them. It is an invitation to surrender our fears to Him, trusting that He will provide the help we need and lead us on a path of courage and growth.

"Calmness is the hallmark of those who are mighty." - Escanor

April 30

Bearing with one another and, if one has a complaint against another, forgiving each other; as the Lord has forgiven you, so you also must forgive. Colossians 3:13

Shun Shun Rikka

(Bleach)

In Bleach, Orihime Inoue encounters numerous challenges and experiences betrayal and loss. Despite these hardships, she consistently exemplifies a forgiving heart, choosing to extend grace and mercy to those who have wronged her. Her actions mirror the biblical principle of forgiving others as we ourselves have been forgiven by the Lord.

In Colossians 3:13, we are reminded of our call to bear with one another and forgive. It acknowledges that conflicts may arise in our relationships, but it encourages us to respond with a forgiving heart. Just as the Lord has forgiven us, we are to forgive others. Orihime's example demonstrates the strength and healing that come from extending forgiveness.

Through Orihime's forgiveness, we are reminded of God's immeasurable mercy and grace towards us. The forgiveness we receive from the Lord is the foundation for our own ability to forgive others. By extending forgiveness, we reflect the character of Christ and participate in the work of reconciliation. Orihime's forgiveness challenges us to let go of resentment, bitterness, and the desire for revenge. It invites us to embrace forgiveness as a means of experiencing personal freedom and restoration in our relationships.

By relating Orihime's forgiveness, we are prompted to consider the significance of forgiveness in our own lives. We are encouraged to forgive others as we have been forgiven by the Lord. Through forgiveness, we can experience healing, reconciliation, and the restoration of relationships, reflecting the love and grace of our Heavenly Father.

"It's impossible to feel exactly the same as someone else... but when you both care for each other, your hearts are able to draw a little closer together. I think that's what it means to make your hearts as one." - Orihime Inoue

May 1

A man of many companions may come to ruin, but there is a friend who sticks closer than a brother. Proverbs 18:24

Besto Freindos

(Jujutsu Kaisen)

In the world of Jujutsu Kaisen, Todo and Itadori's friendship stands out amidst the multitude of companions they encounter. While Itadori has other friends and allies, Todo distinguishes himself as the one who sticks closer than a brother. Their friendship goes beyond superficial connections. They share a deep understanding and camaraderie founded on mutual respect and trust. Despite their differences in personality and background, they form an unbreakable bond that withstands adversity and challenges.

Proverbs 18:24 warns against relying solely on a large circle of friends, as they may not provide the same depth of support and loyalty. Instead, it emphasizes the significance of a friend who remains steadfast and committed even in difficult times. We need to cultivate friendships that go beyond surface-level interactions and provide genuine support and care.

Todo and Itadori have unwavering support for each other. They have each other's backs, provide encouragement and guidance, and are willing to make sacrifices to ensure the other's well-being. Their friendship transcends conventional boundaries and becomes a bond akin to that of family. They exemplify the essence of a true friend, one who not only walks alongside you but also remains faithful during the highs and lows of life.

We can learn from Todo and Itadori's friendship and apply these principles in our own relationships. The deep bond, unwavering support, and intimate connection reflect the essence of true friendship. By observing their relationship, we can strive to cultivate similar friendships that withstand the test of time and provide a sense of loyalty and support that goes beyond what we might expect from ordinary companions.

"You should use your strength to help others." - Wasuke Itadori

May 2

Do not be conformed to this world, but be transformed by the renewal of your mind, that by testing you may discern what is the will of God, what is good and acceptable and perfect. Romans 12:2

Prince of all Saiyan

(Dragon Ball)

Vegeta's character arc in Dragon Ball is marked by his journey from a prideful, ruthless warrior to a more compassionate and selfless individual. Initially, Vegeta is driven by a desire for power and dominance, conforming to the pattern of the world he grew up in, where strength is valued above all else. However, as the series progresses, Vegeta undergoes a transformation, both in his mindset and his actions.

The verse Romans 12:2 encourages believers to break free from the patterns and values of the world and seek transformation through the renewing of their minds. Vegeta's growth can be seen as a result of a shift in his perspective and values. Through his growth, we witness his ability to recognize the significance of love, sacrifice, and the value of protecting others.

As Vegeta experiences personal losses, challenges, and encounters with characters who embody selflessness and compassion, his mindset begins to shift. He starts to appreciate the importance of protecting and caring for others, even at great personal cost. Vegeta's transformation is a testament to his ability to break free from the patterns of his past and embrace a new way of thinking and living.

The transformation of Vegeta from a prideful warrior to a more compassionate and selfless individual reflects the importance of renewing one's mindset and breaking free from the patterns of the world. Just as the verse encourages believers to seek transformation, Vegeta's character serves as a reminder that personal growth and change are possible, leading to a better understanding of God's will and a more virtuous way of life.

"There's only one certainty in life. A strong man stands above and conquers all!" - Vegeta

May 3

Delight yourself in the Lord, and he will give you the desires of your heart. Psalm 37:4

Joy Boy

(One Piece)

Throughout the anime series, Luffy's pursuit of becoming the Pirate King and finding the One Piece brings him great joy and fulfilment. His happiness stems from his unwavering passion and love for the adventurous life of a pirate. Luffy delights in the freedom, excitement, and camaraderie he experiences on his journey with his crew, the Straw Hats.

Psalm 37:4 encourages believers to find their ultimate delight in the Lord. When we prioritize our relationship with God and align our desires with His will, we discover true happiness. In Luffy's story, we see that true happiness is not found in material possessions or temporary pleasures but in the pursuit of one's passion, genuine relationships, and living a life in alignment with one's values. When we delight ourselves in God and seek His will, He blesses us with the desires of our hearts, which often include a sense of purpose, meaningful relationships, and fulfilment in our chosen paths.

The joyful spirit of Luffy is contagious, uplifting those around him and inspiring them to embrace their own dreams and pursue what brings them joy. He finds happiness in the simplest of things, cherishing the bonds he forms with his crewmates and celebrating the adventures they embark upon together. He consistently demonstrates a genuine concern for the well-being and happiness of his friends and even strangers he encounters along the way.

Luffy's delight in the adventurous life of a pirate and the pursuit of his dreams reflects the importance of finding joy in our passions and living out our values. His character reminds us to prioritize genuine relationships, selflessness, and the pursuit of our dreams, trusting that when we delight ourselves in the Lord, He will bless us with the desires of our hearts, leading to true and lasting happiness.

"If you don't take risks, you can't create a future."
- Monkey D. Luffy

May 4

Whatever your hand finds to do, do it with your might, for there is no work or thought or knowledge or wisdom in Sheol, to which you are going. Ecclesiastes 9:10

Café Waitress

(The Disastrous Life of Saiki K.)

Mera Chisato's character in the disastrous life of Saiki K. exemplifies the virtue of hard work and wholehearted commitment. She approaches her role in the broadcasting club with unwavering dedication, investing her time and energy into every aspect of her work. Mera understands the importance of giving her best effort and maximizing her potential in everything she does.

The verse Ecclesiastes 9:10 encourages individuals to approach their work diligently and with excellence, recognizing that there will come a time when our opportunities to engage in earthly pursuits will cease. This passage reminds us that our work matters and has significance, even if it seems fleeting. It encourages us to work diligently, knowing that our efforts are not in vain and that we will be rewarded.

Mera's character serves as an inspiration for viewers to embrace a strong work ethic and a wholehearted approach to their responsibilities. She demonstrates that every task, no matter how seemingly insignificant, deserves our utmost dedication and effort. Her commitment to excellence reminds us that our work and endeavours should be approached with a mindset of wholeheartedness and a desire to honor God.

By observing Mera Chisato, we are reminded to approach our own work and endeavours with diligence, excellence, and a mindset that reflects our faith. We are encouraged to give our best effort, knowing that our work has significance and contributes to our personal growth and the fulfillment of our God-given purpose. Mera's dedication and commitment are a testament to the importance of hard work and the pursuit of excellence in all aspects of our lives.

"There's no such thing as a person without thoughts."
- Kusuo Saiki

May 5

Therefore, having put away falsehood, let each one of you speak the truth with his neighbour, for we are members one of another. Ephesians 4:25

Reality Warping AI

(The Melancholy of Haruhi Suzumiya)

As a member of the SOS Brigade, Yuki Nagato consistently portrays integrity and truthfulness in her words and actions. She values transparency and communicates without deceit, even in challenging or uncomfortable situations. Yuki's honesty in the melancholy of Haruhi Suzumiya brings stability and reliability to the story, as she presents information truthfully and without manipulation.

The biblical principle found in Ephesians 4:25 reminds us to put away falsehood and instead speak the truth with one another. In the Christian faith, honesty is highly valued as it aligns with the nature of God, who is the embodiment of truth. The verse emphasizes the importance of living a life of integrity and honesty in our interactions with others, recognizing that we are interconnected as members of the same body of Christ.

Yuki's honesty serves as a powerful reminder of the impact of truthful communication in our lives. Her character highlights the importance of being truthful in our words and actions, even when it may be challenging or uncomfortable. By embracing honesty, we build trust, foster genuine connections, and contribute to a culture of integrity. Honesty not only strengthens our relationships but also reflects our commitment to following the teachings of Christ.

As we reflect on Yuki Nagato's honesty, we are encouraged to examine our own lives and consider how we can cultivate a spirit of truthfulness. By speaking the truth, avoiding deceit, and living with integrity, we can contribute to a world where honesty and authenticity are valued. Ultimately, our commitment to honesty reflects our desire to honor God and live in alignment with His truth.

"Problems that cannot be solved do not exist in this world." - Yuki Nagato

May 6

And now, O Lord, for what do I wait? My hope is in you.
Psalm 39:7

Chaos Creator

(That Time I Got Reincarnated as a Slime)

In that time, I got reincarnated as a slime, Rimuru Tempest's hope is not solely reliant on external circumstances or his own strength but is deeply rooted in his connection with others and his belief in the power of friendship and unity. He consistently seeks to uplift and inspire those around him, leading by example and demonstrating that hope can be found in unity, compassion, and a shared vision for a better future.

Psalm 39:7 encourages believers to place their hope in God, recognizing that He is the ultimate source of strength and guidance. By entrusting our hopes, dreams, and aspirations to God, we acknowledge His sovereignty and understand that our ultimate hope lies in His perfect plan and faithfulness.

The hope of Rimuru is not founded in his own abilities or circumstances but in his faith and reliance on a higher power. He constantly seeks guidance from the Great Sage within him, representing the wisdom and divine inspiration that guides his actions. In our own lives, it is crucial to recognize that our ultimate hope should not rest in our own capabilities, but in the Lord. Rimuru's character reminds us to turn to God for direction and to place our hope in His sovereign plan. By doing so, we find assurance and confidence in the face of uncertainty.

Rimuru works tirelessly to create a world where different races can coexist in harmony, striving to bring about positive change and a brighter future. Similarly, our hope in God should compel us to work towards a better future, where peace, justice, and compassion prevail. Let us anchor our own hope in God, trusting in His wisdom, guidance, and faithfulness. In Him, we find unwavering hope, strength, and a firm foundation for our lives.

"Once you give up, it's all over. So, you gotta do what you can. Don't get your hopes up." - Rimuru Tempest

May 7

For everyone who exalts himself will be humbled, and he who humbles himself will be exalted. Luke 14:11

First Hokage

(Naruto)

Hashirama Senju, a character from Naruto, exemplifies humility despite his immense power and leadership role. He demonstrates a willingness to listen, learn from others, and prioritize the well-being of his comrades over his own desires. Hashirama's humility allows him to form strong alliances, build bridges, and strive for peace. He does not seek personal glory or dominance over others but values the well-being of the entire community.

Luke 14:11 reminds us that those who exalt themselves, seeking recognition and power, will eventually be humbled. In contrast, those who willingly humble themselves, like Hashirama, will be exalted. Hashirama's humility earns him the respect and admiration of his peers and enables him to foster unity and cooperation among different factions.

As Christians, we are called to follow the example of Jesus Christ, who humbled Himself and served others sacrificially. Hashirama's humility serves as a reminder of the transformative power of humility in our own lives. When we humble ourselves before God and others, we open ourselves up to God's grace and favour, becoming vessels through which, His love and compassion can flow.

True greatness, according to Christ's teachings, is found in selfless service and sacrificial love. By reflecting on Hashirama's humility, we are reminded of the importance of humility in our relationships, leadership roles, and interactions with others. May we strive to follow the path of humility, recognizing that true exaltation comes from embracing a servant's heart and seeking the well-being of those around us.

"They believe in me and I believe in them. That's what being a Hokage means." - Hashirama Senju

May 8

But be doers of the word, and not hearers only, deceiving yourselves. James 1:22

Psychotic Stalker

(JoJo's Bizarre Adventure)

Yukako Yamagishi, a character from JoJo's Bizarre Adventure, exemplifies hypocrisy through her actions and behaviour. She portrays a false facade of kindness and love towards others, particularly her romantic interest, Koichi Hirose, while harbouring possessiveness, jealousy, and controlling tendencies. Her hypocrisy lies in the stark contrast between her outwardly sweet demeanour and her hidden manipulative nature.

The verse James 1:22 highlights the danger of being hypocritical by just listening to or professing faith without putting it into action. It emphasizes the importance of aligning our words and actions, avoiding the deception that comes with empty religious practices. When individuals claim to believe certain principles or values but fail to demonstrate them in their behaviour, they deceive themselves and others.

Yukako Yamagishi presents herself as someone who desires love and devotion from others, but her actions reveal a hypocritical nature. She manipulates and controls others, showing a lack of genuine care and concern for their well-being. As Christians, we are called to live out our faith authentically and consistently. Mere words or claims of belief are insufficient; true faith is demonstrated through our actions. We are called to be people of integrity, whose words and actions align in a way that reflects the love and truth of Jesus. Through our consistent witness, we can bring glory to God and be a positive example to those around us.

By reflecting on the hypocrisy of Yukako Yamagishi, we are prompted to evaluate our own lives and ensure that our actions align with our professed beliefs. May we strive to be genuine followers of Christ, embodying His love, compassion, and integrity in all that we do. Let us be doers of the Word, living out our faith with authenticity and avoiding the trap of hypocrisy.

"Not that it matters who might come by... After all, love is invincible." - Yukako Yamagishi

May 9

Put on then, as God's chosen ones, holy and beloved, compassionate hearts, kindness, humility, meekness, and patience. Colossians 3:12

Celestial Spirit Mage

(Fairy Tail)

Lucy Heartfilia, a character from Fairy Tail, exhibits kindness and compassion towards others. She consistently demonstrates a willingness to help and support her friends and even strangers in need. Her acts of kindness often come from a genuine place of empathy and a desire to make a positive difference in the lives of those around her.

Colossians 3:12 reminds us that as believers, we are called to actively clothe ourselves with kindness. It is not merely an occasional action but an intentional choice to consistently demonstrate kindness in our interactions with others. Kindness is one of the defining characteristics of God's chosen people, and we are called to reflect His character in the way we treat others.

The kindness which Lucy demonstrates also points to the transformative power of small acts of love. In a world often plagued by strife and division, simple acts of kindness can have a profound impact on others. They have the power to uplift spirits, heal wounds, and inspire positive change. Lucy's kindness serves as a reminder that our acts of kindness should flow from a place of genuine love, compassion, and humility, just as Christ demonstrated through His sacrificial love on the cross.

Lucy's character in the anime inspires us to embrace kindness as a way of life. It challenges us to be intentional in our words and actions, consistently demonstrating compassion, gentleness, and patience. Let us clothe ourselves with kindness, knowing that through our acts of love, we can be vessels of God's grace and agents of transformation in the world.

"Remember that everyone you meet is afraid of something, loves something, and has lost something." - Lucy Heartfilia

May 10

Let love be genuine. Abhor what is evil; hold fast to what is good. Romans 12:9

Creepy Demon Child

(My Hero Academia)

Himiko Toga's concept of love in My Hero Academia is deeply flawed and destructive. Her infatuation is driven by a desire to consume and possess the essence of those she loves, resulting in harm and danger. While her love is unhealthy and destructive, it serves as a reminder of the consequences of misplaced affections and the need for discernment.

Romans 12:9 reminds us of the genuine nature of love that God calls us to embrace. It states that we should cultivate love that is pure, honest, and rooted in God's principles. It teaches us to detest evil and cling to what is good, steering us away from harmful expressions of love. It also teaches us to cherish and uphold values that promote the well-being of others. It encourages us to love sincerely, without manipulation or harm.

In the case of Himiko Toga, her distorted version of love showcases the dangers of selfishness, manipulation, and harm that can arise when love is misguided. It reminds us that true love is selfless, seeking the well-being and flourishing of others rather than seeking to possess or harm them. Jesus Christ demonstrated the ultimate example of genuine love through His sacrificial death on the cross. His love was selfless, unconditional, and aimed at reconciling humanity with God. It is this love that we are called to emulate in our own lives.

Reflecting on Himiko Toga's distorted love can remind us of the importance of aligning our understanding of love with the principles taught in the Bible. It urges us to examine our own hearts and motives, ensuring that our love is genuine, selfless, and focused on promoting goodness and righteousness. Through our authentic love, we can be a source of light and transformation in the lives of others, reflecting the unconditional love of God and pointing them towards the true source of love and fulfillment.

"When you shut your feeling away, it only grows inside!" - Himiko Toga

May 11

Therefore, if anyone is in Christ, he is a new creation. The old has passed away; behold, the new has come. 2 Corinthians 5:17

Flame Alchemist

(Fullmetal Alchemist: Brotherhood)

The life of Roy Mustang from Fullmetal Alchemist: Brotherhood portrays the transformative power of redemption and the potential for a person to undergo profound change. Initially, Roy is driven by personal ambitions, seeking power and revenge. He embodies the consequences of living in a broken world, where selfish desires and misguided actions lead to pain and suffering.

The verse 2 Corinthians 5:17 speaks of becoming a new creation in Christ. We are called to let go of our old ways, selfish desires, and sinful nature. We are invited to become new creations, transformed by the grace and love of God. Like Roy, we are called to recognize the brokenness of the world and the impact of our own actions. We are empowered to embrace a purpose greater than ourselves, pursuing justice, compassion, and selfless service.

As Roy aligns himself with the pursuit of truth, justice, and protection for the innocent, his character begins to reflect the qualities of Christ-like love and sacrifice. He willingly embraces the responsibility of leadership and devotes himself to the well-being of others. This newfound purpose and selflessness lead him to become a force for good, using his power not for personal gain but to bring about positive change in the world.

Roy Mustang's journey resonates with the transformative journey of a believer. It reminds us that through faith in Christ, we have the capacity to leave behind our old selves and step into a new life. It encourages us to continually examine our hearts, align our values with those of Christ, and strive to make a positive difference in the lives of others.

"Nothing's perfect, the world's not perfect, but it's there for us, trying the best it can. That's what makes it so damn beautiful." - Roy Mustang

May 12

Do not lay up for yourselves treasures on earth, where moth and rust destroy and where thieves break in and steal, but lay up for yourselves treasures in heaven, where neither moth nor rust destroys and where thieves do not break in and steal. For where your treasure is, there your heart will be also. Matthew 6:19-21

Student Council President

(Kill la Kill)

Kaneo Takarada, the heir to the Takarada Conglomerate in Kill la Kill, is a proud and shameless merchant who views money as an all-powerful resource. He places great value on his riches, often flaunting his opulence and pursuing more wealth at any cost, but his pursuit fails to bring him true fulfillment and happiness.

Matthew 6:19-21 encourages believers to prioritize eternal treasures over earthly possessions. The verse reminds us that true value lies in storing up treasures in heaven. These treasures represent spiritual investments, such as acts of kindness, love, and righteousness, which have lasting significance. By shifting our focus from earthly possessions to eternal treasures, we align our hearts with what truly matters in the eyes of God.

Takarada's materialistic pursuits highlight the dangers of allowing our hearts and desires to be consumed by worldly possessions. His insatiable quest for wealth ultimately leaves him unfulfilled and disconnected from deeper, more meaningful aspects of life. This serves as a reminder to Christians to examine their own hearts and evaluate their priorities.

In the context of Kaneo Takarada's materialism, believers are encouraged to seek true treasures in heaven by investing in relationships, pursuing spiritual growth, and using our resources to bless others. It reminds us that our true worth and significance lies in living in alignment with God's kingdom and values. By placing our treasure in heaven, we experience genuine and lasting fulfillment that transcends the fleeting nature of material wealth.

"It is not money that rules men. It is fear." - Satsuki Kiryūin

May 13

Do you not know that in a race all the runners run, but only one receives the prize? So run that you may obtain it.
1 Corinthians 9:24

Strongest Ultimate Decoy

(Haikyu!!)

Shōyō Hinata, the main protagonist of the anime series Haikyu, is a determined and enthusiastic high school student who dreams of becoming a great volleyball player despite his short stature. Hinata possesses remarkable speed, agility, and jumping ability, which he uses to his advantage on the court. One notable aspect of Hinata's character is his unwavering motivation and passion for the sport. Despite facing challenges and setbacks, he remains resilient and never loses sight of his goal. His determination to improve, push his limits, and prove himself against taller opponents is truly inspiring.

The verse 1 Corinthians 9:24 encourages believers to approach life with the same level of dedication and perseverance. It reminds us that in the race of life, we are called to run in such a way as to obtain the prize. Just as Hinata continually pushes himself to improve, we are encouraged to pursue personal growth, strengthen our faith, and live with purpose, always aiming for the ultimate prize of eternal life with God.

Hinata's story also highlights the importance of teamwork and camaraderie. He recognizes that success in volleyball, and in life, is not achieved alone. This teaches us to value and support one another, recognizing that we are part of a larger body of believers and that our collective efforts can bring about greater impact and growth.

Shōyō Hinata's character embodies qualities of motivation, perseverance, and teamwork that can inspire us in our own lives. His passion for volleyball, determination to overcome obstacles, and commitment to continuous improvement can serve as a model for us as we pursue our own goals and navigate our faith journey.

"The future belongs to those who believe in the beauty of their dreams." - Shōyō Hinata

May 14

For I consider that the sufferings of this present time are not worth comparing with the glory that is to be revealed to us. Romans 8:18

Perverted Outer Space Alien

(Maid Sama!)

Takumi Usui, the cool and charismatic character at Seika High in Maid Sama, carries a deep sense of pain and inner turmoil, which he often conceals behind his composed demeanour. His struggles and past experiences have left lasting scars that impact his emotions and relationships.

In Romans 8:18, we find solace and hope amidst our own pain. This verse reminds us that our present sufferings, no matter how intense or prolonged, cannot be compared to the immeasurable glory that God has prepared for His children. It calls us to shift our perspective from the temporary struggles we face in this world to the eternal joy and fulfillment that await us in God's presence.

Takumi's pain serves as a reminder of the fallen nature of humanity and the brokenness caused by sin. However, we are encouraged to anchor our hope in the promise of God's redemption and the restoration of all things. Despite his pain, Takumi's character exhibits resilience, compassion, and a willingness to protect and support those he cares about. His journey shows us that even in the midst of our own pain, God's love can work through us to bring healing, strength, and transformation to ourselves and others.

In light of Takumi Usui's pain, we are encouraged to hold onto our faith, trusting in God's faithfulness and his ultimate plan for our lives. Our pain, though real and challenging, is not the final word. Through God's grace, we can find strength, healing, and a deep sense of purpose even amidst our most profound struggles.

"Strangely, I don't feel resentful.... The fact that I was born like this, I'm actually thankful." - Takumi Usui

May 15

And let steadfastness have its full effect, that you may be perfect and complete, lacking in nothing. James 1:4

Black Reaper

(Darker than Black)

Hei is a skilled assassin known as the Black Reaper who is adept at keeping his cool in high-pressure situations. Hei's character is known for his calm and composed demeanour, even in the face of challenging and dangerous situations. He displays great patience as he carries out his missions and navigates the complex world of Contractors. Hei's patience allows him to make wise decisions and overcome obstacles with precision and effectiveness.

In the verse James 1:4, we are encouraged to let perseverance or patience complete its work in us. It reminds us that patience is not just about enduring difficult circumstances; it is a transformative process that shapes and matures us. Just as Hei's patience allows him to grow and become a more capable and skilled individual, our own patience develops our character and strengthens our faith.

Hei's patience also highlights the significance of self-control which demonstrates the importance of aligning our desires with God's will. Through patient self-control, we learn to rely on the Holy Spirit's guidance, resisting the temptation to rush into hasty decisions or actions. By surrendering our impatience and seeking God's wisdom, we allow perseverance to shape our character, leading to spiritual growth and a deeper reliance on God.

The story of Hei in Darker than Black can inspire us to adopt a long-term perspective in our faith journey. It reminds us that the rewards of patience go beyond immediate gratification. Just as Hei's patience and perseverance yield fruitful results in his missions, our patient endurance through trials leads to spiritual maturity, completeness, and a deeper understanding of God's faithfulness.

"If you pretend to feel a certain way, the feeling can become genuine all by accident" - Hei

May 16

For am I now seeking the approval of man, or of God? Or am I trying to please man? If I were still trying to please man, I would not be a servant of Christ. Galatians 1:10

Figure Skating Legend

(Yuri!!! On Ice)

Victor Nikiforov, a professional figure skater from Yuri on Ice," faces immense pressure as an athlete but remains unfazed and continues to impress audiences with his performances. He possesses natural talent and effortlessly captivates viewers with his skills, demonstrating that excellence can be achieved even under pressure. Despite his achievements, Victor remains humble, constantly seeking self-improvement and new challenges.

In the context of Galatians 1:10, the apostle Paul questions the motives behind seeking the approval of others. He challenges believers to consider whether their actions are driven by a desire to please people or a genuine commitment to serving God. As Christians, we are called to live in a manner that is pleasing to God and aligned with His will. However, the world often pressures us to conform to its standards, desires, and expectations.

Victor faces a dilemma of conforming to the expectations of others or staying true to his own aspirations and desires. However, his authentic self-expression and pursuit of his passion ultimately bring him fulfillment and success. This highlights the importance of prioritizing personal values, convictions, and relationship with God over seeking the approval of others.

Victor's journey in the anime highlights the significance of staying true to oneself and pursuing personal growth and fulfillment rather than solely seeking external validation. By drawing parallels between Victor's struggle and the challenges presented to believers in the Bible, we learn the importance of maintaining authenticity and commitment to God's calling, leading to a meaningful and purposeful life.

"If you don't have the strength to motivate someone who looks up to you, how can you find the strength to motivate yourself?" - Victor Nikiforov

May 17

For we do not wrestle against flesh and blood, but against the rulers, against the authorities, against the cosmic powers over this present darkness, against the spiritual forces of evil in the heavenly places. Ephesians 6:12

Ultimate Vampire

(Hellsing)

Alucard is the protagonist of the Hellsing series and is believed to be the most powerful vampire alive. He is egotistical, fierce, and cruel, but only uses his abilities for the right reasons. His arrogance is one of his only flaws, as it has led to him being caught off guard in battle. His final form is said to be so powerful that he could punch a hole through the world.

The verse Ephesians 6:12 reminds us that our struggle is not merely against physical adversaries but also against spiritual forces of evil. The portrayal of Alucard's battles against supernatural creatures highlights the existence of a spiritual realm where evil forces seek to harm and deceive humanity. As followers of Christ, we are called to be aware of the spiritual warfare and engage in it through prayer, faith, and reliance on God's power.

Alucard's character arc in the anime reflects the transformative power of redemption. Despite his dark nature and past actions, Alucard embarks on a journey of seeking forgiveness and purpose. This reminds us of the redemptive work of Christ in our own lives. Just as Alucard seeks redemption, we are called to recognize our need for forgiveness, turn away from our past sins, and embrace the transformative power of God's grace and mercy.

In contemplating the power of Alucard, we are encouraged to recognize the reality of spiritual warfare, embrace the power of redemption, engage in the inner struggle against sin, and ultimately find our strength in Christ. By applying these spiritual insights, we can grow in our faith, live victoriously, and participate in the greater battle against evil in the world.

"True prayer is forged in battle! Dazzle your Lord with your prayer, and you shall know Him! You shall know Jerusalem!" - Alucard

May 18

God opposes the proud but gives grace to the humble.
James 4:6

Extravagant Manipulator

(Durarara!!)

Izaya Orihara is a charming villain from "Durarara!!" who manipulates people to do his bidding. His character exudes a sense of self-importance and superiority, often looking down on others and manipulating them for his own amusement. He takes pleasure in observing and orchestrating chaos, feeding off the conflicts he instigates.

James 4:6 serves as a reminder that God stands in opposition to those who are proud in their hearts. Pride goes against the values and principles of humility that God desires from His people. In contrast, the verse highlights that God gives grace to the humble. Humility involves recognizing our limitations, acknowledging our dependence on God, and placing the needs and concerns of others before our own. It is through humility that we open ourselves up to receive the abundant grace that God offers.

Izaya's prideful actions and mindset align with the attitude that God opposes, as they promote self-centeredness, manipulation, and a disregard for the well-being of others. His pride isolates him from experiencing the fullness of God's grace. It hinders his ability to form genuine connections and sabotages his relationships, ultimately leaving him unfulfilled and disconnected from the grace that could bring healing and transformation.

The reflection on Izaya's pride can serve as a reminder to examine our own hearts and actions. As followers of Christ, we are called to cultivate humility and surrender our prideful tendencies to God. This means acknowledging our need for His guidance, seeking His will above our own, and embracing a posture of humility in our relationships with others. By doing so, we align ourselves with God's purposes, experience His grace, and reflect His love to the world.

"Everyone's the same, no exceptions. All of them, equal before God." - Izaya Orihara

May 19

For God so loved the world, that he gave his only Son, that whoever believes in him should not perish but have eternal life. John 3:16

Ultimate Defender Saiyan

(Dragon Ball)

In Dragon Ball, Goku is portrayed as a hero who continuously saves the world from powerful enemies and threats. He consistently puts himself in harm's way to defend his loved ones and even the entire world from formidable threats. While Goku's actions may not grant eternal life or address the spiritual condition of humanity, they can inspire us to reflect on the sacrificial love displayed by Jesus Christ.

The verse John 3:16 reveals God's immense love for the world, as He sent His Son, Jesus Christ, to save humanity from sin and offer eternal life to all who believe in Him. Jesus willingly laid down His life on the cross as the ultimate sacrifice, providing a path to salvation and reconciliation with God. Goku's selflessness and willingness to put others before himself can be seen as a reflection of Christ's sacrificial love. His acts of heroism remind us of the importance of selfless love and the call to serve others in our own lives.

It is crucial to recognize the distinction between a fictional character like Goku and the unique role of Jesus Christ as the divine Saviour. While Goku's actions can inspire us to embody virtues such as courage and selflessness, the fullness of salvation and eternal life can only be found in Jesus.

By relating Goku's selfless actions in the anime, we can emphasize the importance of selflessness and sacrificial love in our own lives. Just as Goku fights for the well-being of others, Jesus sacrificed Himself out of love for humanity. This connection can serve as a reminder of the profound love and sacrifice Jesus demonstrated and encourages us to live out similar values in our relationships with others.

"Power comes in response to a need, not a desire."
- Son Goku

May 20

Even as the Son of Man came not to be served but to serve, and to give his life as a ransom for many. Matthew 20:28

Hero of SAO

(Sword Art Online)

In Sword Art Online, Kazuto exemplifies a spirit of selflessness and sacrifice as he puts himself in harm's way to protect and save his friends trapped in the virtual world. He takes on immense challenges, risks his own life, and endures hardships, all for the sake of those he cares about. His actions reflect the selfless nature of Jesus' mission on Earth.

Matthew 20:28 highlights the purpose of Jesus' coming into the world. He did not come seeking to be served but to serve others and give His life as a ransom. Jesus' sacrificial act of laying down His life on the cross serves as the ultimate example of selflessness and love. Kazuto's sacrifice echoes this biblical principle by demonstrating a willingness to sacrifice his own well-being for the sake of others. His actions reflect the transformative power of selfless love and serve as a reminder of Jesus' ultimate sacrifice for humanity.

Kazuto's character encourages us to reflect on the call to service and sacrificial love in our own lives. It reminds us to cultivate a servant's heart, to prioritize the well-being of others, and to be willing to make sacrifices for the sake of love and compassion. It also challenges us to follow the example of Jesus by putting the needs of others before our own, demonstrating acts of love and service that can make a positive impact on those around us.

In contemplating Kazuto's sacrifice, we are encouraged to live out our faith by serving others, following Jesus' example, and embodying sacrificial love in our daily lives. It is through acts of selflessness and love that we can make a difference in the lives of others and reflect the transformative power of Christ's sacrificial love in the world.

"It is pointless to question who someone really is. All you can do is believe and accept. Because the way you perceive someone is their true identity." - Kirito

May 21

For by the grace given to me I say to everyone among you not to think of himself more highly than he ought to think, but to think with sober judgment, each according to the measure of faith that God has assigned. Romans 12:3

Rebellious Exorcist

(Jujutsu Kaisen)

Maki Zenin's character in Jujutsu Kaisen exemplifies humility in her approach to her own abilities and worth. Despite the discrimination and challenges, she faces due to her lack of cursed energy, Maki remains grounded and realistic about her strengths and limitations. She doesn't let her achievements or physical prowess inflate her ego or think of herself more highly than she ought to. Instead, she maintains a sober judgment of herself, recognizing her unique gifts while understanding that they are not the sole measure of her value.

In Romans 12:3, the apostle Paul advises believers not to think of themselves more highly than they should, but rather to have a humble perspective. This teaching reminds us that our true worth does not come from worldly accomplishments or external validation. Instead, our value is rooted in our identity as beloved children of God. Recognizing our own worth and capabilities with sober judgment allows us to maintain a healthy balance in our self-esteem.

The journey of Maki Zenin reminds us of the importance of relying on God's grace. Her resilience and determination are not solely attributed to her own efforts but can also be seen as an expression of God's grace working through her. Like her, we are called to give thanks for the talents and strengths we possess, recognizing that they are blessings from God.

Maki Zenin's self-esteem can serve as a reminder for us to embrace humility, self-acceptance, and gratitude for the gifts God has bestowed upon us. By recognizing our true worth as children of God and having a balanced perspective on ourselves, we can cultivate a healthy self-esteem that aligns with the teachings of Scripture.

"Why are you pretending to be a victim when you're being protected?" - Maki Zenin

May 22

You said in your heart, 'I will ascend to heaven; above the stars of God, I will set my throne on high; I will sit on the mount of assembly in the far reaches of the north; I will ascend above the heights of the clouds; I will make myself like the Most High.' But you are brought down to Sheol, to the far reaches of the pit. Isaiah 14:13-15

Power-Hungry Mastermind

(Bleach)

In Bleach, Sōsuke Aizen is characterized by his ambition for God-like power and his desire to surpass the limitations of mortals. He seeks to elevate himself above others and establish himself as the ultimate authority. His sin in seeking God-like power and desiring to surpass the limitations of mortals reveals the inherent human tendency towards pride.

The verse Isaiah 14:13-15 describes the fall of the king of Babylon, who, in his pride, sought to exalt himself above God and establish his own reign. This passage serves as a reminder that attempting to elevate oneself to a position of authority or divinity, surpassing the limits set by God, is an act of pride and rebellion. It reveals the consequences of such prideful aspirations, leading to a humbling and a descent into destruction.

Sōsuke Aizen's character highlights the dangers of seeking power and authority for one's own self-interest, without regard for the boundaries set by God. It serves as a cautionary message, warning against the sin of pride and the consequences that follow when individuals attempt to place themselves above the Creator.

The story of Sōsuke Aizen emphasizes the importance of humility and acknowledging our rightful place in relation to God. It reminds us to approach power and authority with reverence, recognizing that true wisdom and strength come from a place of humility and obedience to God's will.

"Any betrayal you can see is trivial, what is truly frightening and much more lethal, is the betrayal you cannot see." - Sōsuke Aizen

May 23

And whatever you do, in word or deed, do everything in the name of the Lord Jesus, giving thanks to God the Father through him. Colossians 3:17

Void Mage

(The Familiar of Zero)

In the anime, Louise de la Valliere's thankfulness can be seen in her growth and transformation as she learns to appreciate the people and experiences in her life. She evolves from a character driven by pride and entitlement to someone who recognizes the value of relationships and expresses gratitude for the kindness and support she receives.

Colossians 3:17 reminds believers to approach all aspects of life, whether through words or actions, with the mindset of doing everything in the name of the Lord Jesus. This includes expressing gratitude and giving thanks to God the Father through Him. When Louise experiences challenges, she begins to recognize the value of her relationships and express gratitude for the kindness and support she receives. Her growth in thankfulness is an embodiment of doing everything in the name of the Lord Jesus.

Louise's journey reminds us of the importance of aligning our thoughts, words, and actions with the example of Christ. Her newfound thankfulness demonstrates the transformative power of a grateful heart. As followers of Christ, we are called to live in a manner that reflects our faith, constantly aware of the presence of God in our lives. This includes expressing gratitude for His blessings and goodness.

By following the example of Louise, we can learn to appreciate the blessings and relationships in our lives, recognizing them as gifts from God. This practice deepens our connection with Him and allows us to witness the transformative power of thankfulness in our own spiritual journeys.

"Death comes at the very end, doesn't it? Until that time comes, do your best at living!" - Louise de la Vallière

May 24

Judge not, that you be not judged. For with the judgment, you pronounce you will be judged, and with the measure you use it will be measured to you. Matthew 7:1-2

Black Leg

(One Piece)

In One Piece, Sanji faces judgments and prejudices based on his background and family history. However, as the story progresses, he learns the importance of not judging others and instead focusing on accepting them for who they are. He realizes that true acceptance requires setting aside preconceived notions and embracing the diversity and uniqueness of individuals.

The verse Matthew 7:1-2 cautions against judgment, reminding us that the measure with which we judge others will be applied to us as well. It encourages us to approach others with empathy and understanding, rather than passing harsh judgments. By practicing acceptance, we create an environment where others can also find acceptance and grow.

The acceptance of Sanji exemplifies the transformative power of unconditional love and grace. He learns to see beyond surface-level judgments and embraces the complexities and unique qualities of individuals. His journey teaches us that acceptance involves recognizing the inherent worth of every person, irrespective of their past or present circumstances. As Christians, we are called to follow the example set by Christ. Jesus demonstrated radical acceptance, embracing sinners, outcasts, and those deemed unworthy by society.

Through the example of Sanji, we are reminded of the transformative power of acceptance and the importance of embracing diversity and individuality. By setting aside judgment and choosing acceptance, we can create a space where everyone feels valued and embraced for who they are. May we strive to be like Sanji, reflecting the love and acceptance that Christ has shown us. Let us approach others with empathy, understanding, and an open heart, allowing God's transformative grace to work in both their lives and our own.

"Don't start a fight if you can't end it." - Vinsmoke Sanji

May 25

Good sense makes one slow to anger, and it is his glory to overlook an offense. Proverbs 19:11

Blue Spirit

(Avatar: The Last Airbender)

Zuko's anger is a central aspect of his character arc in Avatar: The Last Airbender. It stems from deep emotional wounds and a desire to prove himself. He carries a burden of resentment and seeks to right the perceived wrongs done to him. However, as the series unfolds, Zuko begins to experience personal growth and learns the value of wisdom and patience.

Proverbs 19:11 reminds us that true wisdom leads to patience. It encourages us to rise above our initial reactions of anger when faced with offenses and instead choose a path of understanding and forgiveness. This verse challenges us to transcend our natural inclinations and respond with grace and compassion. In a Christian context, it serves as a reminder of the teachings of Christ. Jesus exemplified wisdom and patience, even in the face of great injustice and offenses. He calls us to follow His example by responding to anger with understanding and overlooking offenses with grace.

Zuko's journey reflects the transformative power of wisdom and patience. As he matures, he realizes that holding onto anger and seeking revenge only perpetuate pain and hinder personal growth. Through his experiences, he discovers the importance of understanding others, finding common ground, and extending forgiveness.

By reflecting on Zuko's character, we are reminded of the transformative potential of wisdom and patience in our own lives. We are challenged to examine our responses to anger, seeking the guidance of the Holy Spirit to respond with wisdom and extend forgiveness. Let us choose to overcome anger with wisdom, overlooking offenses for the sake of peace and reconciliation. In doing so, we reflect the character of Christ and bring glory to His name.

"You have to try every time. You can't quit because you're afraid you might fail." - Zuko

May 26

Now there are varieties of gifts, but the same Spirit; and there are varieties of service, but the same Lord; and there are varieties of activities, but it is the same God who empowers them all in everyone. 1 Corinthians 12:4-6

Ice-make Mage

(Fairy Tail)

Gray Fullbuster has dedicated himself to building a strong and muscular physique, but his focus lies solely on becoming the most formidable member of the Fairy Tail guild. He shows little concern for his physical appearance and displays no shame as he often appears scantily clad. It is evident that Gray's priority lies in his strength and abilities, rather than how he is perceived by others.

1 Corinthians 12:4-6 emphasizes the diversity of gifts given by the Holy Spirit to believers within the body of Christ. It highlights that although there are different gifts, services, and activities, they all originate from the same Spirit, Lord, and God. This passage encourages unity among believers while recognizing and celebrating their unique contributions.

Just as Gray's ice magic sets him apart from others, the diversity of gifts within the Christian community allows each believer to contribute in their own unique way. The analogy here is that, just as Gray's appearance reflects his individuality, we are called to embrace our God-given gifts and talents, recognizing that they are part of a larger body where each person's contributions are valued.

Gray Fullbuster's appearance reminds us of the importance of embracing our individual gifts, celebrating the diversity within the Christian community, and working together in unity and service. It encourages us to recognize that our unique contributions, like Gray's ice magic, are given by the same Spirit and should be used for the greater good and the glory of God.

"Sadness is just another wall that blocks you from moving on. I know it's hard to get past it, but you got to break through." - Gray Fullbuster

May 27

Again, I saw that under the sun the race is not to the swift, nor the battle to the strong, nor bread to the wise, nor riches to the intelligent, nor favour to those with knowledge, but time and chance happen to them all.
Ecclesiastes 9:11

Speed-o'-Sound

(One-Punch Man)

Speed-o'-Sound Sonic is an aggressive character in One Punch Man who exhibits heightened behaviour when faced with formidable opponents. He possesses a deep passion for combat and thrives on the thrill of a good fight. Even in the face of defeat, Sonic's determination only intensifies, motivating him to push himself harder. His arrogant attitude remains undeterred, regardless of how many times he may lose to Saitama.

In Ecclesiastes 9:11, we are reminded that success in life is not solely determined by our swiftness, strength, or intelligence. It teaches us that there are factors beyond our control and that chance plays a role in our outcomes. As followers of Christ, we are called to recognize that our achievements and victories are ultimately in God's hands.

Just as Speed-o'-Sound Sonic places excessive confidence in his own talents and abilities, we are also prone to falling into the trap of self-reliance. It serves as a reminder that even the most skilled and capable individuals can encounter setbacks or unforeseen circumstances that can significantly impact their lives.

Sonic's attitude of relying solely on his speed and prowess is challenged by Saitama, urging him to consider the importance of strategy, adaptability, and humility. When we acknowledge our reliance on God's wisdom and providence, we can navigate the uncertainties of life with trust and humility, understanding that true success and fulfillment come through our relationship with Him.

"If you are too confident in your fighting style but lose, the result will always be the same." - Speed-o'-Sound Sonic

May 28

Affliction will slay the wicked, and those who hate the righteous will be condemned. Psalm 34:21

Passione Hitman

(JoJo's Bizarre Adventure)

Cioccolata's character and actions in JoJo's Bizarre Adventure showcase the depths of wickedness and cruelty. His sadistic nature and pleasure in inflicting pain on others reflect the darkness and corruption that can reside in the human heart. His cruel deeds and disregard for human life ultimately led to his own downfall and condemnation.

Psalm 34:21 offers us a reminder of the ultimate justice that awaits the wicked. This verse assures us that evil will not prevail and that the wicked will eventually face the consequences of their actions. We are called to examine our own hearts and ensure that we are not harbouring any tendencies towards wickedness or cruelty. Instead, we are encouraged to live according to God's principles of love, compassion, and justice.

The wicked deeds and sadistic nature of Cioccolata eventually catch up to him. The consequences of evil choices and actions will lead to the downfall and condemnation of those who perpetrate them. God brings comfort to the righteous, sees their struggles, and understands the injustices they may face. He will bring condemnation upon those who oppose righteousness and inflict harm upon others.

Cioccolata's circumstances, as portrayed in JoJo's Bizarre Adventure, prompt us to reflect on the darkness that can lurk within the human heart and emphasize the importance of seeking God's guidance and transforming our lives through His grace. It reminds us of the significance of living in accordance with God's principles, actively resisting wickedness, and striving for righteousness in all aspects of our lives.

"The more curious someone is, the stronger they become mentally. Humans are far more curious than any other creature, and that's why they evolved." - Cioccolata

May 29

So, whether you eat or drink, or whatever you do, do all to the glory of God. 1 Corinthians 10:31

Sound Five Leader

(Naruto)

Kimimaro's commitment in the Naruto anime, despite the questionable nature of Orochimaru's intentions, can be seen as an example of unwavering dedication and loyalty. He devotes himself entirely to Orochimaru's cause, prioritizing his goals and objectives above all else. Kimimaro's loyalty and commitment can be seen as a reflection of his faith in Orochimaru's plans and goals. In this sense, his commitment, although misplaced, demonstrates his willingness to sacrifice and give his all for a higher purpose.

The verse 1 Corinthians 10:31 calls believers to dedicate all aspects of their lives to the glory of God. It encourages individuals to align their actions, even in mundane activities like eating and drinking, with the overarching purpose of bringing glory to God. This verse emphasizes the idea that commitment should extend beyond specific religious activities and encompass every aspect of one's life.

While Kimimaro's commitment may not align with the teachings of the Bible due to Orochimaru's malevolent nature, we can still reflect on the idea of wholehearted devotion and commitment that he exemplifies. It serves as a reminder of the importance of dedicating ourselves to noble and righteous causes, seeking to bring glory to God in all that we do.

The commitment which Kimimaro demonstrates encourages us to evaluate the nature and objectives of our commitments, ensuring they align with God's will and bring Him glory. It reminds us of the transformative power of God's grace and the importance of discernment, avoiding idolatry, and utilizing our gifts for noble and righteous causes.

"Finding our purpose is the meaning. That's why we're here. And the ones who find it... They're the only ones who are truly free." - Kimimaro Kaguya

May 30

For as in one body, we have many members, and the members do not all have the same function, so we, though many, are one body in Christ, and individually members one of another. Romans 12:4-5

U.A. Homeroom Class

(My Hero Academia)

In the anime series My Hero Academia, we witness a group of young aspiring heroes attending U.A. High School to cultivate their abilities and become professional superheroes. Class 1-A represents a diverse group of students with unique Quirks, talents, and personalities. As the series progresses, their rankings evolve, with Deku and his classmates facing new challenges, growing stronger, and developing new techniques and mindsets.

Romans 12:4-5 encourages believers to recognize their belongingness to one another, fostering camaraderie and mutual support. Class 1-A exemplifies this by forging bonds, friendships, and a shared sense of belonging as they confront adversities together, underscoring the significance of teamwork and reliance on each other's strengths.

Class 1-A beautifully portrays the unity found within diversity. Each student brings forth distinct abilities and strengths, contributing to the overall prowess of the class. Similarly, as believers, we are called to recognize and appreciate the diverse gifts and talents present among fellow Christians. Learning from the example set by Class 1-A, we ought to value and respect the unique contributions of our brothers and sisters in Christ.

Reflecting upon Class 1-A from My Hero Academia serves as a reminder of the utmost importance of unity, diversity, collaboration, and servanthood within the Christian community. It prompts us to cherish the distinctive contributions of fellow believers, work harmoniously, and utilize our gifts for the glory of God and the betterment of others.

"Remember why you started down this path, and let that memory carry you beyond your limit." - All Might

May 31

No, in all these things we are more than conquerors through him who loved us. Romans 8:37

Half Elf's Knight

(Re: Zero)

Of all the heroes in the Re: Zero franchise, protagonist Subaru Natsuki is one of the weakest. Despite this, he displays great bravery as he faces his untimely death over and over. His journey is filled with trials, despair, and moments where he confronts his deepest fears. Despite facing countless setbacks, he continues to persevere and push forward. His courage lies in his refusal to be defeated by the challenges he encounters.

In a similar way, Romans 8:37 reminds believers that we are more than conquerors through Christ's love for us. It encourages us to face the trials and tribulations of life with unwavering determination, knowing that we are not alone in our struggles. By relying on Christ's love and strength, we can overcome any obstacle that comes our way.

Subaru demonstrates unwavering resolve, resilience, and courage to rise above his circumstances, refusing to be defined by his failures or setbacks. Similarly, we are called to embrace the truth that, through Christ's love and power, we are not merely survivors but conquerors in every aspect of life. Subaru's courage reminds us that our identity as believers goes beyond being mere survivors. We are called to live as conquerors, knowing that Christ has already secured the victory for us. Our courage stems from the understanding that we are deeply loved by God and empowered by His Spirit.

Subaru's courage in the anime inspires us to embrace our own challenges with boldness and confidence. It reminds us that, regardless of the difficulties we face, we have the assurance of victory through our faith in Christ. Like Subaru, we can find the courage to press on, knowing that we are more than conquerors through Him who loved us.

"Rely on those around you instead of thinking about stuff alone." - Subaru Natsuki

June 1

For everything there is a season, and a time for every matter under heaven. Ecclesiastes 3:1

Britannia's Greatest Sorcerer

(Seven Deadly Sins)

In the Seven Deadly Sins, Merlin demonstrates wisdom by understanding the importance of timing and choosing the right moment to reveal certain information. She recognizes that there is a season for everything, including when to disclose her true identity. By keeping her past hidden, she ensures that the timing is appropriate, considering the potential consequences and the impact it may have on her companions.

The verse from Ecclesiastes 3:1 reminds us that God has ordained specific seasons and times for every activity under heaven. It encourages us to trust in His divine plan and timing, even when it may seem counterintuitive to us. Just as Merlin exercised wisdom in choosing the appropriate time to reveal her true identity, we too are called to seek God's guidance and discernment in determining when to act, speak, or make significant decisions.

The decision of Merlin in the anime encourages us to trust in God's sovereignty and timing, even when it requires patience and the temporary withholding of information. It reminds us that our lives are in God's hands, and He orchestrates each season and moment for His purposes. By following His leading and exercising wisdom in discerning the appropriate time, we can navigate life's challenges and make decisions that align with His will.

Merlin understands the significance of revealing her identity at the right moment. Similarly, we should also seek God's guidance and exercise wisdom in discerning the appropriate timing for various aspects of our lives. By aligning ourselves with God's timing, we can navigate situations and make choices that align with God's greater purpose for our lives.

"Meaning can be found in something that appears meaningless, think, and find the answer for yourselves."
- Merlin

June 2

Let not steadfast love and faithfulness forsake you; bind them around your neck; write them on the tablet of your heart. So, you will find favour and good success in the sight of God and man. Proverbs 3:3-4

Hawk's Eye

(Fullmetal Alchemist: Brotherhood)

Riza Hawkeye exemplifies the essence of love and faithfulness through her unwavering commitment to Roy Mustang. Her actions are driven by a deep care for his well-being and a shared belief in their mission. Riza's love for Roy is not limited to personal affection but extends to her dedication to their shared ideals and the betterment of their country.

Proverbs 3:3-4 encourages us to let love and faithfulness be constant companions in our lives. Riza Hawkeye exemplifies this principle through her unwavering love and faithfulness towards Colonel Roy Mustang. As followers of Christ, we are called to reflect the love and faithfulness of God in our interactions with others.

In Fullmetal Alchemist: Brotherhood, Riza exercises wisdom in choosing the right moment to act or reveal certain information. She understands the significance of timing and aligning herself with a higher purpose. This echoes the biblical principle of seeking God's guidance and trusting in His timing. It reminds us that our lives are in God's hands, and by following His leading, we can navigate life's challenges and make decisions that align with His will.

Riza Hawkeye's devotion to Colonel Roy Mustang shows the importance of embodying love and faithfulness in our relationships. Her selfless love, unwavering commitment, and trust in God's timing inspire us to emulate these virtues in our own lives. By doing so, we reflect the character of Christ and fulfil His commandment to love one another, while also experiencing the favour and blessing that come from living in accordance with God's wisdom.

"Humankind cannot gain anything without first giving something in return." - Riza Hawkeye

June 3

For just as the body is one and has many members, and all the members of the body, though many, are one body, so it is with Christ. 1 Corinthians 12:12

The Forgers

(Spy x Family)

In spy x family, Twilight, also known as Loid, Yor, and Anya are unique individuals with distinct abilities and backgrounds. Twilight is a skilled spy, Yor is a formidable assassin, and Anya is an intelligent and perceptive young girl. While they may seem like separate entities, they come together to form a cohesive and functional family unit.

In the verse 1 Corinthians 12:12, the Apostle Paul uses the analogy of a body to describe the unity and interconnectedness of believers in Christ. Similarly, the Forger's family operates as a single unit despite their diverse roles. Moreover, the verse mentions that it is the same with Christ. This verse reminds believers that, as followers of Christ, they are part of a greater body, the Church. The Forger's family demonstrates unity and support for one another, mirroring the concept of a unified body of believers.

Just as the various parts of a body work together harmoniously, the Forger's family combines their different abilities to overcome challenges. Twilight's intelligence and strategic thinking, Yor's combat skills, and Anya's ability to gather information all play crucial roles in their missions. They understand that their individual contributions are essential and rely on each other's strengths for the family's well-being.

The Forger's family showcases the unity, collaboration, and interdependence of different parts working together towards a common goal, whether it's in the context of a physical body or a family unit. They recognize that their individual strengths are interconnected and necessary for achieving their shared goals. Similarly, we are encouraged to embrace our unique roles, collaborate purposefully, and foster unity in the family of believers.

"All people have a side of themselves they can't reveal to others" - Loid Forger

June 4

Fear not, therefore; you are of more value than many sparrows. Matthew 10:31

High School Madonna

(Komi Can't Communicate)

In Komi Can't Communicate, Shouko Komi is depicted as a character with social anxiety, which hinders her ability to communicate effectively with others. This social anxiety and fear of interacting with people stem from her desire to be understood and accepted. She worries about being judged, misunderstood, or rejected by others, which amplifies her fear.

The verse Matthew 10:31 is part of a larger passage where Jesus is encouraging his disciples, reassuring them of God's care and love for them. It emphasizes that humans are valued and significant to God, even more so than insignificant creatures like sparrows. Additionally, the verse reminds us that our identity and worth are not defined by the opinions or judgments of others. Rather, our value comes from being beloved children of God.

Shouko Komi's fear can be seen as a struggle that many people face in a broken world. It highlights the need for compassion, understanding, and acceptance within the Christian community and society at large. We are also called to support and encourage individuals who struggle with fear, just as Komi finds solace and support from her friends in the story. By extending a helping hand and creating a safe and accepting environment, we can play a role in helping others overcome their fears and find healing and restoration.

As we reflect on the fear experienced by Shouko Komi, we can find inspiration to extend love, grace, and understanding to those who struggle with social anxiety and fear. We can seek to create inclusive communities where individuals feel accepted and valued, reminding them of their worth in the eyes of God. Furthermore, we, as believers, can strive to overcome our own fears and trust in God's guidance and love, knowing that we are called to embrace and support those who face similar struggles.

"I think it's ok, even if I don't understand it" - Shouko Komi

June 5

Judge not, and you will not be judged; condemn not, and you will not be condemned; forgive, and you will be forgiven. Luke 6:37

Rookie Hunter

(Hunter x Hunter)

Gon Freecss, the main protagonist of Hunter x Hunter, exhibits a forgiving nature throughout the series, emphasizing his growth as a character. Despite Killua's troubled past and involvement with a notorious family of assassins, Gon befriends him without hesitation. He sees beyond Killua's history and values him as a loyal companion. Gon's forgiving nature allows him to form a deep bond with Killua and support him in his personal growth.

Luke 6:37 reminds believers to let go of judgment and condemnation, as these attitudes hinder the flow of forgiveness. By forgiving others, we open ourselves up to receiving forgiveness and experiencing liberation from the burdens of resentment and anger. The verse serves as a reminder that forgiveness is not solely an act of kindness towards others but also a means of personal transformation.

Gon's forgiveness challenges us to embrace forgiveness as a means of fostering reconciliation and personal growth. His forgiveness reminds us of the radical love and forgiveness exemplified by Jesus Christ. His sacrifice on the cross paved the way for the forgiveness of our sins and reconciliation with God. Through His teachings, Jesus calls us to follow His example, extending forgiveness to others as we ourselves have been forgiven.

Gon's ability to forgive reflects the transformative power of extending grace and mercy to others, aligning with the biblical principle of forgiving as the Lord has forgiven us. By reflecting on his journey, we are encouraged to live out forgiveness as an expression of Christ's love, allowing it to shape our attitudes, actions, and relationships.

"You can do whatever you want to hide your feelings...you still have a heart." - Gon Freecss

June 6

Above all, keep loving one another earnestly, since love covers a multitude of sins. Show hospitality to one another without grumbling.1 Peter 4:8

Deadly Sin Duo

(Seven Deadly Sins)

The friendship of Meliodas and Ban in the anime Seven Deadly Sins is marked by unwavering loyalty and acceptance of each other, despite their past mistakes and flaws. They exemplify the transformative power of love and forgiveness as they continually extend grace and understanding to one another, even in challenging circumstances.

1 Peter 4:8 encourages believers to love one another deeply because love covers a multitude of sins. When we observe the friendship between Meliodas and Ban, we witness a profound example of this deep love and forgiveness in action. It reminds us to love our friends deeply, without judgment or condemnation, just as Christ loves us. Their friendship challenges us to look beyond the surface-level flaws of our friends and extend grace and forgiveness, knowing that we too have received God's forgiveness.

Furthermore, their friendship serves as a reminder of the redemptive nature of love. Meliodas and Ban's bond becomes a source of healing and restoration for both of them. Through their connection, they find strength, support, and the ability to overcome their personal struggles. It reflects the power of godly friendships in aiding our spiritual growth and helping us become better individuals.

The friendship of Meliodas and Ban compels us to extend grace, understanding, and forgiveness to our friends, even when they fall short. Their friendship also reflects the profound love and forgiveness that Christ has shown us. It inspires us to embody these qualities in our own friendships, showcasing the transformative power of God's love in our lives and the lives of others.

"No matter how much you bleed and even if your tears run dry, you stick to it." - Meliodas

June 7

But the fruit of the Spirit is love, joy, peace, patience, kindness, goodness, faithfulness, gentleness, self-control; against such things there is no law. Galatians 5:22-23

Lightning Mage

(Fairy Tail)

In the Fairy Tail anime, Laxus Dreyar is driven by a thirst for power and seeks validation through dominance. However, as he undergoes character development, he learns the value of love and friendship, developing genuine care and concern for his fellow guild members. He experiences joy in the bonds he forms and the support he receives from his friends. He learns forbearance, becoming more patient and understanding towards others.

The verse from Galatians 5:22-23 describes the qualities that are produced in a person's life through the work of the Holy Spirit. This verse serves as a reminder that true growth involves the transformation of character, allowing the fruit of the Spirit to manifest in one's life. Laxus's journey reflects this transformation as he evolves into a more compassionate, selfless, and emotionally balanced character throughout the Fairy Tail anime.

Laxus demonstrates kindness and goodness as he protects and supports his friends, showing acts of selflessness and compassion. He becomes more faithful, not only to the guild but also to the principles of camaraderie and teamwork. He develops gentleness in his interactions, showing a softer side that he once kept hidden. Lastly, he gains self-control over his pride and anger, learning to channel his power responsibly.

The transformation of Laxus Dreyar in Fairy Tail inspires us to embrace the transformative power of the Spirit as we strive to manifest the fruit of the Spirit in our own lives. We are called to display love, joy, peace, forbearance, kindness, goodness, faithfulness, gentleness, and self-control to bring glory to God and bless those around us.

"Open your eyes it's easy to see... just take your time and look around you. Never forget that this is a beautiful world." - Laxus Dreyar

June 8

Go, eat your bread with joy, and drink your wine with a merry heart, for God has already approved what you do.
Ecclesiastes 9:7

Culinar y School Student

(Food Wars!)

Sōma Yukihira's happiness in Food Wars is deeply intertwined with his love for food and cooking. He approaches each dish with enthusiasm, creativity, and a desire to bring delight to those who taste his creations. He takes pleasure in the process of preparing meals, experimenting with flavours, and presenting his dishes in unique and appealing ways.

Ecclesiastes 9:7 encourages individuals to savour the enjoyment of food and drink. It reminds us that God approves of and delights in our appreciation of His provisions. Sōma embraces the opportunity to explore different ingredients, techniques, and cuisines, always seeking to create memorable and satisfying dining experiences. He embodies the spirit of relishing food and drink with gladness, recognizing that God's approval is found in the pursuit of our passions and the joy we bring to others through our talents.

Sōma's happiness in cooking can be seen as a reflection of his gratitude for the gifts and talents he possesses. He recognizes that cooking is not merely a task but a form of artistry and self-expression. His happiness in the kitchen extends beyond his personal enjoyment. His joy is multiplied when he can share his food with others and witness their delight. Through his culinary creations, he brings people together, fosters connections, and creates moments of happiness and enjoyment for those who partake in his meals.

By following Sōma Yukihira's example, we are reminded to approach the gifts and pleasures God has given us with gladness, recognizing that they are ultimately a reflection of His goodness and love. As we find happiness in our pursuits, we are called to use them to honor God, foster relationships, and spread joy in the world around us.

"The journey is no fun if you know where you are going." -
Sōma Yukihira

June 9

Do your best to present yourself to God as one approved, a worker who has no need to be ashamed, rightly handling the word of truth. 2 Timothy 2:15

Japanese Hawk

(Hajime no Ippo)

Mamoru Takamura from the anime Hajime no Ippo demonstrates unwavering commitment and an unrelenting work ethic in his pursuit of becoming a skilled and respected boxer. His dedication to his craft serves as an inspiration for us as believers, reminding us of the importance of giving our best in all areas of our lives.

The verse from 2 Timothy encourages believers to do their best in their pursuits, not only for their own sake but also to honor God. Furthermore, the verse emphasizes the importance of correctly handling the word of truth. While Takamura's dedication is focused on his boxing career, the principle can be extended to our lives as well. It reminds us to align our actions and attitudes with the truth of God's word, ensuring that our hard work is in line with His principles and values.

Takamura's hard work reflects his desire to honor God through the use of his talents and opportunities. Just as he strives to offer his best efforts in the boxing ring, we are called to offer our best to God in everything we do. Whether it is in our careers, relationships, or service to others, our work should be driven by a desire to bring glory to God and serve as a testimony of His grace in our lives.

By relating Mamoru Takamura's hard work in Hajime no Ippo, we are reminded of the importance of diligently pursuing excellence, handling the truth of God's word with care, and striving to present ourselves as approved workers who bring glory to Him in all that we do.

"It's way harder when someone is supremely more talented. But at the end it doesn't matter because even then you're still based and judged on the results you produce, regardless of your starting point." - Mamoru Takamura

June 10

Lying lips are an abomination to the Lord, but those who act faithfully are his delight. Proverbs 12:22

Child of Brightness

(Demon Slayer)

Tanjiro Kamado's character in the Demon Slayer anime consistently upholds the value of truthfulness and displays integrity in his words and actions. He speaks truthfully, keeps his promises, and holds steadfast to his beliefs and values. His commitment to honesty extends even to difficult situations, where he chooses to confront the truth rather than resorting to deception. Tanjiro's unwavering dedication to the truth reflects his desire to do what is right and to honor the values he holds dear. His commitment to honesty reflects a deep respect for the principles of righteousness and aligns with God's desire for His people to be trustworthy.

Proverbs 12:22 emphasizes God's detestation of lying and His delight in those who are trustworthy. Our words and actions should reflect a commitment to truth, both in our interactions with others and in our relationship with God. By being trustworthy and truthful, we honor God and foster an environment of trust, authenticity, and righteousness in our lives.

Tanjiro's commitment to honesty aligns with God's heart as he strives to embody the virtue of truthfulness. By exemplifying trustworthiness, he reflects God's character and brings delight to Him. Through his character, we are reminded of the importance of being trustworthy individuals who reflect God's delight and bring honor to His name.

In a world where dishonesty often prevails, the example of Tanjiro Kamado encourages us to stand firm in our commitment to truth. By embracing honesty and integrity, we reflect God's delight and strive to create a culture of trust and righteousness. Let us, like Tanjiro, be known as people who are trustworthy and honor God with our words and actions.

"Life can be as fickle as the weather. Constantly changing, never stagnating. It won't always stay sunny, but snowfall doesn't last forever either." - Tanjiro Kamado

June 11

But they who wait for the Lord shall renew their strength; they shall mount up with wings like eagles; they shall run and not be weary; they shall walk and not faint. Isaiah 40:31

Air bending Instructor

(Avatar: The Last Airbender)

Avatar Aang is yet another animated protagonist who will never give in to despair or give up on the people who need him. He is burdened with the responsibility of restoring balance to the world and ending the war. Despite the challenges he faces, he maintains hope in the future and believes in the potential for a better world. He trusts in the greater purpose and plan set before him, knowing that his actions will ultimately lead to a brighter future.

The verse Isaiah 40:31 assures us that when we place our hope in the Lord, our strength is renewed. It speaks of soaring on wings like eagles, running without growing weary, and walking without fainting. This verse speaks to the transformative power of hope in God, empowering us to rise above our circumstances and endure with resilience.

Aang embraces his role as the Avatar and trusts that his actions will contribute to a better world. He finds strength, courage, and perseverance through his connection with the spiritual world and his unwavering faith. When we place our hope in the Lord, we experience a renewal of strength that transcends our human limitations. We find the ability to soar above our circumstances, run the race of life without growing weary, and walk with steadfast faith, knowing that God is with us.

The story of Avatar Aang in the anime reminds us that hope in the Lord is not passive or futile; it is an active and transformative force. By placing our hope in God, we tap into His unlimited power and receive the strength, courage, and endurance needed to face life's challenges. We are reminded to trust in His promises, knowing that He is faithful to renew our strength and guide us through every step of our journey.

"When we hit our lowest point, we are open to the greatest change." - Avatar Aang

June 12

The reward for humility and fear of the Lord is riches and honor and life. Proverbs 22:4

Wizard King

(Black Clover)

Julius Novachrono from the anime Black Clover exemplifies humility through his leadership and character. Despite being one of the most powerful mages in the Clover Kingdom, he remains humble and respectful towards others. He doesn't boast about his abilities or use his power to dominate others, but instead, he uses his strength to protect and guide his kingdom.

Proverbs 22:4 highlights the connection between humility and the fear of the Lord. It teaches us that humility, which stems from the fear of the Lord, leads to blessings and honor. By humbling ourselves before God and recognizing His sovereignty, we open ourselves up to His abundant provision, spiritual riches, and a life lived in alignment with His will. Julius exemplifies this by acknowledging the spiritual realm and the higher power at work in his role as the Magic Emperor. He approaches his responsibilities with reverence and humility, recognizing that his authority and abilities are ultimately derived from God.

Julius's humility enriches his own life. It opens him up to the wisdom and guidance of God, allowing him to make sound decisions and lead with integrity. His humility also fosters a spirit of selflessness, making him more aware of the needs of others and enabling him to bring positive change to the world around him.

As we reflect on Julius Novachrono's humility, we are reminded of the transformative power of humility in our own lives. By humbling ourselves before God, acknowledging His authority, we can experience the richness, honor, and fulfillment that come from walking in humility. Julius's example challenges us to cultivate a humble heart, allowing God to work through us for the betterment of others and the advancement of His kingdom.

"You can't protect others with pride, and the trust of others comes with merit." - Julius Novachrono

June 13

Beware of the leaven of the Pharisees, which is hypocrisy.
Luke 12:1

Shinobi of Darkness

(Naruto)

Danzō Shimura, a character from Naruto, presents himself as a loyal and dedicated leader, but his actions behind the scenes contradict this image. He manipulates events, betrays trust, and pursues his personal agenda while claiming to act in the best interest of the village. His hypocrisy damages relationships and undermines trust and unity within the community.

Luke 12:1 serves as a warning from Jesus to be on guard against the leaven of the Pharisees, which refers to hypocrisy. The verse reminds us to be vigilant, continually assessing our thoughts, attitudes, and behaviours. We must guard against the subtle infiltration of hypocrisy into our lives and strive for sincerity and authenticity. This requires aligning our inner convictions with our outward actions, ensuring that our words and deeds reflect the love and truth of Christ.

Danzō Shimura's example challenges us to examine our hearts and actions. As Christians, we are called to live lives of authenticity and integrity, reflecting the character of Christ. Hypocrisy goes against the essence of our faith, which is built on truth, love, and genuine transformation. When we succumb to hypocrisy, we tarnish the name of Christ and hinder our witness to the world.

The hypocrisy of Danzō Shimura encourages us to be mindful and discerning, avoiding the allure of hypocrisy, and pursuing lives characterized by genuine faith, integrity, and sincerity. By living with transparency and integrity, we bear witness to the transformative power of the gospel. We become instruments of God's grace and truth in the world, shining a light in the midst of darkness. Let us heed Jesus' warning, be on guard against hypocrisy, and allow His Spirit to shape us into people of genuine faith and consistent character.

"Emotion leads one to hate... and hate leads one to conflict and war." - Danzō Shimura

June 14

Love is patient and kind; love does not envy or boast; it is not arrogant. 1 Corinthians 13:4

Mechanical Soldier

(Black Bullet)

Rentaro's character exhibits kindness in various ways throughout the Black Bullet series. He shows compassion and empathy towards those who are suffering or marginalized, and goes out of his way to help and protect them. Despite facing numerous challenges and dangers, he maintains a kind heart and seeks to bring comfort and hope to those around him.

The verse from 1 Corinthians describes love as being patient and kind. Rentaro's kindness reflects this patience. He remains calm and understanding even in difficult circumstances, taking the time to listen and empathize with others. As Christians, we are called to imitate the love of Christ. This challenges us to examine our own hearts and actions, urging us to cultivate a love that is patient, kind, and selfless.

Rentaro's character is characterized by genuine care and concern for the well-being of others. His actions consistently reflect a selfless love that seeks the good of those around him. Whether it is protecting the weak, offering encouragement, or providing a helping hand, Rentaro shines brightly as a beacon of hope. His kindness is also free from envy, boasting, and pride. He does not seek personal gain or recognition through his acts of kindness. Instead, his focus is solely on the well-being and happiness of others. His humility allows his kindness to flow naturally, without any ulterior motives.

In a world where selfishness and self-centeredness often prevail, Rentaro's kindness reminds us of the transformative power of love. It encourages us to extend kindness to those around us, regardless of their circumstances or background. By embodying love, we can make a positive impact in the lives of others and reflect the love of Christ to a world in need.

"Just what is right and what is wrong? To begin with, just who is the enemy I must defeat?" - Rentaro Satomi

June 15

Beloved, let us love one another, for love is from God, and whoever loves has been born of God and knows God. 1 John 4:7

Humanoid Heroine

(My Hero Academia)

Mina Ashido's love in My Hero Academia reflects agape love, which is selfless and unconditional, originating from God. Her love is not based on personal gain or convenience but is freely given to others, regardless of their circumstances or background. Similarly, the love that comes from God is offered to everyone without discrimination or favouritism.

In 1 John 4:7, believers are encouraged to show love and compassion towards one another, emphasizing that love originates from God. This verse emphasizes that love is not merely a sentiment but a tangible expression of care and concern for others. When we allow God's love to flow through us, it brings about a positive change in our interactions with others and enhances their well-being.

The actions of Mina Ashido reflect the active nature of love. Love is not meant to be a passive feeling but rather an active force that drives us to show compassion and kindness towards others. Mina actively seeks out opportunities to help and support her friends, going the extra mile to make a positive impact in their lives. This challenges us to examine how we can actively demonstrate love in practical ways in our own lives.

By observing Mina Ashido's character, we are reminded of the importance of embodying God's love in our interactions with others. Just as Mina's love brings joy, unity, and encouragement, our love should reflect the transformative power of God's love, creating an atmosphere of acceptance, compassion, and unity. As followers of Christ, we are called to love one another selflessly and unconditionally, following the example of His love for us.

"Whether you win or lose... you can always come out ahead by learning from the experience." - All Might

June 16

For by grace, you have been saved through faith. And this is not your own doing; it is the gift of God, not a result of works, so that no one may boast. Ephesians 2:8-9

Black Wizard

(Fairy Tail)

Zeref Dragneel from Fairy Tail epitomizes the human struggle with sin and guilt. He embodies the challenges faced by a deeply troubled and burdened character who seeks redemption and salvation. Throughout his journey, he wrestles with the weight of his past actions and the consequences they have brought upon himself and others. He yearns for a way to break free from the cycle of darkness and find forgiveness.

Ephesians 2:8-9 reminds us that salvation is not something we can earn or achieve through our own efforts. It is solely by the grace of God that we are saved. It emphasizes that our own actions or merits cannot bring about redemption, but rather it is through faith in God's grace that we receive salvation. This verse also highlights the humbling aspect of salvation; no one can boast about their own efforts or accomplishments when it comes to being saved.

Zeref's relentless pursuit of redemption reflects the futility of relying on one's own works or abilities to obtain salvation or forgiveness. His quest for forgiveness and freedom aligns with the truth that salvation is a gift bestowed upon us through God's grace. Zeref's struggles and search for forgiveness also teach us the importance of humility and recognizing our desperate need for God's mercy and grace.

By contemplating Zeref's life in Fairy Tail, we are reminded of the central message of the gospel. Salvation is a gift of God's grace, which is received through faith in Jesus Christ. Zeref's struggles and quest for redemption serve as a poignant reminder of our own need for God's saving grace and the transformative power of His forgiveness.

"There are things in this world that you cannot oppose, no matter how hard you try." - Zeref Dragneel

June 17

Take care, and be on your guard against all covetousness, for one's life does not consist in the abundance of his possessions. Luke 12:15

Cat Burglar

(One Piece)

In One Piece, Nami's materialistic nature is evident in her relentless pursuit of wealth, treasures, and financial security. She often prioritizes the accumulation of material possessions above all else, believing that they hold the key to happiness and security. While she initially joins Luffy's crew for her own personal gain, she evolves throughout the series.

In light of Luke 12:15, we are called to shift our focus from the accumulation of possessions to cultivating a heart of contentment, gratitude, and generosity. This challenges us to seek treasures that have eternal significance, such as love, compassion, and acts of service. By detaching ourselves from the grip of materialism, we can discover the joy and freedom that comes from finding our true worth and security in our relationship with God.

Nami's pursuit of material possessions often leads to a sense of emptiness and dissatisfaction. Her actions demonstrate the temporary nature of worldly treasures and the insatiable appetite that materialism can create within us. It reminds us that placing our hope and identity solely in material wealth can never truly satisfy the deepest longings of our hearts.

Nami's materialistic tendencies can serve as a reminder for us to be mindful of our own desires for material wealth and to strive for a balanced perspective. It encourages us to prioritize the values of God's kingdom, investing in relationships, personal growth, and spiritual well-being. By aligning our hearts with God's purposes and seeking His kingdom above all else, we can find genuine fulfillment and experience a life that transcends the temporary allure of material possessions.

"Life is like a pencil that will surely run out, but will leave the beautiful writing of life." - Nami

June 18

Do not be slothful in zeal, be fervent in spirit, serve the Lord. Romans 12:11

Red Pineapple

(Bleach)

In the Bleach series, Renji's motivation stems from his deep sense of loyalty and commitment to his friends and the Soul Society. He demonstrates unwavering fervour in his determination to protect them and fulfil his duty as a Soul Reaper. Renji also displays great zeal in his training and battles, constantly pushing himself to improve and serve his cause.

The verse Romans 12:11 encourages us to never lack in zeal and to maintain our spiritual fervour. This means approaching our relationship with God and our responsibilities as disciples with enthusiasm and passion. We should have a fervent desire to grow in our faith, protect and care for our spiritual family, and fulfil the purposes God has for us.

Renji's character challenges us to reflect on our own level of zeal and fervour in our Christian walk. His determination and perseverance in the face of challenges remind us of the importance of pressing on in our faith journey. Just as he never gives up, even when faced with formidable foes, we should not grow weary or be discouraged in our pursuit of a deeper relationship with God. Our zeal and fervour should fuel us to overcome obstacles and continue serving the Lord with passion and determination.

Relating to Renji's motivation, we are reminded of the importance of remaining zealous, passionate, and engaged in our faith. It prompts us to examine whether we are truly serving the Lord wholeheartedly or if we have become complacent or apathetic. Renji's motivation serves as a reminder that our faith journey should be marked by fervour, enthusiasm, and wholehearted commitment. It challenges us to evaluate our level of zeal and encourages us to pursue spiritual growth and service with passion. By doing so, we can more fully live out our calling as disciples of Christ and bring glory to God through our lives.

"It's easier to crush a dream than realize one." - Gin Ichimaru

June 19

The sacrifices of God are a broken spirit; a broken and contrite heart, O God, you will not despise. Psalm 51:17

Crystal Alchemist

(Fullmetal Alchemist: Brotherhood)

Dr. Tim Marcoh from Fullmetal Alchemist: Brotherhood experiences deep pain and remorse for his past actions as a State Alchemist. He was involved in conducting unethical experiments and developing destructive weapons, causing immense suffering and loss of life. Over time, he becomes burdened by guilt and seeks redemption for his past deeds.

Psalm 51:17 teaches us that God does not despise a broken and contrite heart; instead, He welcomes it. This reveals God's desire for true repentance and sincere acknowledgement of our sins. This verse also reminds us that our sacrifices to God are not in the form of material offerings but rather in the form of a broken spirit and a contrite heart. It is through genuine repentance and a humble attitude that we find favour in His sight.

Dr. Marcoh's story reflects the broader theme of redemption present in the Bible. Despite his past actions, he seeks to rectify the wrongs he committed and uses his knowledge for good. This echoes the transformative work of God's grace as He takes broken and flawed individuals and moulds them into instruments of His love and righteousness.

In contemplating the pain of Dr. Tim Marcoh, we are called to examine our own hearts and confront the areas in our lives where we have fallen short. It encourages us to approach God with sincerity and humility, trusting in His forgiveness and the healing power of His grace. Through repentance, we can experience the restoration of our relationship with God and be empowered to live transformed lives, serving Him and others with renewed purpose and compassion. Dr. Marcoh's journey towards repentance reminds us of the profound impact of genuine contrition and the boundless love and mercy of our Heavenly Father.

"How can you move forward if you keep regretting the past." - Edward Elric

June 20

For you have need of endurance, so that when you have done the will of God you may receive what is promised.
Hebrews 10:36

Antagonist Angel

(Angel Beats!)

Throughout the anime series Angel Beats, Kanade Tachibana displays an exceptional degree of patience. Despite finding herself in a mysterious afterlife school, with fragmented memories and uncertain circumstances, she remains resolute in her purpose. Her patience is evident as she diligently carries out her duties as the student council president and seeks to understand the truth of her existence.

In Hebrews 10:36, believers are encouraged to endure and remain patient in their faith journey, trusting in God's promises. This endurance and patience are essential for us as we navigate the challenges and trials of life, striving to align ourselves with God's will. We are called to patiently persevere in our faith, even when faced with uncertainty and adversity. Kanade's patience serves as a reminder that the journey of faith requires trust in God's timing and purposes, even when circumstances are unclear or challenging.

The patience of Kanade Tachibana is also displayed in her interactions with others. She often demonstrates kindness and understanding, taking the time to listen and support her fellow students. This aspect of her character reflects the Christian value of patience in relationships, as believers are encouraged to bear with one another, extend grace, and demonstrate love even in difficult circumstances.

Kanade's character can serve as a source of inspiration for us, encouraging us to cultivate patience in our faith, trusting in God's timing and persevering through challenges, as we strive to live out His will and experience the rewards, He has prepared for us.

"We have no choice but to accept the one and only life we're given, no matter how cruel and heartless it might be." - Yuri Nakamura

June 21

Be watchful, stand firm in the faith, act like men, be strong. 1 Corinthians 16:13

Volley Ball Captain

(Haikyu!!)

In the volleyball anime Haikyu, Daichi Sawamura faces tremendous peer pressure as the captain of the Karasuno High School volleyball team. He encounters opponents who constantly challenge him, teammates who look up to him, and the weight of expectations to lead his team to victory. His journey can be seen as a reflection of the challenges we face in our own lives when confronted with peer pressure.

The verse 1 Corinthians 16:13 begins with the call to be watchful. We are called to be aware of the world's values and ideologies that may conflict with our faith. By being on guard, we can discern when peer pressure seeks to divert us from God's truth. The next exhortation in the verse is to stand firm in the faith, encouraging us to hold steadfast in our belief in Christ. Additionally, the verse urges us to be courageous and strong. When faced with peer pressure, it requires courage and strength to remain faithful to our convictions.

As a captain, Daichi was mindful of the strategies and tactics employed by opposing teams. His commitment to his team and the sport of volleyball provides an analogy to standing firm in our faith as Christians. Just as he remains resolute in leading his team to success, we are encouraged to stand firm in our belief in Christ.

By reflecting on Daichi's experiences, we can learn important lessons. We are reminded to be vigilant and discerning, aware of the influences that may lead us astray. We are called to be courageous and strong, relying on God's power and grace to overcome the pressures that come our way. Like Daichi, we can overcome peer pressure, remaining steadfast in our beliefs and shining as a light in the world, living out our faith with courage and strength.

"Even if we're not confident that we'll win, even if others tell us we don't stand a chance, we must never tell ourselves that." - Daichi Sawamura

June 22

He gives power to the faint, and to him who has no might he increases strength. Isaiah 40:29

Gourmet Hunter

(Toriko)

In the world of Toriko, the protagonist possesses incredible physical power and culinary prowess. He showcases immense strength, allowing him to overcome formidable challenges and adversaries. This power is a central aspect of Toriko's character and plays a significant role in his journey to discover rare ingredients and become a renowned gourmet hunter.

Isaiah 40:29 invites us to recognize our dependence on God's strength. It calls us to acknowledge our limitations, weariness, or weaknesses and to turn to God for renewal and empowerment. Furthermore, this verse encourages us to seek God's strength when we face challenges in life. We may encounter physical, emotional, or spiritual obstacles that leave us feeling weary or weak. However, Scripture assures us that God is ready to provide the strength we need. He is there to uplift us, grant us endurance, and empower us to overcome any adversity we may face.

Just as Toriko relies on his incredible power to face formidable adversaries, we are encouraged to recognize that our true strength lies in our relationship with God. It is through His strength that we can face life's challenges, overcome obstacles, and accomplish the tasks set before us. Our own abilities and power have limits, but with God's empowerment and guidance, we can overcome obstacles and achieve great things.

The power of Toriko serves as a reminder of our reliance on God's strength. By seeking His power and aligning our abilities with His will, we can become vessels for His work in the world. We must always remember that our true strength lies in Him, and through Him, we can accomplish great things for His glory.

"As long as you never stop walking forward, all there is... is growth!" - Toriko

June 23

As for the rich in this present age, charge them not to be haughty, nor to set their hopes on the uncertainty of riches, but on God, who richly provides us with everything to enjoy. 1 Timothy 6:17

145th King

(Attack On Titan)

In Attack on Titan, Karl Fritz's pride and arrogance are evident in his actions as the ruler of the Fritz royal family. He places his trust and hope in his own authority and the wealth he possesses. His pride blinds him to the true source of fulfillment and leads him down a path of self-centeredness and oppression.

The verse 1 Timothy 6:17 advises those who are rich in this present age not to be haughty or arrogant, and not to set their hopes on the uncertainty of riches. Instead, it calls them to place their hope in God, who is the ultimate source of provision and enjoyment. As followers of Christ, we are called to cultivate humility, recognizing that everything we have is ultimately a gift from God.

Karl Fritz's pride led him to rely on his own authority and wealth, neglecting the true source of fulfillment and security found in a relationship with God. His arrogance blinded him to the needs of others and resulted in the oppression and suffering of countless individuals within the Attack on Titan storyline.

Reflecting on Karl Fritz's pride prompts us to examine our own hearts and attitudes toward wealth and power. It encourages us to seek contentment in God, using our resources and abilities for His purposes and the well-being of others. True fulfillment and security come from placing our hope in God in all aspects of our lives. Ultimately, our true value and significance lie not in the accumulation of wealth or power, but in our relationship with God and our commitment to living out His love and grace in our interactions with others.

"You can't change anything unless you can discard part of yourself too." - Armin Arlert

June 24

I am the good shepherd. The good shepherd lays down his life for the sheep. John 10:11

Crazy Slots Nen-user

(Hunter x Hunter)

Kite from the anime Hunter x Hunter exhibits traits that align with the sacrificial nature of a saviour. He acts as a mentor and protector for Gon, the main protagonist, guiding him and shielding him from harm. Kite's unwavering dedication to Gon's well-being and growth echoes the selflessness and bravery required to guide and protect others, just as Jesus laid down his life for the salvation of humanity.

In John 10:11, Jesus emphasizes His willingness to lay down His life for His sheep, signifying His ultimate act of sacrificial love. Similarly, Kite's guidance and protection of Gon symbolize the role of Jesus as our shepherd. Jesus, the Good Shepherd, leads and protects us, nurturing our spiritual growth and guiding us along the right path. Kite's relationship with Gon reflects the care and guidance that Jesus provides to His followers.

Kite's role as a saviour figure in Hunter x Hunter allows us to recognize the importance of having someone who selflessly sacrifices themselves for our benefit. It serves as a reminder of Jesus' sacrificial love on the cross, where He gave His life to save us from sin and offer eternal life. Kite puts himself in danger and risks his own life to ensure the safety and progress of Gon. This parallel invites us to reflect on the profound love and sacrifice that Jesus made for humanity's salvation.

As we contemplate Kite's character, we are encouraged to appreciate and embrace Jesus as our ultimate saviour. Just as Kite's actions show his love and sacrifice for Gon, Jesus' sacrifice on the cross demonstrates His incomparable love for us. We can find comfort and assurance in knowing that Jesus, the Good Shepherd, is always there to guide, protect, and lay down His life for us, offering us salvation and eternal life.

"If you aren't satisfied, then all the more reason to become stronger." - Kite

June 25

I appeal to you therefore, brothers, by the mercies of God, to present your bodies as a living sacrifice, holy and acceptable to God, which is your spiritual worship.
Romans 12:1

Mechanically Modified Elder

(Inuyashiki)

Ichirō Inuyashiki was always the unlikely hero in the anime Inuyashiki, but he shows from the very beginning that he is an honest hero. Despite facing a life of being unappreciated and unfair circumstances, he remained committed to protecting the lives of others. The anime concludes with his ultimate sacrifice, where he selflessly chooses to destroy a meteor heading towards Earth, which posed a threat to humanity.

The verse in Romans 12 encourages believers to present their bodies as living sacrifices. It challenges us to align our lives with God's will, seeking to serve and bless others with the gifts and abilities we have been given. It also calls us to surrender our lives, desires, and ambitions to God, dedicating ourselves wholly to His purposes. This act of surrender is seen as an act of worship where we acknowledge God's mercy and respond with selfless devotion.

Ichirō's sacrifice also serves as a reminder of the ultimate sacrifice made by Jesus on the cross. Just as Jesus laid down His life for the salvation of humanity, Ichirō lays down his own safety and comfort for the sake of others. This parallel invites us to reflect on the immeasurable love and sacrifice of Jesus and how His sacrifice serves as the ultimate example of selflessness and redemption.

As we contemplate Ichirō's character and his sacrificial acts in Inuyashiki, we are challenged to examine our own lives and consider how we can follow his example. It calls us to a life of selfless devotion, recognizing God's mercy and responding with wholehearted dedication to His service. Through our sacrificial acts of love and service, we can reflect the character of Christ and bring glory to God.

"Death is what makes life so precious and dear to us." - Ichirō Inuyashiki

June 26

Fear not, for I have redeemed you; I have called you by name, you are mine. Isaiah 43:1

Revolver Toting Sorcerer

(Jujutsu Kaisen)

In the story of Jujutsu Kaisen, Mai Zenin, unlike her confident sister Maki, struggles with low self-esteem and bitterness due to the prejudice and rejection from their family. She feels unworthy of being a sorcerer and lacks faith in her own powers, despite her arrogant facade. Mai's insecurities lead her to envy her sister and hide her true feelings. She often battles feelings of inadequacy and a sense of worthlessness due to her family's expectations and her perceived lack of strength.

Isaiah 43:1 reminds us that our worth is not determined by our abilities or the opinions of others. Instead, our true value comes from being created and loved by God. We can find solace in the knowledge that God has created us uniquely and purposefully, and He has redeemed us through the sacrifice of Jesus Christ. We are called by name, chosen, and cherished by God Himself.

Mai Zenin's self-esteem is characterized by deep-seated feelings of inadequacy and worthlessness. To mask her insecurities, Mai adopts an arrogant facade, but internally, she harbors bitterness and envy toward her own sister Maki. Her journey in Jujutsu Kaisen involves grappling with these self-esteem issues and finding ways to overcome them, ultimately discovering her own value and embracing her true self.

When reflecting on Mai Zenin's self-esteem journey in Jujutsu Kaisen, we are reminded of the powerful truth that our worth as individuals is not based on our accomplishments or the opinions of others. Instead, our true value lies in being created and loved by God, who calls us by name. This understanding can guide us to overcome self-esteem issues and live confidently, embracing our identity as cherished children of God.

"Searching for someone to blame is just a pain." - Gojo Satoru

June 27

For all have sinned and fall short of the glory of God.
Romans 3:23

Next New Hitler

(Monster)

Johan Liebert, the antagonist in the anime series Monster, embodies a complex and deeply sinful nature. His actions and manipulation throughout the series reveal a sinister and destructive character. Johan commits various sins, including murder, manipulation, and the destruction of lives. His malevolent intentions and disregard for the sanctity of human life highlight the depths of his wickedness.

In Romans 3:23, we are reminded of the reality that no one can save themselves or earn their way into God's favour. We all need God's grace and forgiveness. Through the sacrifice of Jesus Christ on the cross, God offers redemption and reconciliation to all who believe in Him. Johan Liebert's sins prompt us to reflect on our own need for forgiveness and the transformative power of God's grace. They also deepen our appreciation for the magnitude of God's love, demonstrated through Jesus' sacrifice.

Johan's sins are particularly abhorrent because they involve the deliberate taking of innocent lives, often with calculated planning and manipulation. His actions reflect a complete disregard for the sanctity of human life and a desire for power and control. He uses deceit and manipulation to further his own agenda, causing immense suffering and pain to those around him. His sins highlight the darkness and brokenness that can exist within the human heart. They also expose the need for redemption and transformation.

Reflecting on the sin of Johan Liebert from the anime highlights the universal nature of sin and the need for God's grace and redemption. It reminds us of our own fallenness and the transformative power of Christ's sacrifice. It prompts us to approach our own shortcomings with humility and gratitude, seeking forgiveness and extending compassion to others.

"How weak the mind is when it wants to forget." - Johan Liebert

June 28

But they soon forgot his works; they did not wait for his counsel. But they had a wanton craving in the wilderness, and put God to the test in the desert; he gave them what they asked, but sent a wasting disease among them. Psalm 106:13-15

Power-Hungry Vampire

(JoJo's Bizarre Adventure)

Dio Brando's character in JoJo's Bizarre Adventure is marked by ambition, selfishness, and a constant desire for power. He is never satisfied with what he has and is always seeking more. This insatiable hunger for control leads him to make destructive choices and harm those around him. In a way, Dio Brando embodies the ungratefulness and discontentment that the Israelites displayed in the wilderness.

Psalm 106:13-15 describes how the Israelites quickly forgot God's works, lusted after worldly desires, and tested God's patience. Despite their ungratefulness, God still provided for their needs. However, the consequences of their unappreciative attitudes were spiritual emptiness and dissatisfaction. As believers in Christ, we are called to live lives of gratitude, recognizing and appreciating God's blessings and provisions.

The lack of gratitude and constant pursuit of power by Dio Brando lead to his downfall and a sense of spiritual emptiness. He never finds true fulfillment because his focus is solely on his own desires and ambitions, disregarding the blessings and opportunities around him. Dio Brando's ungratefulness prompts us to examine our motives and desires, ensuring that we are not consumed by selfish ambitions but instead humbly acknowledge God's blessings and respond with gratitude.

The ungratefulness of Dio Brando's character serves as a cautionary tale, inspiring us to embrace thankfulness as a fundamental aspect of our Christian walk. Through gratitude, we can experience true fulfillment, peace, and a deeper relationship with God.

"The more carefully you scheme, the more unexpected events come along." - Dio Brando

June 29

A new commandment I give to you, that you love one another: just as I have loved you, you also are to love one another. By this all people will know that you are my disciples, if you have love for one another." John 13:34-35

Byakugan Princess

(Naruto)

Hinata Hyūga, the heiress of the Hyūga clan, initially faces doubts, criticism, and even self-doubt due to her shy and reserved nature. However, as the story unfolds, her unwavering love and acceptance of others, particularly towards Naruto Uzumaki, become apparent. Her actions reflect a deep care for others, devotion, and a genuine desire for their well-being.

In John 13:34-35, Jesus gives His disciples a new commandment to love one another, just as He has loved them. The verse emphasizes that this love should be a distinguishing characteristic of Jesus' disciples. Hinata's acceptance and love for others, even in the face of adversity, exemplify this teaching. Through her actions, she becomes a testament to her identity as a follower of Christ, embodying the transformative power of love in fostering acceptance and unity.

Hinata's journey also reminds us of our call as Christians to emulate Christ's love in our own lives. We are called to see beyond external appearances and flaws, extending love and acceptance to others, just as Christ has loved and accepted us. By doing so, we become living testimonies of the Gospel, demonstrating the transformative power of love to the world.

Reflecting on Hinata's story challenges us to examine our own capacity to love and accept others. It invites us to show genuine compassion, kindness, and understanding, embodying the love of Christ in our relationships. Through our love, we can create a safe space where others feel accepted, valued, and embraced for who they are.

"You make mistakes. But because of those mistakes... You get the strength to stand up." - Hinata Hyūga

June 30

A fool gives full vent to his spirit, but a wise man quietly holds it back. Proverbs 29:11

10th Espada

(Bleach)

Yammy Llargo's character in Bleach demonstrates the destructive consequences of uncontrolled anger. His rage leads to chaos, violence, and harm to others. It serves as a reminder that when we allow anger to consume us without restraint, it can lead us down a destructive path, causing harm to ourselves and those around us.

The verse Proverbs 29:11 emphasizes the importance of wisdom and self-control in managing anger. As followers of Christ, we are called to exercise self-discipline and seek the guidance of the Holy Spirit in controlling our emotions. The verse encourages us to reflect on the consequences of our actions and strive to respond to anger with measured, calm, and thoughtful attitudes, seeking resolution and reconciliation.

While Yammy Llargo represents the fool who gives full vent to rage, as Christians, we are called to pursue peace and bring calm in the midst of anger. Instead of allowing anger to drive us to destructive behaviour, we are called to seek God's wisdom, pray for guidance, and choose a path of reconciliation and peace. By emulating the wise who bring calm in the end, we reflect the character of Christ, who Himself exemplified forgiveness and love even in the face of anger. Through a relationship with God, we can experience a transformation of our hearts and learn to manage anger in healthier ways, guided by His wisdom and grace.

In reflecting on the anger of Yammy Llargo, we are encouraged to cultivate self-control, seek peaceful resolutions, and allow God's transformative work in our lives to guide us in managing our emotions. Ultimately, it is an invitation to become more Christ-like in our responses, demonstrating love, forgiveness, and wisdom even in the face of anger.

"Change is inevitable. Instead of resisting it, you're better served simply going with the flow." - Shunsui Kyoraku

July 1

But when you fast, anoint your head and wash your face, that your fasting may not be seen by others but by your father who is in secret. And your Father who sees in secret will reward you. Matthew 6:17-18

Eraser Head

(My Hero Academia)

In My Hero Academia, Shōta Aizawa is a teacher at U.A. High School who often appears tired, with dishevelled hair, and his eyes covered by his signature goggles. His unkempt appearance shows his dedication and commitment to his role as a hero and teacher. Despite his weariness, Aizawa continues to persevere and fulfil his responsibilities.

In Matthew 6:17-18, Jesus teaches about the importance of humility and authenticity when engaging in acts of devotion, such as fasting. He advises those who fast to maintain a presentable appearance, not drawing attention to their sacrifice but seeking the approval of God, who sees what is done in secret. Just as the verse calls for inward sincerity, Aizawa's appearance may mask his true commitment, skill, and care for his students. This prompts us to look beyond surface-level judgments and value the character and actions of individuals rather than being swayed by external appearances.

Furthermore, Aizawa's dishevelled appearance may symbolize the burdens and sacrifices he carries in his hero work. It illustrates the cost of his dedication and his willingness to put others' well-being before his own comfort. This can be seen as a reflection of Christ's sacrificial love, who humbly took on the burdens of humanity on the cross.

By relating Shōta Aizawa's appearance, we can reflect on the importance of genuine humility, selflessness, and devotion in our own lives. It prompts us to evaluate our motives and intentions, ensuring that our actions are rooted in a desire to serve others and please God, rather than seeking recognition or praise from the world.

"There's nothing crueller than letting a dream end midway." - Shōta Aizawa

July 2

Whoever despises his neighbour is a sinner, but blessed is he who is generous to the poor. Proverbs 14:21

Black Sister

(The Promised Neverland)

In the anime, Sister Krone initially displays an attitude of despising her fellow caretakers and the children in her care. She is driven by personal ambition and seeks to advance her own position within the orphanage, often resorting to manipulative tactics. Her actions demonstrate a lack of compassion and a disregard for the well-being of those around her.

Proverbs 14:21 highlights the sinfulness of despising one's neighbour, emphasizing the importance of treating others with kindness and generosity. It calls for a mindset of compassion and a willingness to extend help to those in need, particularly the poor and vulnerable. We are called to embody the virtues of love, compassion, and generosity.

Sister Krone's attitude serves as a cautionary example of the negative consequences of selfish ambition and disregard for others. It reminds us to examine our own attitudes and actions, ensuring that we do not fall into similar patterns of despising or manipulating others for personal gain. Instead, we are called to follow Christ's example, who consistently showed kindness, mercy, and selfless love towards others. By embodying these virtues, we not only avoid sin but also bring blessings to our own lives and the lives of those around us.

The character of Sister Krone in The Promised Neverland highlights the importance of aligning our actions with the teachings of Christ, treating others with genuine love, and being generous to those in need. This serves as a reminder of the importance of valuing and caring for our neighbours, treating them with respect and kindness rather than harbouring disdain or seeking personal gain at their expense.

"So Beautiful. I think you and I can do this. To change the world... and we just have to start with ourselves." - Emma

July 3

For everyone who exalts himself will be humbled, but the one who humbles himself will be exalted. Luke 18:14

Homunculus Pride

(Fullmetal Alchemist: Brotherhood)

Homunculus Pride is a character in the Fullmetal Alchemist: Brotherhood anime series. As one of the seven Homunculi, Pride represents the sin of pride itself. He exhibits a sense of superiority, arrogance, and a desire to dominate others. This haughty spirit blinds him to his own limitations and leads him down a destructive path.

In Luke 18:14, Jesus shares a parable about two individuals praying in the temple. The Pharisee exalts himself before God, boasting about his own righteousness and looking down on others. In contrast, the tax collector humbly acknowledges his sins, seeking God's mercy. Jesus concludes that it is the humble tax collector who goes home justified, while the proud Pharisee is not. This verse reminds us of the dangers of pride and the importance of humility in our relationship with God.

The story of Homunculus Pride in the anime serves as a cautionary tale, highlighting the negative consequences of pride and self-exaltation. It challenges us to examine our own hearts and attitudes, ensuring that we do not fall into the same trap of seeking personal glory and power. Instead, we are called to cultivate a spirit of humility, acknowledging our dependence on God and recognizing the inherent worth of every individual.

The circumstances of Homunculus Pride invite us to reflect on the dangers of pride and the importance of humility in our faith journey. It reminds us to approach God and others with a humble heart, seeking His forgiveness and extending grace to those around us. By doing so, we align ourselves with the teachings of Jesus and embrace a life that reflects His love, compassion, and humility.

"Appearances rarely show the whole truth." - Pride

July 4

You shall love the Lord your God with all your heart and with all your soul and with all your mind. This is the great and first commandment. And a second is like it: You shall love your neighbour as yourself. Matthew 22:37-39

Realistic Joestar

(JoJo's Bizarre Adventure)

Jonathan Joestar, the protagonist of the first part of JoJo's Bizarre Adventure, is a character known for his strong sense of justice, unwavering commitment, and compassionate nature. Throughout his journey, he faces numerous challenges, including conflicts with supernatural entities and personal adversaries. However, Jonathan remains steadfast in his pursuit of justice, always striving to protect the innocent and stand up against evil.

Matthew 22:37-39 is a summary of Jesus' teachings about the two most important commandments. The first emphasizes the love and devotion we should have towards God, encouraging us to give our whole selves to Him. The second emphasizes the importance of loving others as we love ourselves, treating them with kindness, compassion, and respect.

Jonathan's commitment extends beyond his immediate circle, as he shows kindness and understanding to those who may be considered adversaries. He seeks to understand their motivations and, if possible, offers them a chance for redemption and change. This showcases his belief in the transformative power of compassion and forgiveness.

Jonathan's character reminds us of the transformative power of love. We can cultivate a deep relationship with God, strive for righteousness, and extend love and kindness to our neighbours. Just as Jonathan's commitment brought about positive change and impacted the lives of those around him, our own commitment to these commandments can contribute to the flourishing of our communities and the furthering of God's kingdom on Earth.

"There are times when a gentleman has to be courageous and fight, even when his opponent is bigger than he is and he knows he's going to lose!" - Jonathan Joestar

July 5

And no wonder, for even Satan disguises himself as an angel of light. So, it is no surprise if his servants, also, disguise themselves as servants of righteousness. Their end will correspond to their deeds. 2 Corinthians 11:14-15

Elite Rogue Ninjas

(Naruto)

In the Naruto series, Akatsuki can be seen as a community that embodies deception in various ways. They present themselves as a group with noble ideals, aiming to bring peace to the world by eliminating corrupt leaders and oppressive regimes. However, their methods involve violence, manipulation, and even sacrificing innocent lives for their own gain. Their true nature is often hidden behind a façade of noble intentions.

In 2 Corinthians 11:14-15, the Apostle Paul cautions the Corinthians that Satan himself can masquerade as an angel of light, and his followers can appear as ministers of righteousness. This passage emphasizes the need for discernment within the Christian community, as not everyone who claims to represent truth and goodness genuinely does so.

The Akatsuki group presents itself as a group striving for peace and justice, but their actions often contradict these stated goals. The organization consists of rogue ninjas who employ manipulation, violence, and even acts of terrorism to achieve their objectives. Members like Pain and Itachi Uchiha, for instance, commit heinous acts in the name of their supposed vision for a better world. This parallel to false apostles reflects the theme of deception and the dangers it poses within communities.

Akatsuki from Naruto highlights the theme of deception within a community. It serves as a reminder for us to exercise discernment, evaluate the actions and motives of those around us, and stay grounded in God's truth to avoid being led astray by false teachings or individuals who present themselves as righteous but act contrary to God's will.

"Life's only beautiful because it's so fleeting, so transient."
- Deidara

July 6

What then shall we say to these things? If God is for us, who can be against us? Romans 8:31

Death Goddess

(Bleach)

In Bleach, Rukia Kuchiki is a Shinigami (Soul Reaper) who possesses exceptional courage and determination. She often finds herself in dangerous situations and faces formidable enemies, yet she never backs down. Rukia's courage is evident in her unwavering commitment to her duties and her willingness to put herself at risk to protect others.

In Romans 8:31, the verse reassures believers that if God is on their side, nothing can ultimately stand against them. Rukia's courage reflects a similar trust in a higher power, as she consistently relies on her training and the support of her fellow Soul Reapers. Her willingness to put herself at risk for the sake of protecting others echoes the self-sacrificial love exemplified by Jesus Christ. Christians are called to imitate Christ's love, which involves selflessly serving and caring for others. Rukia's courage in risking her own safety to protect those in need can be seen as a reflection of this sacrificial love.

Rukia often finds strength and support in her relationships with her friends and allies. This highlights the importance of community and the assurance that we are not alone in our battles. As Christians, we can find solace in the fact that we have a supportive and loving God who is always with us, empowering us to face our challenges with courage.

The courage of Rukia Kuchiki from Bleach emphasizes the themes of trust in God's presence and support, dedication to one's calling, sacrificial love, and the importance of community. Her example serves as an inspiration for believers to face their own trials with unwavering faith, knowing that they are not alone and that God is with them in every circumstance.

"Even if no one in the world believes you, stick out your chest and scream in defiance." - Rukia Kuchiki

July 7

If anyone would come after me, let him deny himself and take up his cross and follow me. For whoever would save his life will lose it, but whoever loses his life for my sake will find it. Matthew 16:24-25

One-Eyed King

(Tokyo Ghoul)

In Tokyo Ghoul, Ken Kaneki faces numerous challenges and undergoes a significant transformation. Initially, he is a shy and bookish character who is thrust into the dark world of ghouls after becoming one himself. Throughout the series, Kaneki wrestles with his sense of self, facing the challenge of reconciling his human and ghoul identities. Ultimately, he makes the decision to embrace his ghoul nature and fight for the survival and rights of his fellow ghouls, even if it means forsaking his humanity and facing immense hardships.

Matthew 16:24-25 speaks to the idea of self-denial and taking up one's cross to follow Jesus. This passage suggests that by willingly surrendering one's life, or sacrificing personal ambitions, individuals can find a deeper, more fulfilling purpose. The verse also highlights the paradoxical nature of finding life through losing it for the sake of Christ.

Kaneki's journey can be seen as a metaphor for the Christian walk. Just as Kaneki faces persecution and hardship in his quest to protect and serve his fellow ghouls, Christians may encounter difficulties and opposition when living out their faith. The decision to follow Christ is not always easy or comfortable, but it requires a willingness to endure hardships and make sacrifices for the sake of God's kingdom.

The decision of Ken Kaneki in Tokyo Ghoul emphasizes the importance of self-denial, embracing challenges, and finding new life through sacrifice. It encourages believers to prioritize their commitment to Christ over their own desires and comforts, knowing that in doing so, they can discover a deeper sense of purpose and fulfilment.

"The pain you feel today will be the strength you'll have tomorrow." - Ken Kaneki

July 8

The plans of the diligent lead surely to abundance, but everyone who is hasty comes only to poverty. Proverbs 21:5

Pirate Hunter

(One Piece)

Zoro's devotion in One piece anime is exemplified through his diligent training and constant pursuit of improvement in his swordsmanship skills. He spends countless hours practicing, pushing himself to the limits, and honing his abilities. He is also diligent in honing his skills as a swordsman and constantly pushes himself to become stronger, all for the sake of Luffy and their shared goal of finding One Piece.

In the context of Proverbs 21:5, Zoro's devotion can be seen as a reflection of diligence in his pursuit of his goal to become the world's greatest swordsman. This verse emphasizes the importance of diligence and careful planning in achieving success. Similarly, we are called to be diligent and devote ourselves wholeheartedly to God. This devotion involves a commitment to prayer, studying God's Word, and living according to His principles.

Zoro's diligent planning and Luffy's unwavering dedication form a harmonious balance. They rely on each other's strengths and compensate for their respective weaknesses. Zoro's planning provides a solid foundation, ensuring that their efforts are not in vain. Meanwhile, Luffy's enthusiasm motivates the crew and propels them forward, inspiring them to embrace new challenges.

Just as Zoro's devotion contributes to the success of their crew, our devotion to God leads to spiritual growth, transformation, and a life that honours Him. Let us be inspired by Zoro's unwavering devotion to Luffy and seek to apply the principles of diligence, careful planning, and sacrificial love in our own relationship with God and in our interactions with others.

"It's okay to lose your way… just don't lose sight of what you have decided." - Roronoa Zoro

July 9

Look at the birds of the air: they neither sow nor reap nor gather into barns, and yet your heavenly Father feeds them. Are you not of more value than they? Matthew 6:26

Kusakabe family

(My Neighbor Totoro)

In My Neighbor Totoro, the Kusakabe family provides a beautiful depiction of faith, trust, and finding peace in the midst of difficulties. They face their own challenges, particularly with the illness of their mother. Despite their concerns, they find solace in the wonder of nature, in their encounters with the forest spirits, and in the support of their loved ones. This family reflects a childlike faith, relying on the beauty of the world around them, finding peace and joy in the simple things. Their experiences remind us that even in difficult times, we can turn to God, trust in His provision, and find comfort in His creation.

In Matthew 6:26, Jesus directs our attention to the birds of the air, highlighting how God faithfully provides for them. This reminds us of God's provision, deep love, and care for His creation, especially for humanity, including the birds. It reassures us that if God takes care of them, how much more will He care for and provide for us, His valued children.

The Kusakabe family's unity and love for one another serve as a powerful example for us as believers in Christ. Their support and care for each other remind us of the importance of nurturing our family relationships and showing compassion to those around us.

As we reflect on the Kusakabe family's story, we are encouraged to have faith in God's provision, knowing that He values us greatly. We can find peace in His care, just as the family finds peace amidst their challenges. Therefore, let us embrace a childlike trust, appreciate the wonders of creation, and lean on the support of our loved ones. May the journey of Kusakabe family in the anime inspire us to deepen our faith and seek God's provision and comfort in all circumstances.

"Try laughing. Then whatever scares you will go away."
- Tatsuo Kusakabe

July 10

But immediately Jesus spoke to them, saying, "Take heart; it is I. Do not be afraid. Matthew 14:27

Cer ulean Gym Leader

(Pokémon)

Misty, one of the main characters in Pokémon, is known for her fear of bugs. This fear is portrayed throughout the series, particularly when she encounters bug-type Pokémon or situations involving insects. Misty's fear of bugs can be seen as a character trait that adds depth to her personality and highlights her vulnerabilities.

In Matthew 14:27, Jesus speaks to His disciples who were filled with fear as they saw Him walking on water. He tells them to take courage and not to be afraid. This verse resonates with Misty's experiences as it reminds us that Jesus's presence can bring comfort and dispel fear. In the midst of the disciples' fear, Jesus assures them that He is with them. His words encourage them to have courage and not let fear overpower them.

In the context of Misty's fear of bugs, we can reflect on the universal experience of fear in our own lives. Fear is a natural human emotion that can arise from various sources, whether they are rational or irrational. It is important to recognize that everyone has fears and that they can differ from person to person. For us as believers, a timeless truth is that Jesus is always with us, even in the midst of our fears and uncertainties. We can find comfort and strength by turning to Him, knowing that His presence brings peace and assurance.

Misty's fear of bugs in Pokémon serves as a reminder that fear is a natural part of being human. This prompts us to consider the role fear plays in our lives as believers. It is an opportunity for growth, resilience, and relying on God's strength. May Misty's journey inspire us to confront our own fears with courage and faith, knowing that we are not alone in our struggles and that God is always there to help us through.

"Don't you know that love is the most important thing in the whole world?" - Misty

July 11

Then Peter came up and said to him, "Lord, how often will my brother sin against me, and I forgive him? As many as seven times?" Jesus said to him, "I do not say to you seven times, but seventy-seven times." Matthew 18:21-22

Fairy King

(Seven Deadly Sins)

In the Seven Deadly Sins anime, the theme of forgiveness is prominently explored through the character of the Fairy King. King exhibits a profound capacity for forgiveness, which plays a crucial role in the story's narrative and character development. Throughout the series, he encounters various situations where he has been wronged or betrayed by his fellow characters. Despite the pain and anger, he may initially feel, King consistently chooses forgiveness over revenge or holding grudges.

In Matthew 18:21-22, Jesus emphasizes the importance of unlimited forgiveness. He teaches that forgiveness is not about keeping score or setting a finite limit. By employing the metaphor of "seventy times seven,"Jesus emphasizes the limitless nature of forgiveness, urging His followers to emulate His boundless mercy.

King's forgiveness also reflects the transformative work of God's grace in our lives. As followers of Christ, we believe in the power of God's forgiveness through Jesus Christ. Through His sacrifice, we are offered the opportunity to receive forgiveness and extend it to others. King's forgiveness can be seen as an embodiment of this divine grace, as he exemplifies the Christian virtues of mercy and reconciliation.

The portrayal of forgiveness by Fairy King in the anime resonates with Christian teachings on forgiveness. It serves as a reminder of the transformative power of extending grace, the potential for redemption and restoration in relationships, and the embodiment of God's forgiveness through Jesus Christ.

"Whether you're big or small, you're always you." - King

July 12

Every good gift and every perfect gift is from above, coming down from the Father of lights, with whom there is no variation or shadow due to change. James 1:17

Childhood Frenemies

(Gintama)

In Gintama, Gin and Katsura have distinct personalities and ideologies, but they appreciate and respect one another's perspectives. Their friendship transcends these differences and fosters a deep sense of connection. They serve as pillars of support for each other during difficult times, providing a listening ear, offering words of encouragement, and providing strength and comfort when needed.

James 1:17 reminds us that every good and perfect gift comes from God. This verse reflects God's goodness and grace, illustrating His provision of meaningful and fulfilling relationships in our lives. It also reminds us of the unchanging nature of God's gifts. While circumstances may shift and friendships may evolve, God's blessings remain constant.

The friendship of Gin and Katsura in Gintama demonstrates the power of God's provision to meet our relational needs. As humans, we are wired for connection and community, and God graciously supplies us with friends who encourage, challenge, and uplift us. Gin and Katsura's friendship serve as a reminder that true friends are a manifestation of God's love and care in our lives.

When we reflect on the friendship of Gin and Katsura, we are prompted to cherish and cultivate the friendships we have. We are reminded to recognize them as gifts from God and to appreciate the ways in which they contribute to our well-being and spiritual growth. Their friendship in Gintama inspires us to value and nurture the friendships we have, recognizing them as divine provisions that reflect the unchanging goodness of our Heavenly Father.

"If you have time to fantasize about a beautiful end, then just live beautifully 'til the end." - Gintoki Sakata

July 13

For his anger is but for a moment, and his favour is for a lifetime. Weeping may tarry for the night, but joy comes with the morning. Psalm 30:5

Hikikomori Guy

(Anohana)

The growth of Jinta Yadomi in Anohana: The Flower We Saw That Day is a powerful narrative of redemption, healing, and discovering hope amidst pain. At the beginning of the series, Jinta carries the heavy burden of guilt, grief, and a deep sense of isolation. His unresolved emotions and past actions weigh him down. However, as the story unfolds, we witness a gradual transformation in Jinta, fuelled by the love and support of his friends.

In Psalm 30:5, we find a verse that beautifully encapsulates God's character and his redemptive nature. It reminds us that God's anger is momentary, but His favour and love are everlasting. The verse acknowledges the existence of seasons of weeping, sorrow, and hardship in our lives. However, it also offers a message of hope, assuring us that joy will come in the morning, just as the night gives way to the dawn.

Jinta's growth in Anohana resonates with the transformative power of God's love and grace in our own lives. It teaches us that no matter how broken or burdened we may feel, there is always hope for redemption and restoration. Like Jinta, we can experience healing and find joy through genuine connections and the support of our community. God's favour is readily available to us, and His promise of rejoicing can infuse new life into our circumstances.

Jinta's character serves as a reminder that even in our darkest moments, God's light can break through. His story encourages us to place our trust in God's unwavering faithfulness and embrace the journey of healing and transformation. Just like him, we too can discover solace and restoration through God's everlasting love and favour.

"I thought I could just apologize tomorrow. But that tomorrow... never came." - Jinta Yadomi

July 14

Rejoice and be glad, for your reward is great in heaven, for so they persecuted the prophets who were before you.
Matthew 5:12

Superhero Lemillion

(My Hero Academia)

Mirio's character, also known as Lemillion, in My Hero Academia, exemplifies the qualities of perseverance, selflessness, and a strong sense of purpose. Despite facing numerous challenges and setbacks, he remains resilient and maintains an unwavering determination to protect others and uphold justice. Mirio's happiness stems from his deep conviction and commitment to his hero's duty, finding joy in the opportunity to make a positive difference in the lives of those around him.

The verse Matthew 5:12 encourages believers to rejoice and be glad in the face of persecution and difficulties. It reminds us that our reward in heaven is significant, just as it was for the prophets who faced persecution before us. Mirio finds fulfilment and contentment in knowing that his actions align with his values and contribute to the greater good.

Mirio's character invites us to reflect on our own pursuit of happiness. His happiness stems from his selflessness and dedication to serving others, reminding us of the joy that comes from sacrificial love and living according to God's commandments. Just as Mirio faces trials and setbacks, we too may encounter challenges in our faith journey.

In light of Mirio's happiness, we are encouraged to find joy in fulfilling our purpose, serving others, and remaining faithful to God's calling. By aligning our lives with Christ's teachings, we can experience a deeper and lasting happiness that transcends worldly circumstances. Mirio's character reminds us that true happiness is found in selflessness, perseverance, and the knowledge that our ultimate reward awaits us in heaven.

"Wanting to do what you can to help those in trouble...Is part of the basics for a hero." - Mirio Togata

July 15

The hand of the diligent will rule, while the slothful will be put to forced labor. Proverbs 12:24

Delivery God

(Noragami)

Yato the main character from Noragami, embodies the value of hard work and determination. Despite being a minor deity and facing numerous obstacles, Yato tirelessly strives to become a renowned and respected god. He takes on odd jobs and goes to great lengths to fulfil the wishes of those who seek his help. His hard work and perseverance demonstrate his unwavering commitment to his goals and the lengths he is willing to go to make a difference.

Proverbs 12:24 reminds us that diligence is not in vain and brings about positive outcomes. It highlights the principle that those who are diligent in their work are more likely to achieve positions of authority and influence. In contrast, laziness leads to unproductive and burdensome circumstances. God calls us to steward the gifts and talents we have been given, which includes being diligent in our work and responsibilities.

Yato is very dedicated to his tasks, no matter how small or menial they may seem. He understands that success and fulfilment come through putting in the necessary effort and taking responsibility for his actions. His diligence propels him forward and allows him to navigate the challenges he faces, ultimately shaping his growth as a character.

Yato's character encourages us to approach our responsibilities and tasks with diligence, recognizing that our efforts can lead to personal growth, fulfilment, and even positions of influence. Just as his hard work paves the way for his journey, we too can apply the principles of diligence and hard work to pursue our dreams and goals, knowing that our efforts are not in vain.

"Even if things are painful and tough, people should appreciate what it means to be alive." - Yato

July 16

Do not lie to one another, seeing that you have put off the old self with its practices. Colossians 3:9

Student House Pet

(Kakegurui)

The character Ryota Suzui from the anime series Kakegurui embodies the value of honesty. Despite being in a school where gambling and deception are prevalent, Ryota consistently upholds his integrity and remains truthful in his actions. He resists the temptations of cheating and dishonesty, choosing to maintain his moral principles even when faced with challenging situations.

The verse Colossians 3:9 emphasizes the importance of truthfulness in our interactions with others. It encourages believers to reject the old self, which is characterized by dishonesty, and instead embrace a new way of living in Christ. This verse also highlights the significance of our actions and words in relationships with others.

Ryota's honesty demonstrates the transformative power of Christ's work in our lives. Through his adherence to truthfulness, he exemplifies the change that occurs when we put off our old selves and embrace the new life we have in Christ. His honesty also highlights the impact that truthfulness can have on relationships. As Christians, we are called to build relationships based on truth and love, reflecting the character of Christ and creating spaces where others can feel safe and valued.

The example of Ryota's commitment to honesty encourages us to put off deceitful practices and embrace a life marked by truth, reflecting the transformation that comes through our relationship with Christ. By following his example, we can strive to build relationships based on trust and honesty, cultivating a positive and authentic environment in our own lives.

"If you lose your nerve once you've been driven back this far, it's even harder to make a comeback." - Ryota Suzui

July 17

So now faith, hope, and love abide, these three; but the greatest of these is love. 1 Corinthians 13:13

Sky Sorceress

(Fairy Tail)

In Fairy Tail, Wendy Marvell, the Sky Dragon Slayer, faces challenges and hardships, but she consistently demonstrates a resilient spirit and an unwavering belief in a better future. Her hope can be seen as an expression of faith, as she puts her trust in the idea that things will improve and that there is always a chance for redemption and happiness.

In 1 Corinthians 13:13, hope is mentioned alongside faith and love. These three qualities are seen as enduring virtues that hold great significance. Additionally, the verse highlights that the greatest of these virtues is love. Christian hope is ultimately grounded in the love of God, which is demonstrated through the sacrifice of Jesus Christ.

Wendy's hope is deeply intertwined with her faith. She places her trust in her friends, her guild, and the power of love to overcome challenges. She also exemplifies the transformative power of love. In Fairy Tail, Wendy's hope is often driven by her love for her friends and her desire to protect and support them. Wendy's hopeful nature, fuelled by her love for others, serves as a reminder of the transformative impact love can have in our lives. In the face of adversity, Wendy's hope serves as an inspiration to keep pressing on, trusting that God is with us and that He will bring about a better outcome.

Wendy Marvell's character in Fairy Tail reflects the interplay of faith, hope, and love. She reminds us of the importance of trusting in God's promises, the transformative power of love, and the need to persevere in hope even when faced with challenges. Wendy's hope serves as an encouragement for Christians to cultivate a hopeful spirit, rooted in faith and anchored in God's unfailing love.

"Bravery awakens when you're being consumed by fear." - Wendy Marvell

July 18

Whoever humbles himself like this child is the greatest in the kingdom of heaven. Matthew 18:4

Zoldyck Assassin

(Hunter x Hunter)

Zeno Zoldyck from Hunter x Hunter is an extraordinarily powerful Nen-user and world-renowned assassin. He is known for his remarkable humility, despite being a member of the infamous Zoldyck family of assassins. His humility is demonstrated through his calm and composed demeanour, his willingness to listen to others, and his lack of arrogance despite his immense strength and skills.

Matthew 18:4 is a verse which reminds us that humility is a virtue highly esteemed in the kingdom of heaven. Jesus calls his disciples to humble themselves, like a child, in order to enter and experience the fullness of God's kingdom. Zeno embodies this call to humility by setting aside his pride, recognizing that true greatness comes from a posture of humility and a willingness to serve others.

Zeno's humility serves as an example for Christians to follow. It reminds us to approach our relationships and interactions with others with humility and a childlike faith. By humbling ourselves and recognizing our reliance on God, we can experience the blessings and joy that come from living in alignment with His kingdom.

Reflecting on Zeno's character, we are encouraged to examine our own attitudes and actions. We must be willing to set aside our pride, ego, and desire for recognition in order to humbly serve others. We also need to be open to learning from those around us, regardless of their social status or background. Zeno's example reminds us that humility is not a sign of weakness but rather a pathway to true greatness in God's kingdom.

"An apology is a promise to do things differently next time, and to keep the promise." - Ging Freecss

July 19

Why do you see the speck that is in your brother's eye, but do not notice the log that is in your own eye? Or how can you say to your brother, 'Let me take the speck out of your eye,' when there is the log in your own eye? You hypocrite, first take the log out of your own eye, and then you will see clearly to take the speck out of your brother's eye. Matthew 7:3-5

Beast King

(Inuyasha)

Sesshōmaru's hypocrisy in the anime is evident in his disdain for Inuyasha's human and demon heritage, considering it impure. He looks down upon Inuyasha for his perceived weaknesses yet fails to acknowledge and confront his own arrogance and pride. This hypocrisy blinds him from recognizing his own inner conflicts and growth opportunities.

The verse Matthew 7:3-5 addresses the issue of hypocrisy and the need for self-reflection before judging or criticizing others. It emphasizes the importance of self-awareness and humility. When we fail to recognize our own faults and weaknesses, we become blinded by pride and self-righteousness, hindering our ability to extend compassion and understanding to those around us.

Initially driven by a desire for power and dominance, Sesshōmaru fails to recognize the importance of emotional connections and empathy. However, through self-reflection and the influence of others, he learns that true strength lies not only in physical abilities but also in compassion and understanding.

The reflection on Sesshōmaru's hypocrisy prompts us to examine our own hearts and actions. It encourages us to confront our own shortcomings and seek God's transformation in our lives. Through self-reflection and the guidance of the Holy Spirit, we can cultivate humility, genuine love, and a spirit of grace towards others.

"In the hearts of men lies both good and evil. The two coexist. Some men become good, and others become evil. It is the way of this world." - Kikyō

July 20

And as you wish that others would do to you, do so to them. Luke 6:31

Octopus Teacher

(Assassination Classroom)

In Assassination Classroom, Koro-sensei, who is initially portrayed as a powerful and seemingly invincible creature, becomes a teacher to a group of students tasked with assassinating him. Despite this unique situation, Koro-sensei consistently demonstrates kindness towards his students. He genuinely cares for their well-being, encourages their growth, and helps them overcome their personal challenges.

Luke 6:31 is a verse from the Bible, often referred to as the Golden Rule, which teaches the importance of treating others with kindness and respect. It emphasizes the idea that we should treat others in the same way that we would want to be treated ourselves. Jesus emphasized the importance of showing love and compassion to others, even to those who may be different or challenging to us. Koro-sensei's example challenges us to extend our kindness beyond our comfort zones and to reach out to those who may need it the most.

Koro-sensei's kindness is not limited to his students but extends to other characters in the series as well. This echoes the Biblical principle of loving our neighbours as ourselves, showing kindness and compassion to all people, regardless of their backgrounds or circumstances.

By reflecting on Koro-sensei's kindness, we are reminded of the Christian call to imitate Christ's love and kindness in our own lives. We are encouraged to treat others with the same care, empathy, and respect that we desire for ourselves. Just as Koro-sensei's kindness impacts the lives of his students, our acts of kindness can have a positive influence on those around us, showing them the love of Christ through our actions.

"The name doesn't make the person. The name simply remains gently within the footprint left on the path a person walks." - Koro-Sensei

July 21

Love does no wrong to a neighbor; therefore love is the fulfilling of the law. Romans 13:10

Cur e a Cute Waitress

(Happy Sugar Life)

Satō Matsuzaka's love in Happy Sugar Life is deeply flawed and distorted. She becomes consumed by obsessive and possessive love, which leads her to manipulate and harm those around her. Her actions demonstrate the destructive consequences of selfish and self-centred love that disregards the well-being of others.

From Romans 13:10, we can recognize the biblical ideal of love. The verse teaches us that love should be characterized by kindness, compassion, and a genuine desire for the well-being of others. It also emphasizes the idea that true love fulfils the law. In the context of the Bible, the law refers to the commandments and teachings that guide righteous living. Satō's actions disregard moral boundaries and harm others, highlighting the contrast between her distorted love and the biblical understanding of love as fulfilling the law.

Satō's love falls short of this ideal, as she consistently causes harm and pain to those she claims to love. Her actions serve as a cautionary example, highlighting the consequences of love driven by selfish desires and lacking consideration for the well-being of others. As followers of Christ, it is essential to reflect on the damaging effects of distorted love and strive to embody the kind of love that Scripture encourages. We are called to love our neighbours, seeking their welfare and treating them with kindness and respect.

By examining Satō's flawed love, we can reinforce the importance of selflessness, empathy, and genuine concern for the well-being of others in our own lives. This reflection serves as a reminder of the transformative power of true love, which brings healing and fulfilment, in contrast to the destructive consequences of love that harms and manipulates others.

"Love is something your heart feels by itself. It's sweet, it sparkles, and it makes you realize what makes you happy without anyone telling you." - Satō Matsuzaka

July 22

Come now, let us reason together, says the Lord: though your sins are like scarlet, they shall be as white as snow; though they are red like crimson, they shall become like wool. Isaiah 1:18

Boar Hat Owner

(Seven Deadly Sins)

In the anime series, Meliodas has a dark and troubled past, having committed grave sins as the leader of the Ten Commandments. He carries the weight of his sins and the guilt associated with them. However, he demonstrates a strong desire for redemption and continually seeks opportunities to make amends and protect those he cares about.

The verse Isaiah 1:18 speaks of God's willingness to forgive and cleanse our sins, no matter how deep or scarlet they may be. It conveys the idea that through God's grace and forgiveness, our sins can be washed away, leaving us purified and renewed. The imagery of sins as scarlet or crimson being made white as snow or like wool portrays the transformative power of God's forgiveness.

Meliodas's story resonates with this message of forgiveness and transformation. Through his actions, he demonstrates a genuine desire to protect and serve others, working to make amends for the sins of his past. He seeks redemption, aiming to change the course of his life and find forgiveness. It serves as a reminder that no matter how deep or severe our sins may be, God's grace can wash them away, offering us a fresh start and a new identity.

By relating Meliodas's journey in Seven Deadly Sins, we are reminded of the transformative power of God's forgiveness and grace. It highlights the hope and possibility for redemption, even for those burdened by deep-seated guilt and a history of wrongdoing. Meliodas's story serves as a reminder that no matter the darkness of our past, we can find forgiveness and restoration through God's mercy, leading to a new life and a renewed sense of purpose.

"No matter what lies you tell, you can't fool your own heart." - Meliodas

July 23

He who loves money will not be satisfied with money, nor he who loves wealth with his income; this also is vanity.
Ecclesiastes 5:10

Mankanshoku Family

(Kill la Kill)

The Mankanshoku family in Kill la Kill spends most of their time being dead broke. They are portrayed as a happy, loving family, and their financial situation is more comical than genuinely difficult. However, their materialistic tendencies are still evident through their constant desire for food and insatiable appetite. They are frequently shown indulging in large meals, driven by their love for satisfying their hunger.

Ecclesiastes 5:10 highlights the emptiness of relentlessly pursuing wealth and possessions. The Mankanshoku family's pursuit of food can be seen as a metaphor for the never-ending quest for material possessions. Despite their continuous consumption, they never seem to be fully satisfied. This parallels the message of the Bible verse, which suggests that those who love money or wealth will always desire more, finding no true fulfilment in their pursuit.

The materialism of Mankanshoku family reminds us of the fleeting nature of material possessions. It emphasizes the idea that seeking satisfaction solely through material means is ultimately meaningless and can leave one feeling unfulfilled. Instead, the focus should be on finding meaning and contentment in deeper and more meaningful aspects of life.

The portrayal of the Mankanshoku family in the anime serves as a reminder of the importance of seeking a balanced perspective on wealth and possessions, recognizing their limitations, and prioritizing the eternal over the temporal. By acknowledging the temporary nature of material possessions and directing our hearts towards heavenly treasures, we can find true fulfilment and purpose in our lives.

"And everyone on the planet knows that if you win with friendship, you win at life!" - Mako Mankanshoku

July 24

For the righteous falls seven times and rises again, but the wicked stumble in times of calamity. Proverbs 24:16

Bushy Brows

(Naruto)

Rock Lee's unwavering determination and motivation in Naruto can be seen in his ability to rise again after experiencing setbacks or failures. Throughout the series, he faces numerous challenges and defeats, yet he never allows them to deter him from pursuing his goal of becoming a skilled ninja. He embodies the spirit of this verse by demonstrating resilience in the face of adversity.

The verse Proverbs 24:16 reminds us that as righteous individuals, we may experience setbacks and even fall multiple times. We encounter obstacles and trials that can lead us to stumble or even question our purpose. However, the verse encourages us to maintain hope and resilience. It reminds us that setbacks do not define our ultimate worth or destiny.

Despite his initial limitations and numerous defeats, Rock Lee never allows these setbacks to define him. Instead, he finds the courage to pick himself up, learn from his failures, and persistently pursue his goal of becoming a skilled ninja. As believers, we find strength in God's presence and His promises. When we face challenges, we can draw upon His grace and the power of the Holy Spirit to rise again. God's faithfulness and love enable us to push through adversity and continue pursuing righteousness.

Rock Lee's motivation serves as a reminder that our faith journey is not exempt from difficulties but rather an opportunity for growth and spiritual development. We can find hope in the knowledge that even when we stumble, our faith and the support of God will empower us to rise again and continue pursuing the abundant life He has planned for us.

"A hero is not the one who never falls. He is the one that who gets up, again and again, never losing sight of his dreams." - Rock Lee

July 25

Blessed be the God and Father of our Lord Jesus Christ, the Father of mercies and God of all comfort, who comforts us in all our affliction, so that we may be able to comfort those who are in any affliction, with the comfort with which we ourselves are comforted by God. 2 Corinthians 1:3-4

Icy Hot Superhero

(My Hero Academia)

In My Hero Academia, Shoto Todoroki carries deep emotional pain and trauma due to his abusive upbringing. His father, Endeavor, pushed him to his limits and used him as a tool to surpass All Might. This experience left Todoroki scarred and conflicted, as he struggled to reconcile his powerful Quirk inherited from his father with his desire to be his own person.

In 2 Corinthians 1:3-4, we find a Christian reflection that offers hope and guidance in the midst of such pain. The verse reminds us that God is the ultimate source of comfort and compassion. He is described as the Father of mercies and the God of all comfort. This means that when we are hurting, feeling broken, or experiencing affliction, God is there with us, offering His love, solace, and healing touch.

As Christians, we can identify with Todoroki's journey because we, too, have experienced pain and brokenness in our lives. However, we are not left alone in our suffering. God's comforting presence surrounds us, providing strength and hope even in the darkest moments. He understands our pain intimately and offers the comfort that only He can provide.

In reflecting on Todoroki's pain, we are reminded of the transformative power of God's comfort in our lives. We are called to embrace our own healing, drawing strength from God's presence, and allowing His comfort to mend our brokenness. And as we experience this comfort, we are compelled to share it with others, bringing hope and healing to those who are struggling.

"Never forget who you want to become." - Shoto Todoroki

July 26

Be still before the Lord and wait patiently for him; fret not yourself over the one who prospers in his way, over the man who carries out evil devices! Psalm 37:7

Noble Shinigami Captain

(Bleach)

Throughout the Bleach series, Byakuya exhibits a calm and composed demeanour, even in challenging situations. His patient nature allows him to carefully assess his surroundings, make wise decisions, and persevere through difficult trials. Byakuya's patience is rooted in his understanding of the bigger picture and his unwavering commitment to justice.

The verse Psalm 37:7 encourages believers to be still before the Lord and wait patiently for His guidance and intervention. It reminds us not to be troubled or envious when we see others succeeding through unjust means. Instead, we are called to trust in God's sovereignty and have patience as we wait for His timing and justice to prevail. We are also encouraged to cultivate patience in our own lives, trusting that God is working behind the scenes and that His justice will ultimately prevail.

Byakuya Kuchiki's patient character in the anime aligns with the biblical teaching of waiting patiently for the Lord. He demonstrates a willingness to trust in the bigger plan, even when faced with seemingly insurmountable obstacles. Similarly, as followers of Christ, we are encouraged to cultivate patience in our own lives, trusting that God is working behind the scenes and that His justice will ultimately prevail.

In moments of impatience or when we witness injustice, we can draw inspiration from Byakuya's example. We can choose to be still before the Lord, trusting in His timing and aligning ourselves with His will. Byakuya's patience serves as a reminder that through patience and trust in God, we can navigate challenging situations with wisdom, grace, and a steadfast commitment to justice.

"Arrogance destroys the footholds of victory." - Byakuya Kuchiki

July 27

Do not be deceived: "Bad company ruins good morals." 1 Corinthians 15:33

Random Diary Holder

(Future Diary)

Yukiteru's character arc in the anime demonstrates the dangerous consequences of succumbing to negative peer influences. He faces immense pressure from Yuno Gasai, whose manipulative actions and distorted values lead him down a dark and destructive path. Despite his initial reluctance, Yukiteru becomes entangled in a web of violence and deceit, compromising his own morals and endangering others.

In 1 Corinthians 15:33, the apostle Paul urges believers to exercise discernment in choosing their companions. It serves as a reminder that the company we keep can have a profound impact on our character and spiritual well-being. We are called to be discerning and intentional about the company we keep, seeking relationships that nurture our spiritual growth and challenge us to live according to God's standards.

Yukiteru's experiences highlight the detrimental effects of succumbing to negative peer pressure. His association with Yuno, who embodies deceit and manipulation, gradually compromises his own character and decision-making. This serves as a reminder to us as Christians to carefully choose our companions and influences, ensuring they align with our values and encourage our growth in faith.

The reflection on Yukiteru's story aligns with the call to be transformed by the renewing of our minds and to walk in a manner worthy of our calling. By relying on God's strength, seeking His wisdom, and choosing companionship that aligns with His truth, we can withstand negative peer pressure and grow into individuals of godly character, positively impacting the world around us.

"If there's a miracle that can be reached by fighting to the end, then I want to see it." - Yukiteru Amano

July 28

Once God has spoken; twice have I heard this: that power belongs to God. Psalm 62:11

World's Strongest Man

(One Piece)

In One Piece, Edward Newgate, also known as Whitebeard, is hailed as the strongest man in the world and the captain of the Whitebeard Pirates. His imposing stature and countless battle scars attest to his incredible resilience. Even in his old age, his physical strength surpasses that of giants. His abilities, such as causing earthquakes, command respect and evoke fear from others. However, it is essential to remember that Whitebeard's power is merely a fraction of the power that belongs to God.

Psalm 62:11 emphasizes that ultimate power and authority reside with God alone. It reminds us that God's power surpasses any earthly strength or force we may encounter. We are called to align ourselves with God and surrender to His authority. We should not place our ultimate trust or reliance on our own strength or the powers of this world. Instead, we are encouraged to acknowledge that true power comes from God and seek His guidance and wisdom.

Reflecting on Whitebeard's power leads us to recognize the greatness and supremacy of God's power. It reminds us that God's power is limitless and transcends the physical realm, extending into the spiritual and supernatural. We should hold God's power in the highest regard and not take it lightly or attempt to manipulate it for selfish purposes. Instead, we are to respect and utilize God's power in alignment with His will, which is rooted in love, justice, and righteousness.

The power of Whitebeard from One Piece prompts us to acknowledge the greatness of God's power and place our trust in His unlimited might. We should not rely solely on human strength or earthly forces but instead recognize that true power rests in God. Let our awe and reverence for God's power inspire us to live in alignment with His divine will.

"You can't live in this world without a code of conduct" - Whitebeard

July 29

Therefore, let anyone who thinks that he stands take heed lest he fall. 1 Corinthians 10:12

Dwarf in the flask

(Fullmetal Alchemist)

The character Father aka the Dwarf in the Flask from Full metal Alchemist: Brotherhood represents a being consumed by pride and the desire for ultimate power. He seeks to obtain the knowledge and abilities of the Homunculi to transcend human limitations and become a god-like being. This insatiable pride blinds him to the consequences of his actions and leads to his downfall.

1 Corinthians 10:12 serves as a wake-up call, urging us to be cautious and vigilant. It reminds us that even the most faithful and devoted followers of Christ can fall if they let pride take hold. We must guard against complacency and remember that our spiritual strength and growth come from God alone. We should approach our faith with a sense of awe and reverence, understanding that we are not immune to temptation or failure. By acknowledging our vulnerabilities and staying rooted in God's Word, we can avoid the pitfalls of pride and continue to grow in our relationship with Him.

Pride often tempts us to rely solely on our own abilities, wisdom, and achievements, leading us to believe that we are strong and invulnerable. The Dwarf in the Flask's excessive pride blinded him to the potential consequences of his actions, and he paid a heavy price for his hubris. Similarly, when we become overly confident in our own spiritual journey, we risk neglecting our dependence on God and His guidance.

The story of the Dwarf in the Flask reminds us that pride is a dangerous trap that can lead us astray. By embracing humility, relying on God's strength, and seeking accountability within our Christian community, we can navigate our spiritual journey with wisdom and discernment, avoiding the pitfalls of pride and remaining faithful to our calling in Christ.

"You can't change reality, just your perception!" - Father

July 30

By this we know love, that he laid down his life for us, and we ought to lay down our lives for the brothers. 1 John 3:16

Elderly Legend

(Hunter x Hunter)

Isaac Netero from the anime Hunter x Hunter can be seen as a saviour figure in certain aspects. He dedicates his life to protecting humanity from the threat of the Chimera Ants and willingly sacrifices himself to ensure their defeat. His selflessness, courage, and unwavering determination to protect others align with qualities often associated with saviours.

The verse 1 John reminds us of the ultimate act of love demonstrated by Jesus Christ, who willingly laid down his life for us. It emphasizes that love is not just a sentiment or feeling but an action that requires self-sacrifice. Just as Jesus' sacrifice on the cross brought redemption and salvation, Isaac Netero's sacrifice in the anime serves as a symbol of hope and protection for humanity. Both instances remind us of the profound impact that selfless acts of love and sacrifice can have on others.

Isaac Netero's role as a saviour figure serves as an inspiration for us as believers in Christ. It reminds us of the call to love sacrificially, to put the needs of others before our own, and to be willing to lay down our lives, not just in physical terms but also in terms of our time, resources, and personal desires.

In contemplating Isaac Netero's character in Hunter x Hunter, we are challenged to examine our own lives and consider how we can more fully embody sacrificial love in our relationships and service to others. It invites us to lay down our lives, comforts, and desires for the well-being and salvation of those around us, mirroring the love demonstrated by Christ Himself.

"A prayer comes from the heart. If the heart achieves the correct form, it becomes emotions and emotions can be manifested." - Isaac Netero

July 31

In this the love of God was made manifest among us, that God sent his only Son into the world, so that we might live through him. In this is love, not that we have loved God but that he loved us and sent his Son to be the propitiation for our sins. Beloved, if God so loved us, we also ought to love one another. 1 John 4:9-11

Scarf Girl

(Attack On Titan)

Mikasa's actions reflect a profound love and devotion towards her friends, particularly Eren, in the Attack on Titan anime series. She demonstrates selflessness and a willingness to lay down her life for their well-being. Her sacrifice mirrors the sacrificial love shown by God when He sent His Son, Jesus Christ, into the world to save humanity.

1 John 4:9-11 encourages us to respond to God's love by loving one another in the same way. It challenges us to examine our own lives and consider how we can imitate the love of Christ by putting the needs and well-being of others above our own. When we embody this sacrificial love, we have the potential to bring healing, restoration, and hope to others.

Mikasa demonstrates a sacrificial love that goes beyond mere words or feelings. Her willingness to give up her own desires, safety, and comfort for the sake of others embodies the essence of selfless love. Her sacrifice also speaks to the transformative power of love. Her actions have a profound impact on those around her, inspiring them to persevere and find hope in the face of adversity.

In reflecting on Mikasa's sacrifice, we are invited to examine the depth of God's love for us and how that love should inform and shape our own relationships with others. It encourages us to step outside of ourselves, to lay down our own interests, and to love sacrificially, just as Christ has loved us. Let Mikasa's example inspire us to live out the selfless love of God in our own lives, making a difference in the lives of those around us.

"Believe in your own power." - Mikasa Ackerman

August 1

The Lord will fulfil his purpose for me; your steadfast love, O Lord, endures forever. Do not forsake the work of your hands. Psalm 138:8

Brainwashing Anti-Hero

(My Hero Academia)

Hitoshi Shinso from My Hero Academia is a character who initially struggles with low self-esteem and a sense of inadequacy. He possesses a unique quirk called Brainwashing, which allows him to control the actions of those who respond to his voice. However, due to his quirk's limitations and the discrimination he faces as a student in the hero course, Shinso often doubts his abilities and feels inferior to his classmates.

In light of Psalm 138:8, we are reminded of the profound truth that God has a purpose for each individual's life. The psalmist acknowledges that God's steadfast love endures forever and that He never forsakes the work of His hands. This understanding can provide us with a sense of security and comfort, knowing that we are unconditionally loved by our Creator.

Shinso's journey is marked by determination to overcome obstacles and prove himself. He understands that his worth is not defined by others' opinions or limitations. Through perseverance, he works hard to improve and expand his abilities. Support from friends and mentors uplifts him, enabling him to embrace his uniqueness. Recognizing his strengths, he realizes the meaningful impact he can make, empowering him to embrace his individuality with confidence.

Our self-esteem is intricately tied to our understanding of God's love for us and His purpose in our lives. By embracing this truth, we can cultivate a healthy and Christ-centred self-esteem, living with the assurance that we are beloved children of God, equipped to fulfil the purpose God has set before us.

"If you know what you want for your future, then you can't worry about appearances." - Hitoshi Shinso

August 2

Whoever conceals his transgressions will not prosper, but he who confesses and forsakes them will obtain mercy.
Proverbs 28:13

Universal Emperor

(Dragon Ball)

The character Frieza from Dragon Ball represents a figure consumed by sin, known for his wickedness, cruelty, and lust for power. His character exemplifies the consequences of concealing sins. He refuses to acknowledge or take responsibility for his actions, allowing his pride to blind him to the harm he inflicts upon others. In his pursuit of power, he becomes trapped in a cycle of darkness, unable to experience true prosperity or find lasting fulfilment.

Proverbs 28:13 teaches us that concealing sins leads to spiritual decay. When we deny or hide our wrongdoing, we distance ourselves from God's mercy and grace. However, the verse also offers hope and a path towards transformation. It highlights the power of confession and renunciation. When we have the courage to humbly admit our faults, seek forgiveness, and turn away from our sinful ways, we open ourselves to God's mercy and the opportunity for genuine change.

Frieza's refusal to confess his sins ultimately isolates him from the possibility of redemption and restoration. His character serves as a cautionary tale, reminding us of the destructive nature of unrepentant sin. It calls us to examine our own lives and confront the sins we may be concealing, recognizing that only by confessing and renouncing them can we find true healing and restoration in Christ.

The sin of Frieza from Dragon Ball serves as a reminder of the destructive consequences of concealing sins and the transformative power of confession and repentance. It calls us to examine our own lives, seek God's mercy, and embrace the path of genuine transformation and reconciliation.

"Cannon fodder do have their uses, do they not?" - Frieza

August 3

Oh, give thanks to the Lord, for he is good, for his steadfast love endures forever! Psalm 107:1

King of Duelists

(Yu-Gi-Oh!)

Seto Kaiba's character in the Yu-Gi-Oh anime series provides a perspective on thankfulness when considering his growth and transformation throughout the story. Initially driven by ambition and a desire for power, Kaiba's character evolves over time, leading him to appreciate the people and experiences that have shaped him.

Psalm 107:1 encourages us to express gratitude to the Lord, recognizing His love and goodness. Additionally, the verse highlights the enduring nature of God's love. As we express gratitude to Him, we recognize His faithfulness and the countless ways He has shown His goodness throughout our lives. By expressing gratitude to the Lord, we open our hearts to receive His blessings and experience a deeper sense of joy, contentment, and peace. Thankfulness helps us shift our focus from our own ambitions and desires to acknowledging the goodness and provision of God in our lives.

The thankfulness of Seto Kaiba also extends to the Duel Monsters game itself. He appreciates the intricacies and strategic depth of the game, seeing it as a platform for self-expression and personal growth. Kaiba's dedication and relentless pursuit of excellence in Duel Monsters reflect his deep respect and gratitude for the game and the opportunities it provides.

Seto Kaiba's journey teaches us that thankfulness can have a profound impact on our character and outlook. By cultivating a spirit of gratitude, we can develop a deeper sense of humility, appreciation, and joy. Regardless of our circumstances or goals, expressing thankfulness allows us to recognize the blessings in our lives and fosters a heart of contentment and appreciation.

"The future is unlimited and the past is but a trace of a memory." - Seto Kaiba

August 4

Come to me, all who labor and are heavy laden, and I will give you rest. Take my yoke upon you, and learn from me, for I am gentle and lowly in heart, and you will find rest for your souls. For my yoke is easy, and my burden is light.
Matthew 11:28-30

Heterochromia Monster Slayer

(Wonder Egg Priority)

Ai Ohto, a character in Wonder Egg Priority, was born with heterochromia, a condition where one eye has a different colour than the other. Unfortunately, Ai became the target of relentless bullying by her classmates due to this distinctive feature. This constant torment led to poor self-esteem, isolation, and depression. However, through overcoming personal hardships and forming new friendships, Ai gradually began to see herself in a more positive light.

Matthew 11:28-30 extends a profound invitation from Jesus Himself to find rest in Him. Jesus calls us to come to Him with our brokenness, pain, and longing for acceptance. He understands the heaviness of our hearts and the burdens we bear. In Him, we discover the true rest and comfort our souls desperately need.

Ai's story reflects the universal search for solace and acceptance in the world. Like her, we may seek validation and acceptance from others, only to be left disappointed and hurt. However, Jesus invites us to take His yoke upon us, to learn from Him and follow His ways. By embracing His teachings and surrendering to His guidance, we find a genuine sense of belonging and acceptance.

Through Ai's journey, we are reminded that true acceptance and rest are found in Jesus alone. As we bring our struggles, fears, and insecurities to Him, we encounter a loving Saviour who embraces us and offers us a place of belonging. We no longer need to strive for acceptance from the world, for in Him, we are unconditionally accepted and loved.

"I'm done with the me that craved attention. I'm going to believe! If I don't, I can't protect anyone! Can't love anyone!" - Ai Ohto

August 5

A hot-tempered man stirs up strife, but he who is slow to anger quiets contention. Proverbs 15:18

Master Craftsman

(The Rising of The Shield Hero)

Naofumi Iwatani from The Rising of the Shield Hero anime is a character who experiences intense anger and resentment after being falsely accused and betrayed. He becomes filled with a deep sense of injustice and uses his anger as a driving force for vengeance and self-protection. His anger often leads him to isolate himself from others and view the world through a lens of bitterness.

The verse Proverbs 15:18 highlights the value of patience in diffusing quarrels and promoting peaceful interactions. It encourages us to exercise self-control and avoid impulsive outbursts of anger. Instead, we are called to approach conflicts with a patient and composed attitude, seeking resolutions that bring about reconciliation and understanding.

As the story progresses, Naofumi learns the importance of patience and controlling his anger. He begins to realize that his hot-tempered reactions only exacerbate his problems and hinder his ability to find solutions. Through his encounters with others and his personal growth, Naofumi starts to develop a more patient and composed demeanour. He understands that by remaining calm and level-headed, he has a better chance of resolving conflicts and fostering understanding.

Naofumi's character in the anime reminds us of the destructive nature of uncontrolled anger and the importance of cultivating patience and self-control. It encourages us to consider the consequences of our reactions and to strive for peaceful resolutions in our own lives. Through practicing patience and seeking understanding, we can contribute to a more harmonious and reconciled world, aligning ourselves with God's desire for peace among His creation.

"Wherever the waves go, I'll go with my friends." - Naofumi Iwatani

August 6

And why are you anxious about clothing? Consider the lilies of the field, how they grow: they neither toil nor spin, yet I tell you, even Solomon in all his glory was not arrayed like one of these. Matthew 6:28-29

Cor al Peacocks' vice-captain

(Black Clover)

In Black Clover, Kirsch Vermillion is a member of the noble Vermillion family known for their fire magic abilities. He is recognized for his flamboyant and extravagant personality, with a unique sense of style. Kirsch can often be seen wearing elaborate and colourful outfits adorned with jewellery and accessories. His appearance is characterized by his long, flowing blonde hair and confident demeanour.

Matthew 6:28-29 reminds us of Jesus' teaching about worry and the fleeting nature of material possessions. It encourages us to trust in God's provision and care, as exemplified by the flowers of the field. While expressing oneself through fashion and personal style is not inherently wrong, the verse reminds us not to prioritize external adornment excessively. Instead, it encourages us to prioritize inner qualities such as love, compassion, and faithfulness, which hold eternal significance.

The flamboyant appearance of Kirsch Vermillion can serve as a reminder that God's creation is wonderfully diverse. Just as the flowers in the field display a variety of colours, shapes, and forms, Kirsch's appearance showcases the richness of human expression and creativity. It urges us not to judge or dismiss others based on their outward appearance but rather appreciate the unique ways in which individuals reflect the beauty of God's creation.

Kirsch Vermillion's character in Black Clover invites us to celebrate the diversity of God's creation, appreciate individual expression, and focus on the inner qualities that truly matter in our interactions with others and our relationship with God.

"Being weak is nothing to be ashamed of. Staying weak is."
- Fuegoleon Vermillion.

August 7

Better is the end of a thing than its beginning, and the patient in spirit is better than the proud in spirit.
Ecclesiastes 7:8

Eight-Dragon God

(Fairy Tail)

God Serena's attitude in the anime Fairy Tail is characterized by pride, arrogance, and a relentless pursuit of power. He seeks immediate recognition and asserts his superiority over others without considering the consequences of his actions. His behaviour reflects the danger of allowing pride to govern our lives.

In Ecclesiastes 7:8, we are reminded that the end of a matter is more important than its beginning and that patience is better than pride. This verse teaches us the value of patience and humility in our pursuits. It encourages us to have a long-term perspective, recognizing that the ultimate outcome and the growth we experience along the way are more significant than initial successes or appearances.

God Serena's character demonstrates the dangers of pride and emphasizes the importance of humility. It highlights the negative consequences of seeking power and recognition solely for personal gain. In contrast, the Fairy Tail guild, with its emphasis on friendship, unity, and selflessness, serves as a counterbalance to God Serena's arrogance. This encourages us to reflect on our own attitudes and motivations, reminding us to seek humility and place our trust in God rather than seeking power and recognition for our own glory.

By relating God Serena's attitude in the anime, we are reminded of the significance of patience and humility in our own lives. It urges us to embrace a patient and humble attitude, recognizing that true growth and fulfilment come from trusting in God's plan and exercising patience in all aspects of life.

"The mistakes people make are usually labelled as experience. But with a true mistake, there will be no experience gained." - Hades

August 8

"Let the one who boasts, boast in the Lord." For it is not the one who commends himself who is approved, but the one whom the Lord commends. 2 Corinthians 10:17-18

Noveno Espada

(Bleach)

In Bleach, Aaroniero Arurruerie's circumstance reflects his desire for power, control, and recognition. He boasts about his power and abilities, seeking validation from others and elevating himself above his peers. However, his boasting is empty and self-centred, driven by a desire for personal glory rather than acknowledging the true source of his strength.

The verse in 2 Corinthians 10:17-18 highlights the appropriate way to boast or find worth and approval. It emphasizes that boasting should not be in oneself but in the Lord. Our validation and approval do not come from self-promotion or the praises of others, but rather from God's commendation. We are called to cultivate humility and acknowledge that our abilities and achievements are gifts from God. Instead of boasting in ourselves, we are called to boast in the Lord, recognizing His sovereignty, grace, and power working through us. Our validation and approval come from aligning our lives with His will and seeking His commendation.

Aaroniero's boasting and self-commendation ultimately lead to his downfall and expose the emptiness of relying solely on one's own strength. It highlights the emptiness and fleeting nature of seeking validation from worldly sources. His downfall exposes the limitations of relying solely on one's own strength and accomplishments.

By relating Aaroniero's circumstance, we are reminded of the importance of humility and giving glory to God. It prompts us to seek validation and worth in our relationship with Him, acknowledging that our abilities and accomplishments are gifts from Him. Instead of boasting in ourselves, we should boast in the Lord, recognizing His authority in our lives.

"No matter how strong a defence, a stronger offense will always shatter it." - Byakuya Kuchiki

August 9

But seek first the kingdom of God and his righteousness, and all these things will be added to you. Matthew 6:33

SOS Brigade Leader

(The Melancholy of Haruhi Suzumiya)

Haruhi Suzumiya, the main character in the anime "The Melancholy of Haruhi Suzumiya,"exhibits a strong commitment to her desires and ambitions. She is determined to find excitement, supernatural phenomena, and create a world that suits her preferences. Her commitment can be seen as a reflection of her strong will and unwavering determination to shape her reality.

The verse in Matthew 6:33 reminds us of the importance of prioritizing God's kingdom and righteousness above all else. It calls us to seek God's will and His purposes in our lives, placing Him at the centre of our commitments and actions. When we seek God's kingdom first, He promises to provide for our needs and bless us abundantly.

The commitment of Haruhi Suzumiya can prompt us to reflect on our own priorities and motivations. Her journey serves as a cautionary tale, reminding us of the limitations and emptiness of solely pursuing personal fulfilment and excitement. As Christians, our ultimate fulfilment and purpose are found in a deep relationship with God, aligning our lives with His will, and participating in the work of His kingdom. While seeking excitement and fulfilment is not inherently wrong, we should ensure that our commitments and pursuits are in line with God's priorities and honour Him in all that we do.

Haruhi's commitment in the anime can serve as a reminder to reorient our focus, placing God at the centre of our lives and seeking His kingdom above all else. By doing so, we can experience true fulfilment and purpose, knowing that God will provide for our needs and guide us on a path that leads to eternal significance.

"Dreams start by believing." - Haruhi Suzumiya

August 10

From whom the whole body, joined and held together by every joint with which it is equipped, when each part is working properly, makes the body grow so that it builds itself up in love. Ephesians 4:16

Magic Knights Squad

(Black Clover)

The Black Bulls are a ragtag team of misfits from Black Clover who exemplify the beauty and power of unity within a diverse community. Despite their differences in personalities, backgrounds, and magical abilities, they come together as a cohesive unit, supporting and relying on one another. This unity mirrors the ideal of the body of Christ, where believers from various walks of life are joined together by their faith in Christ.

Ephesians 4:16 reminds us that our growth and building up happen in love. Love is the driving force that enables us to extend grace, forgiveness, and understanding to one another. It fosters an environment where unity thrives and where the body of Christ can grow and impact the world around us.

Like the Black Bulls, we each have a unique role to play as a part of the body of Christ. Our individual talents, skills, and experiences contribute to the growth and building up of the body as a whole. Just as the Black Bulls rely on every supporting member as ligaments, we are called to recognize and value the diverse contributions of fellow believers, appreciating the unique gifts and perspectives they bring.

In reflecting on the Black Bulls team from Black Clover, we are encouraged to cultivate unity, embrace diversity, and extend love within the body of Christ. By doing so, we can experience the growth, edification, and transformative power that comes from functioning as a unified and loving community, fulfilling our purpose as followers of Christ.

"Even if you think you might lose, you'll be fine as long as you don't give up. Surpass your limits. Then a path will open up for you." - Yami Sukehiro

August 11

Be strong, and let your heart take courage, all you who wait for the Lord! Psalm 31:24

Intergalactic Bounty Hunter

(Cowboy Bebop)

Spike Spiegel from the Cowboy Bebop anime embodies strength and resilience in the face of adversity. He takes on dangerous missions and confronts his own haunting past with unwavering determination. In moments of uncertainty, Spike remains steadfast and resolute, never losing hope or giving in to despair.

The verse from Psalm 31:24 encourages all who place their hope in the Lord to be strong and take heart. It speaks to the courage that arises from trusting in God's guidance and provision. Our hope lies in the redemptive power and faithful presence of God. This hope becomes the foundation on which we can draw strength and courage. Similarly, Spike's character highlights the transformative power of hope in fostering courage. In the midst of a broken and chaotic world, he carries a sense of hope for a better future. This hope fuels his determination to confront his past and seek justice.

Spike's courage is intertwined with his sense of hope. Despite the challenges and dangers, he encounters, he maintains a belief in the possibility of redemption and justice. This hope fuels his determination and gives him the strength to persevere through difficult circumstances. His unwavering strength amidst challenging circumstances serves as a reminder of the importance of anchoring our hope in the Lord.

As we reflect on the courage of Spike Spiegel, we are reminded to be strong and take heart in our hope in the Lord. His character in the anime serves as an inspiration to remain steadfast and resolute, drawing strength from our faith and trust in God's provision. By embracing this courageous spirit, we can navigate life's challenges with grace and unwavering hope, knowing that the Lord is our stronghold and guide.

"Life will challenge you to do things sometimes. You just have to let go!" - Spike Spiegel

August 12

If any of you lacks wisdom, let him ask God, who gives generously to all without reproach, and it will be given him. James1:5

Mr. Principal

(My Hero Academia)

Principal Nezu from My Hero Academia consistently demonstrates wisdom and discernment in his role as the principal of U.A. High School. His decisions often involve considering the well-being and growth of the students and the school as a whole. He demonstrates a deep trust in his own judgment but also understands the importance of seeking guidance beyond his own understanding.

In James 1:5, believers are encouraged to seek wisdom from God when facing difficult choices or situations. It highlights the generous nature of God, who freely gives wisdom to those who ask without finding fault. As believers, we are called to approach decision-making with a humble heart, acknowledging our dependency on God's wisdom rather than relying solely on our own understanding.

The decision-making process of Principal Nezu reflects the importance of considering multiple perspectives and seeking counsel. By seeking wisdom from various sources, he ensures that he is making informed decisions that prioritize the well-being of the students and the school community. This resonates with the biblical principle of seeking wise counsel and valuing diverse perspectives in order to make sound decisions.

Principal Nezu ensures that U.A. High School operates in a manner that promotes growth, safety, and the overall well-being of its students. His example serves as a reminder for believers to approach decision-making humbly, acknowledging their need for wisdom from God and trusting in His guidance to navigate complex situations.

"The single step... feels like an impossible journey. And I believe... once someone takes that unlikely step and carves a path... the ultimate hero rises up." - Nezu

August 13

If anyone would come after me, let him deny himself and take up his cross daily and follow me. Luke 9:23

Shadow Boy

(Naruto)

Shikamaru Nara from the Naruto anime consistently demonstrates selflessness and humility in his actions and decisions. Despite his own abilities and intellect, he often prioritizes the well-being and interests of his friends and the village over his own desires. He puts the needs of others above his own and makes sacrifices for the greater good.

In Luke 9:23, Jesus speaks to His followers about the requirements of discipleship: denying oneself, taking up the cross daily, and following Him. As followers of Jesus, we are called to deny ourselves, setting aside our selfish ambitions and desires. Shikamaru's devotion encourages us to examine our own lives and consider how we can deny ourselves for the sake of Christ and others. It reminds us that true discipleship involves a daily commitment to put aside our selfish ambitions and follow Jesus with selflessness and dedication.

Shikamaru's commitment to taking up his responsibilities and facing challenges aligns with the concept of carrying our cross daily. In his role as a ninja, he willingly embraces the burdens and hardships that come with his position, just as Jesus carried His cross to Calvary. His example prompts us to consider the challenges we face in our own lives and encourages us to approach them with faith, courage, and a willingness to endure for the sake of our faith.

The devotion of Shikamaru Nara in the anime challenges us to examine our own lives and consider how we can deny ourselves, carry our cross daily, and faithfully follow Jesus. His character also serves as an inspiration for us to live out our faith with selflessness, sacrifice, and unwavering dedication to Christ and others.

"Never avert your eyes, because if an opening arises, even our insignificant power may be enough to determine the fate of the world." - Shikamaru Nara

August 14

'Truly, I say to you, as you did it to one of the least of these my brothers, you did it to me.' Matthew 25:40

Valac Family

(Mairimashita! Iruma-kun)

In the anime, the Valac family extends their love, acceptance, and support to Iruma, a human who finds himself in a demon world. Despite Iruma's differences and vulnerabilities, they treat him as a cherished member of their family, extending kindness and understanding. Their actions remind us that each person has inherent worth, and by showing compassion to others, we express our love for Christ Himself.

Matthew 25:40 calls us to a life of selflessness and empathy, reminding us that our actions towards others hold eternal significance. Through the Valac family's portrayal in the anime, we are encouraged to examine our hearts and consider how we can extend Christ's love and compassion to "the least of these"in our communities and beyond.

By showing love and acceptance to Iruma, the Valac family demonstrates their understanding that their actions towards him ultimately express their love for Christ. They recognize the inherent worth and dignity of Iruma as a person, regardless of his human status in a demon world. God's love extends to all people, irrespective of their background or circumstances. This encourages us to break down barriers, embrace diversity, and extend Christ-like love to those who may be marginalized or in need.

The Valac family from Marimashita Iruma-kun challenges us to examine how we can extend Christ's love to others, recognizing that by serving and caring for them, we are serving and caring for Christ Himself. It encourages us to be agents of love, compassion, and acceptance in a world that desperately needs it.

"Despair won't change anything, nor it would fill my stomach, if I don't move there's nothing will change" - Iruma Suzuki

August 15

I have said these things to you, that in me you may have peace. In the world you will have tribulation. But take heart; I have overcome the world. John 16:33

King of Curses

(Jujutsu Kaisen)

Ryomen Sukuna, known as the King of Curses thousands of years ago, serves as the primary antagonist in Jujutsu Kaisen. He represents a powerful and menacing force that invokes fear and poses great challenges for the characters. They face constant threats and uncertainties in their battles against him. Similarly, in our lives, we often encounter fears and difficulties that can overwhelm us and leave us feeling powerless.

The verse John 16:33 offers a message of hope and reassurance amidst our fears. Jesus, speaking to His disciples, acknowledges that trouble and tribulations are inevitable in this world. However, He encourages them to take heart and find peace in Him. He assures them that He has overcome the world, triumphing over its darkness and fear.

The fear of Ryomen Sukuna in Jujutsu Kaisen represents the things that threaten our peace and security. In our own lives, we encounter various forms of fear and anxiety that can grip our hearts and disturb our peace. Whether it's the fear of the unknown, fear of failure, or fear of the darkness around us, these emotions can overwhelm us and leave us feeling powerless. However, Christ offers us peace that can anchor our souls even in the midst of turmoil.

Just as the characters in Jujutsu Kaisen confront the fear of Ryomen Sukuna, we too face fears that can paralyze us. By shifting our focus from our fears to Jesus, we can find peace. When we trust in Him, we find the peace that surpasses all understanding, enabling us to face our fears with courage and resilience. We can take comfort in His words and find peace in Him, knowing that He is with us in every trial we face. With Jesus as our anchor, we can face our fears head-on, confident in His ultimate victory.

"Stand proud. You are strong." - Ryomen Sukuna

August 16

Who is a God like you, pardoning iniquity and passing over transgression for the remnant of his inheritance? He does not retain his anger forever, because he delights in steadfast love. Micah 7:18

Humanoid Typhoon

(Trigun)

Throughout the Trigun anime series, Vash encounters numerous individuals who have wronged him or caused harm to others. Despite the pain and suffering, he consistently demonstrates a remarkable capacity for forgiveness. He understands that holding onto grudges and seeking revenge only perpetuates a cycle of violence and does not bring true resolution or healing.

Micah 7:18 reminds us of the unmatched character of God, who pardons sin and forgives transgressions. It emphasizes that God's forgiveness is not driven by anger or a desire for retribution but by His delight in showing mercy. This verse highlights the depths of God's love and grace, demonstrating His willingness to extend forgiveness to the undeserving.

Vash's character mirrors divine forgiveness as he consistently chooses to let go of anger and resentment, embracing a spirit of mercy and compassion. He seeks the redemption of those who have wronged him rather than seeking revenge. In doing so, he exemplifies the transformative power of forgiveness. His portrayal of forgiveness reminds us that extending forgiveness is not a sign of weakness but a manifestation of strength, love, and grace. It requires us to let go of bitterness, resentment, and the desire for retaliation.

The journey of Vash the Stampede in Trigun encourages us to embrace forgiveness as a vital component of our faith. It calls us to extend mercy, grace, and love to others, just as God has extended them to us. By embodying the forgiveness of God, we participate in His work of reconciliation and offer a testimony of His transformative power to the world around us.

"The ticket to the future is always open." - Vash the Stampede

August 17

If one member suffers, all suffer together; if one member is honoured, all rejoice together. 1 Corinthians 12:26

Hunter Duo

(Hunter x Hunter)

Gon and Killua's friendship in the Hunter x Hunter anime reflects the spirit of unity and empathy, as they share a deep emotional connection where they genuinely care for each other's well-being. Their friendship demonstrates remarkable solidarity and mutual compassion. They understand that they are on this journey together and genuinely share each other's joys and sorrows. Their bond goes beyond superficial companionship, as they are intimately connected on an emotional and spiritual level.

In 1 Corinthians 12:26, the apostle Paul reminds us that as members of the body of Christ, we are intricately connected. The suffering of one part affects the whole body, and we all share in that suffering. Similarly, when one part is honoured, we all rejoice together. This verse emphasizes the unity and shared experiences within the body of Christ. It highlights the significance of true companionship, where friends genuinely care for each other's well-being.

Gon and Killua exhibit humility and a willingness to set aside their own interests for the sake of their friendship. They support each other's dreams and goals, celebrating each other's successes without envy or rivalry. Their friendship is characterized by mutual respect, trust, and a shared sense of purpose.

By relating the friendship of Gon and Killua in Hunter x Hunter, we are reminded of the value of genuine friendship and the impact it can have on our lives. It encourages us to be deeply invested in the well-being of our friends, showing compassion in their struggles and celebrating their successes. It reminds us that true friendship involves actively sharing in each other's journey, walking together as a unified and supportive community.

"If you want to get to know someone, find out what makes them angry." - Gon Freecss

August 18

We are afflicted in every way, but not crushed; perplexed, but not driven to despair; persecuted, but not forsaken; struck down, but not destroyed; 2 Corinthians 4:8-9

Selfless crusader

(Erased)

In Erased, Satoru faces numerous challenges, including the pursuit of a serial killer and the need to change the past to save lives. Despite being hard-pressed on every side, he remains resilient and determined, refusing to be crushed by the weight of his circumstances. He navigates through moments of confusion and despair, yet he never loses hope. Even when faced with persecution and setbacks, he finds the strength to keep going.

The verses in 2 Corinthians 4:8-9 highlight the human capacity to endure and overcome challenges. They emphasize our ability to persevere through difficult circumstances with God's strength and guidance. These verses remind us that even when we face overwhelming odds, we are not alone. God's presence sustains us and empowers us to rise above our trials.

Satoru's character serves as a reminder that our weaknesses can become opportunities for God's strength to be revealed. Just as he undergoes growth and transformation through his struggles, we can find similar growth and transformation in our own lives when we allow God to work through our challenges. God's power is made perfect in our weakness, and His grace is sufficient for us.

The growth that Satoru Fujinuma experiences throughout Erased serves as an example for us to trust in God's faithfulness and rely on His strength during challenging times. Just like him, we too can find growth and transformation when we lean on God's grace and navigate through life's obstacles. We can draw inspiration from Satoru's journey, knowing that despite the hardships we encounter, we can find the strength to persevere and ultimately thrive.

"The future is always blank. Only your willpower can leave footsteps there." - Satoru Fujinuma

August 19

Rejoice in the Lord always; again, I will say, rejoice.
Philippians 4:4

Potato girl

(Attack on Titan)

Sasha Braus from Attack on Titan finds happiness in simple pleasures and cherishes the joy of living. Despite the harsh and dangerous world, she inhabits, she maintains a positive and light-hearted outlook, often finding happiness in the smallest of things. Her love for food and her genuine appreciation for the beauty of nature bring her great delight.

Philippians 4:4 encourages us to find lasting joy in our relationship with God. It reminds us that true happiness is found when we anchor our hearts in the Lord's goodness, faithfulness, and love. When we embrace this message, our own happiness becomes a testimony to the transformative power of God's love. By radiating joy, we become agents of hope and light in a world that is often clouded by darkness.

Sasha's character serves as a reminder that even in the midst of chaos and despair, we can choose to rejoice in God's presence and find comfort in His promises. Her happiness extends beyond herself. Her infectious joy positively impacts those around her, uplifting their spirits and reminding them of the goodness in life. Sasha's happiness also reminds us to appreciate the simple blessings in life. She finds delight in the basic necessities, such as food and companionship, teaching us to cultivate a spirit of gratitude and contentment. Through her character, we are encouraged to take a step back and find joy in the ordinary moments, recognizing that every good gift comes from God.

In reflecting on Sasha's happiness, we are reminded to prioritize our relationship with God, cultivate a heart of gratitude, and embrace a joyful spirit that impacts both ourselves and those around us. By finding our ultimate source of joy in the Lord, we can experience a happiness that transcends circumstances and brings light into a world in need of hope.

"It's alright if you're weak, there are people who will come and rescue you." - Sasha Braus

August 20

As each has received a gift, use it to serve one another, as good stewards of God's varied grace. 1 Peter 4:10

Dedicated Mangaka

(Bakuman)

The hard work of Moritaka Mashiro from the anime Bakuman reflects his determination and pursuit of his dreams. Despite facing challenges and setbacks, he tirelessly dedicates himself to his passion for manga and strives to become a successful artist. His commitment to honing his skills, pushing through failures, and continuously improving is an inspiration.

The verse 1 Peter 4:10 reminds us of the importance of recognizing and utilizing the unique gifts and talents that God has blessed us with. It calls us to be good stewards of these gifts, using them not for our own selfish ambitions but for the service and benefit of others. By embracing the call to use our gifts for the service of others, we become vessels of God's grace, spreading His love, joy, and creativity to the world.

Moritaka's journey of hard work and dedication reminds us of the importance of stewardship. As faithful stewards of God's grace, we are called to wisely and responsibly use the gifts and talents bestowed upon us. Moritaka's example encourages us to identify our own abilities, whether they are in the arts, sciences, communication, or any other area, and invest them diligently for the betterment of others and the glory of God.

Through Moritaka's character, we see the transformative power of hard work, perseverance, and a heart focused on serving others. His story reminds us that our work, no matter how ordinary or unconventional it may seem, can be an avenue for God's grace and love to touch people's lives. By emulating his dedication, we can make a meaningful impact in the world and fulfil our calling as faithful stewards of God's gifts.

"Those who don't give up no matter how many walls they run into; those are the ones who'll make their dreams come true." - Moritaka Mashiro

August 21

These are the things that you shall do: Speak the truth to one another; render in your gates judgments that are true and make for peace; Zechariah 8:16

Japanese Police Head

(Death Note)

Soichiro Yagami from the Death Note anime is a character who embodies the importance of honesty in relationships, recognizing that trust and transparency are foundational to healthy interactions. As the chief of the NPA and Light Yagami's father, he upholds a strong moral compass and maintains integrity in his pursuit of solving crimes and holding criminals accountable, even when faced with difficult decisions and personal sacrifices.

Zechariah 8:16 is part of a prophecy given by the prophet Zechariah to the people of Israel during their return from exile in Babylon. It emphasizes the importance of truthfulness, honesty, and integrity in their dealings with one another and in the administration of justice in their courts. The verse encourages the people to uphold these principles and to act justly in their relationships and legal proceedings.

Soichiro's honesty reminds us of the importance of upholding truth in our interactions, relationships, and decision-making processes. It prompts us to evaluate our own lives and ask ourselves if we are faithfully living out the call to be people of truth and integrity. By emulating Soichiro's commitment to truth and sound judgment, we contribute to a more just and compassionate society.

Reflecting on Soichiro's character reminds us of the importance of speaking truthfully and pursuing justice in our own lives. It encourages us to be people of integrity, guided by the principles of truth and righteousness. Just as Soichiro's honesty had an impact on the story, our commitment to truth and justice can contribute to a more just and righteous society, reflecting the character of God and bringing honour to His name.

"Laws are evidence of the human struggle to be righteous."
- Soichiro Yagami

August 22

Hope deferred makes the heart sick, but a desire fulfilled is a tree of life. Proverbs 13:12

Pre-Emptive Strike Leader

(Kuroko's Basketball)

Ryō Sakurai is a character from the anime series "Kuroko's Basketball"known for his incredible shooting skills and unwavering determination. He is often depicted as having a hopeful and optimistic outlook, constantly striving to improve himself and achieve success in the sport. He consistently overcomes obstacles and contributes to the success of his team.

The verse Proverbs 13:12 also highlights the transformative power of fulfilled longing, comparing it to a tree of life. As followers of Christ, we can find hope in the assurance that God is faithful to His promises. The verse also emphasizes the transformative power of the fulfilment of longing. When our hopes and longings are realized, they bring a sense of joy, satisfaction, and vitality. It compares the fulfilment of desires to a tree of life, symbolizing abundant growth, nourishment, and flourishing.

Just like Ryō Sakurai, who may experience moments of frustration and doubt when his hopes seem far off, we need to understand the impact of deferred hope. It reminds us that the journey towards achieving our desires may involve seasons of waiting and obstacles that can test our resolve. We must surrender our desires to God, trusting that He knows what is best for us, and remain hopeful even in the face of delays or setbacks, knowing that God is at work, shaping us and fulfilling His purposes in our lives.

By relating Ryō Sakurai's hope in the anime, we are reminded of the significance of enduring through seasons of deferred hope. It encourages us to hold onto our dreams and aspirations, even when faced with challenges and setbacks, knowing that the eventual fulfilment will bring abundant life and joy. This verse reminds us to remain resilient and hopeful, trusting that the fruition of our desires will bring about a renewed sense of purpose and fulfilment.

"When you come to hate something, you liked it is incredibly painful." - Tetsuya Kuroko

August 23

For all that is in the world—the desires of the flesh and the desires of the eyes and pride of life—is not from the Father but is from the world. 1 John 2:16

Sword Saint

(Re: Zero)

In the world of Re: Zero, Reinhard stands out as a character who exemplifies humility. He consistently demonstrates a willingness to put others before himself, serving with a selfless attitude. Reinhard's humility is seen in his rejection of personal ambition and the pursuit of worldly recognition. Instead, he focuses on his duty to protect and help those around him.

When we examine 1 John 2:16, we understand that it warns about the dangers of pride and the pursuit of worldly desires. It reminds us that the pride of life, seeking personal glory and recognition, is not aligned with God's purposes. True humility requires us to surrender our own desires and align our hearts with God's will, putting Him and others before ourselves.

Reinhard's character serves as a reminder that true strength lies in humility. In a world that often glorifies pride and self-promotion, his example encourages us to embrace humility as a virtue and seek to reflect Christ's character in our lives. His humility also reminds us of the importance of setting aside our own desires and ambitions, and instead, seeking to serve and uplift those around us. It challenges us to examine our motives and actions, ensuring that we are not driven by selfish desires or the pursuit of worldly recognition.

When we relate Reinhard's humility in the anime, we are reminded of the significance of humility in our relationship with God and others. It prompts us to examine our own hearts and attitudes, striving to cultivate humility and avoid the pitfalls of pride. Just as Reinhard's humility allows him to experience favour and support from those around him, our humility can open the doors to God's grace and blessings in our lives.

"I have only one wish, for all to be equal, I desire to create a nation where all citizens are equal." - Emilia

August 24

Beware of false prophets, who come to you in sheep's clothing but inwardly are ravenous wolves. You will recognize them by their fruits. Are grapes gathered from thornbushes, or figs from thistles? Matthew 7:15-16

Witch Doctor

(Soul Eater)

Medusa Gorgon is a deceptive and manipulative character from Soul Eater who poses as a caring and nurturing nurse. However, her true nature is revealed as she works to achieve her own sinister agenda, using others as pawns in her schemes. Her hypocritical behaviour showcases her willingness to deceive and harm others for personal gain.

In Matthew 7:15-16, Jesus warns his followers to be cautious of such individuals. He emphasizes that false prophets may appear outwardly righteous, but their true character is revealed by their actions or fruits. The verse urges us to exercise discernment and not be easily deceived by appearances. It reminds us to look beyond surface-level impressions and evaluate the consistent actions and intentions of individuals. By doing so, we can identify those who claim to be righteous but actually perpetrate deceit and harm.

Medusa's character highlights the potential dangers of allowing deceit and selfishness to take root in our lives. It serves as a cautionary tale, reminding us of the importance of aligning our thoughts, motives, and actions with the teachings of Jesus. Hypocrisy undermines the credibility of our witness and hinders the Gospel. Therefore, it is important for us to examine our own hearts and actions, ensuring that we are not engaging in hypocritical behaviour.

The hypocrisy of Medusa Gorgon in the Soul Eater anime series serves as a reminder of the dangers and consequences of deceit and false appearances. It challenges us to be discerning, live with integrity, and ensure that our actions align with the teachings of Jesus. By doing so, we can strive for authenticity, strengthen our witness, and bring glory to God.

"It will be alright, have faith in yourself." - Medusa Gorgon

August 25

Whoever brings blessing will be enriched, and one who waters will himself be watered. Proverbs 11:25

Cotton Candy Lover

(One Piece)

Tony Tony Chopper from the One Piece anime is a kind and compassionate character. Despite being a reindeer with a tragic past, he displays unwavering kindness towards others, especially those in need. His generosity goes beyond material possessions. He gives his time, energy, and emotional support to those in need, consistently refreshing and rejuvenating their spirits. In return, he experiences his own refreshing moments, finding fulfilment and happiness through his selfless acts.

Proverbs 11:25 reminds us that when we generously pour out our kindness and refresh others, we also receive blessings and refreshment in return. It reinforces the principle that acts of kindness are not only beneficial to the recipient but also bring about personal growth, satisfaction, and spiritual well-being.

Chopper 's character challenges us to examine our own hearts and actions. It prompts us to reflect on how we can be more generous and refreshing to others in our daily lives. It encourages us to move beyond self-interest and extend a helping hand to those in need. It reminds us that acts of kindness not only become a blessing for others but also bring blessings into our own lives.

The kindness of Tony Tony Chopper in One Piece reminds us of the reciprocal nature of generosity and refreshment, highlighting the transformative power of acts of kindness. Chopper's character challenges us to cultivate a spirit of generosity, seeking opportunities to refresh and uplift those around us. By doing so, we not only bring blessings to others but also experience our own spiritual and emotional refreshment.

"There's no disease in this world that can't be cured!" - Tony Tony Chopper

August 26

But I say to you, Love your enemies and pray for those who persecute you. Matthew 5:44

Rain Woman

(Fairy Tail)

In the early parts of the Fairy Tail anime series, Juvia's love for Gray Fullbuster is characterized by possessiveness and jealousy. She sees other female characters as her rivals and often clashes with them due to her strong affection for Gray. However, as the story progresses, she undergoes a transformation and learns to love not only Gray but also her enemies and those who have persecuted her.

The verse Matthew 5:44 challenges us to examine our own attitudes towards those who mistreat us. It prompts us to respond with love and prayer instead of retaliation or bitterness. By following this teaching, we can contribute to healing and reconciliation, allowing God's love to work through us. We are called to imitate Christ's love, which extends to everyone, even those who oppose us.

Juvia's character arc focuses on her personal growth and transformation. She learns to overcome her obsession with Gray and develops a more selfless and mature love for him. Additionally, she becomes more open and caring towards her friends and allies, displaying strong loyalty and a willingness to protect them. Her journey highlights the transformative power of love and the importance of personal growth and selflessness.

Juvia's story showcases the capacity for change and the power of love to overcome obstacles and bring people together. Her growth reflects the principle that love can transcend animosity and personal interests. By learning to love her enemies, she shows that genuine love has the power to bridge gaps and heal conflicts. Juvia's journey serves as a reminder of the transformative power of love, to extend love and compassion even to those who may seem unworthy or opposed to us.

"It doesn't matter what day it is as long as you are happy."
- Juvia Lockser

August 27

When you pass through the waters, I will be with you; and through the rivers, they shall not overwhelm you; when you walk through fire you shall not be burned, and the flame shall not consume you. Isaiah 43:2

Magic Fish Heroine

(Ponyo)

In the anime, Ponyo is a fish who yearns to become human and embarks on an extraordinary journey to fulfil her desire. Along the way, she encounters tumultuous waters and faces various challenges. Despite the dangers and uncertainties, Ponyo remains determined and displays unwavering love and devotion for the human boy she befriends.

Isaiah 43:2 reassures believers that when we pass through the waters, God is with us and will prevent us from being overwhelmed. This verse reminds us of God's faithfulness and His promise to be present in our lives, providing guidance and protection through turbulent times. As believers in Christ, we are called to navigate the challenges of life with unwavering faith, knowing that God is by our side. Just as Ponyo's love for the human boy propels her through the waters, our love for God and others can be a guiding force that helps us overcome obstacles and find peace amidst the storms of life.

Ponyo's journey parallels the challenges we face in our own lives. Her character in the anime serves as a reminder that, in times of trial, we can find solace and assurance in God's presence. By embracing deep trust in Him, we can experience His protection and guidance, knowing that He will not allow the waters to overwhelm us.

The story of Ponyo reminds us that even in the midst of difficulties, we are not alone. God promises to be with us, protecting us from being overwhelmed. By embracing love, determination, and trust, we can find strength and resilience to face the challenges that come our way, knowing that God is by our side.

"You should never judge others by their looks." - Lisa

August 28

Do not toil to acquire wealth; be discerning enough to desist. When your eyes light on it, it is gone, for suddenly it sprouts wings, flying like an eagle toward heaven.
Proverbs 23:4-5

Poker Alice

(Cowboy Bebop)

Faye Valentine is a character from the anime series Cowboy Bebop who initially embodies a materialistic lifestyle. She is driven by a desire for wealth, often seeking quick riches and engaging in activities motivated by personal gain. Faye's materialistic tendencies lead her to make choices that prioritize worldly possessions and temporary pleasures over deeper, more meaningful aspects of life. Therefore, she frequently faces disappointment and setbacks in her quest for material possessions.

The verse Proverbs 23:4-5 cautions against becoming consumed by the pursuit of wealth and relying solely on our own abilities to amass riches. It reminds us that wealth is transient and can easily vanish, much like an eagle soaring away in the sky. It also warns against placing too much trust in our own cleverness.

Faye's journey throughout the series involves confronting the emptiness and fleeting nature of her materialistic pursuits. As she faces various challenges and develops relationships with her fellow crew members, she gradually learns the importance of deeper connections and genuine human experiences.

The character arc of Faye Valentine in the anime serves as a cautionary tale about the potential emptiness and disillusionment that can come from pursuing material wealth without considering the deeper aspects of life. It prompts us to seek contentment in the things that truly matter and find purpose beyond the accumulation of possessions.

"The past is the past and the future is the future. A man is a man and a woman is a woman. The present is the present. I am who I am and you are who you are. That's all there is to it. Does it really matter? Or do we just think it does?" - Faye Valentine

August 29

For whoever would save his life will lose it, but whoever loses his life for my sake will save it. Luke 9:24

Magical Red Girl

(Puella Magi Madoka Magica)

Kyoko Sakura is a character from the anime series Puella Magi Madoka Magica who initially acts out of self-interest and personal gain. Motivated by her own survival and the accumulation of grief seeds, which fuel her powers as a magical girl, Kyoko is driven by a desire for material comfort and security. She is cynical and distrustful of others, often using her powers to manipulate situations to her advantage.

The verse Luke 9:24 is part of a larger passage where Jesus is teaching his disciples about the cost of discipleship. He emphasizes the importance of prioritizing their commitment to him over their own desires and self-preservation. In this particular verse, Jesus encourages his followers to be willing to sacrifice their own lives and desires for the sake of following him, indicating that true life and salvation come from a selfless dedication to him.

In the series, Kyoko's journey involves a gradual shift in her motivations as she forms a connection with the main character, Madoka, and learns the importance of self-sacrifice and genuine care for others. She discovers that true fulfilment and purpose come not from pursuing personal gain but from selflessness and sacrificing oneself for the greater good.

Kyoko Sakura's journey in Puella Magi Madoka Magica serves as a Christian reflection on the transformative power of self-sacrifice. It demonstrates that true fulfilment and meaning can be found by giving up one's own ambitions and priorities in favour of a higher purpose. It invites us to examine our own motivations and consider how we can let go of our selfish desires, align our lives with the selflessness of Christ, and find true fulfilment and salvation by losing our lives for His sake.

"You take what you've got and figure out how to get something out of it." - Kyoko Sakura

August 30

My flesh and my heart may fail, but God is the strength of my heart and my portion forever. Psalm 73:26

Rabbit Mask Manager

(Tokyo Ghoul)

The pain experienced by Touka Kirishima in Tokyo Ghoul reflects the deep and complex nature of human suffering in our fallen world. In her journey, we witness her physical and emotional struggles, her grief, and her search for meaning and purpose amidst the chaos of her circumstances.

In Psalm 73:26, the psalmist acknowledges the frailty and limitations of our human existence. He directs our focus to the source of true strength. The verse proclaims that even when our own strength fails us, God remains the strength of our hearts. He is the unwavering foundation upon which we can rely. He offers us the spiritual fortitude, perseverance, and endurance we require to face the trials and pains of life.

While Touka's pain in the anime is specific to her fictional character, this can be applied in a metaphorical sense to anyone who is experiencing emotional or spiritual anguish. It reminds us that even in our darkest moments, we are not alone, and there is potential for comfort and salvation.

By relating the pain that Touka Kirishima faces in Tokyo Ghoul, we can find solace in the understanding that God is with her in her struggles and can provide the strength she needs to face her challenges. It reminds us that even in the darkest moments, God is present, ready to provide comfort, strength, and a sense of purpose. By aligning our hearts with His, we can discover a peace that transcends our circumstances and find the strength to persevere in the face of pain.

"There's no way someone who can't even protect himself can protect anyone else, is there?" - Touka Kirishima

August 31

The Lord is not slow to fulfil his promise as some count slowness, but is patient toward you, not wishing that any should perish, but that all should reach repentance. 2 Peter 3:9

Painting Shinobi

(Naruto)

Sai from Naruto initially portrays a lack of emotional understanding and struggles to connect with others. However, through his experiences and interactions with his teammates, he begins to cultivate patience within himself. This patience enables him to learn, understand, and empathize with others, ultimately leading to deeper connections and personal growth.

2 Peter 3:9 reminds us of God's patience and His desire for everyone to come to repentance. It emphasizes that God's timing may not align with our expectations, but His patience is rooted in His love and mercy. God's patient nature allows for opportunities of repentance and redemption, as He desires that no one should perish. We are called to emulate God's patience in our interactions with others by extending patience, understanding, and love. Through this, we create an environment that fosters growth, forgiveness, and repentance.

Sai's journey reminds us that patience is not an easy or instantaneous virtue to cultivate. He gradually discovers the importance of emotional bonds and seeks to understand and connect with his teammates. Similarly, in our faith journeys, we are called to exercise patience as we wait upon the Lord and His timing. We trust that God's promises will be fulfilled in His perfect timing and that He is working in and through our lives, even when we cannot see it.

Through Sai's transformation, we are reminded of the power of patience in fostering personal growth, empathy, and meaningful connections. In turn, 2 Peter 3:9 encourages us to embrace God's patient nature and extend that patience to others, trusting in His perfect timing and His desire for all to come to repentance.

"A smile is the best way to get oneself out of a tight spot, even if it's a fake one. Surprisingly enough, everyone takes it at face value." - Sai

September 1

Let no one despise you for your youth, but set the believers an example in speech, in conduct, in love, in faith, in purity. 1 Timothy 4:12

Healing Soul Reaper

(Bleach)

Retsu Unohana is known for her exceptional skills, wisdom, and strength as a character. As the captain of the Soul Society's 4th Division, she faces various challenges and pressures. Yet she refuses to let others belittle her abilities or make her feel inferior due to her age or gender. Instead, she sets an example for others through her speech, conduct, love, faith, and purity. She demonstrates leadership qualities, compassion, and dedication to her duties, gaining respect from her peers and becoming a role model for others.

The verse 1 Timothy 4:12 emphasizes that age or any other external factors should not hinder us from living out our faith boldly. It encourages individuals not to allow others to disregard them based on their age or any other factor. We are called to embrace our identity in Christ and use our gifts and abilities to make a difference, shining His light in the world.

Retsu Unohana's demonstration of speech, conduct, love, faith, and purity serves as a model for us. Similarly, in our interactions with others, we are called to exhibit grace, kindness, and compassion. Retsu's dedication to her duties and the care she shows for others reflect the character traits we are encouraged to cultivate as followers of Christ. We are reminded to be a positive influence and set an example through our actions and words, showing God's love and reflecting His light to those around us.

The peer pressure faced by Retsu Unohana encourages us as believers to stand firm in our faith, set an example in our words and actions, and embrace our identity in Christ. We are reminded that regardless of our age or circumstances, we can make a positive impact by living out our faith with love, integrity, and a steadfast commitment to God's truth.

"You shouldn't let your feelings dictate what you say." - Retsu Unohana

September 2

For I am not ashamed of the gospel, for it is the power of God for salvation to everyone who believes, to the Jew first and also to the Greek. Romans 1:16

Selfless Doctor Hunter

(Hunter x Hunter)

Leorio Paradinight from the anime Hunter x Hunter may not possess extraordinary powers like some other characters, but he exemplifies a unique form of power that extends beyond physical strength or abilities. His power transcends his physical skills as a doctor and lies in his unwavering sense of justice, empathy, and deep desire to help those in need. He demonstrates the virtue of putting others' needs before his own and strives to use his abilities and knowledge for the betterment of society.

Romans 1:16 highlights the transformative power of the gospel and the salvation it brings to all who believe. It emphasizes the confidence and boldness that believers have in sharing the good news of Jesus Christ. Leorio's power in the anime aligns with the transformative power of the gospel, which brings salvation and healing to all who believe.

As followers of Christ, we can be inspired by Leorio's character and apply it to our own lives. We are called to recognize and utilize the unique gifts and abilities that God has given us, just as Leorio employs his medical skills to bring healing. We can also seek to bring positive change and transformation to the lives of others, displaying the power of the gospel through our actions and words.

The power of Leorio Paradinight from Hunter x Hunter reflects the transformative power of the gospel. His dedication to justice, empathy, and service aligns with the heart of Jesus, showcasing the power of the gospel in action. As Christians, we can draw inspiration from Leorio's character to live out our faith boldly, recognizing the power of the gospel to bring salvation and transformation to the lives of those around us.

"Human potential for evolution is limitless." - Isaac Netero

September 3

Have this mind among yourselves, which is yours in Christ Jesus, who, though he was in the form of God, did not count equality with God a thing to be grasped, but emptied himself, by taking the form of a servant, being born in the likeness of men. And being found in human form, he humbled himself by becoming obedient to the point of death, even death on a cross. Philippians 2:5-8

God of Skypiea

(One Piece)

In One Piece, Eneru, as a character, embodies excessive pride and arrogance. He considers himself a god and believes that he is invincible and superior to others. This prideful mindset leads him to underestimate his opponents and disregard their worth. However, as the story progresses, Eneru's pride becomes his downfall as he is eventually defeated and humbled.

In Philippians 2:5-8, we see the humility of Jesus Christ as the perfect example for us to follow. Despite being in the form of God and having equal status with God, He chose not to cling to His rights and privileges. Instead, Jesus willingly humbled Himself, taking on the form of a servant and even sacrificing His life on the cross for the redemption of humanity.

Eneru's pride is characterized by a sense of superiority, entitlement, and a desire for control. His prideful mindset leads him astray and causes harm to those around him. As Christians, we are called to humble ourselves before God and others, recognizing our dependence on Him and seeking His will above our own. By embracing humility, we can find true power, purpose, and the blessings of God's grace.

The character of Eneru from One Piece anime reminds us of the destructive nature of pride. Christ's humility and selfless sacrifice serve as a reminder for us to let go of our own pride and embrace a servant's heart. By doing so, we can reflect the character of Christ and bring honour to His name.

"No matter how they struggle, can humans defeat thunder?" - Eneru

September 4

The Lord is my rock and my fortress and my deliverer, my God, my rock, in whom I take refuge, my shield, and the horn of my salvation, my stronghold. Psalm 18:2

Water Hashira

(Demon Slayer)

In the world of Demon Slayer, Giyu Tomioka can be seen as a saviour-like figure within the context of the anime series. As a demon slayer, he dedicates his life to protecting humanity from the threat of demons. His exceptional skills, unwavering determination, and selfless acts of heroism make him a symbol of hope and salvation for those in need.

The psalmist describes the Lord in Psalm 18:2 as his rock, fortress, deliverer, shield, and stronghold. These powerful metaphors depict God as a source of protection, refuge, and salvation. We can find comfort in knowing that our true saviour, God Himself, is our rock, fortress, and deliverer. His love and protection are always available to us, and we can rely on Him to be our shield in times of trouble.

As a demon slayer, Giyu becomes a vessel through which the attributes of God are demonstrated. He becomes a symbol of protection, a guardian who stands as a rock against the demonic forces threatening humanity. Just as God is described as a fortress and stronghold, Giyu provides a safe haven for those in need, fighting relentlessly to shield them from harm. His sacrifice and selflessness remind us of the ultimate sacrifice made by Jesus Christ, who laid down His life to deliver us from sin and provide eternal salvation.

Giyu Tomioka, as a saviour-like figure in the Demon Slayer anime, invites us to reflect on the attributes of God and the significance of His role as our ultimate protector and deliverer. His unwavering commitment to defending others encourages us to stand firm in our faith and protect those around us from the spiritual battles we face. It encourages us to seek refuge in Him and to emulate His qualities of strength, protection, and salvation in our own lives.

"Do not let others hold the right to decide if you live or die!" - Giyu Tomioka

September 5

But he was pierced for our transgressions; he was crushed for our iniquities; upon him was the chastisement that brought us peace, and with his wounds we are healed.
Isaiah 53:5

Goddess of Magical Girls

(Puella Magi Madoka Magica)

In the anime, Madoka makes the ultimate sacrifice by choosing to become a magical girl, also known as a Puella Magi, in order to save others. She willingly gives up her own existence and takes on the suffering and despair of all magical girls throughout history, effectively erasing herself from the world. This act of self-sacrifice is driven by her love and desire to protect her friends and countless others from the tragic fate of becoming witches.

In Isaiah 53, the prophet foretells the suffering and sacrifice of the Messiah, who would bear the sins of humanity to bring about peace and healing. Jesus Christ, the ultimate sacrificial lamb, took upon Himself the sins of the world. He willingly suffered and died on the cross, bearing the punishment that humanity deserved. Through His sacrifice, He made it possible for us to experience peace with God and receive spiritual healing and restoration.

Madoka's sacrifice exemplifies the transformative power of selfless love. She takes on the suffering and despair of her fellow magical girls, offering them the chance to find peace and freedom from their tragic fate. Her sacrifice brings healing to their souls, symbolizing the transformative power of selflessness and love.

In contemplating Madoka's sacrifice in the anime, we are reminded of the redemptive power of selfless love and the incredible price paid for our healing and salvation. It deepens our appreciation for the sacrificial love demonstrated by Jesus Christ and encourages us to reflect upon the ways we can emulate His example in our own lives.

"If someone like me could do that, go around helping people who are in trouble, then I think that would be... truly wonderful." - Madoka Kaname

September 6

Having gifts that differ according to the grace given to us, let us use them: if prophecy, in proportion to our faith; if service, in our serving; the one who teaches, in his teaching; the one who exhorts, in his exhortation; the one who contributes, in generosity; the one who leads, with zeal; the one who does acts of mercy, with cheerfulness.
Romans 12:6-8

Meat Dango

(Komi Can't Communicate)

Himiko Agari is one of the main characters and a close friend of the protagonist, Shouko Komi, in the anime series Komi Can't Communicate. Himiko is a passionate gamer who often hides her face behind a mask, which becomes a symbol of her struggle with social anxiety and difficulty in communicating with others. Throughout the series, her character development revolves around her journey to overcome her insecurities and find her voice.

In Romans 12:6-8, the apostle Paul reminds us that God has bestowed different gifts upon each person within the body of Christ. It is essential to recognize that self-esteem should be rooted in a deep understanding of our identity in Christ. Every person is uniquely designed and has been blessed with distinct gifts and talents.

Himiko's dedication to gaming serves as an outlet for her emotions and a means of connection with like-minded individuals. Like her, we can find confidence and fulfilment by channelling our passions and abilities in ways that bring about positive change and promote the well-being of others. By recognizing our value and embracing our gifts, we can step into our roles within the body of Christ and contribute to the flourishing of the community.

The reflection on Himiko's self-esteem invites us to see ourselves through the lens of God's love and grace. By embracing our unique identities, acknowledging our gifts, and using them to serve others, we can grow in self-esteem and contribute to the work of God's kingdom.

"Just because a person has problems communicating doesn't mean that person doesn't want to communicate with others." - Tomohito Oda

September 7

A man who is kind benefits himself, but a cruel man hurts himself. Proverbs 11:17

Sadistic Ghoul Torturer

(Tokyo Ghoul)

In the anime series Tokyo Ghoul, Yakumo Oomóri, also known as Yamori or Jason, is a sadistic ghoul who inflicts immense pain and torture on others for his own pleasure. His actions demonstrate a profound disregard for the well-being and dignity of others, reflecting the sin of cruelty and the absence of empathy. His cruelty becomes a self-destructive cycle, damaging his own soul and well-being.

The verse Proverbs 11:17 invites us to reflect on the importance of kindness, compassion, and treating others with respect. It reminds us of the consequences of cruelty and mistreatment. The verse also emphasizes that being kind and considerate towards others not only benefits them but also benefits ourselves. Acting with kindness leads to healthier relationships, personal growth, and a sense of fulfilment.

Yakumo's actions reflect a heart that lacks compassion and empathy, indulging in cruelty for personal satisfaction. This behaviour stands in direct opposition to the teachings of Christ, who calls us to love one another, treat others with kindness, and value the dignity and worth of every person. Through Christ's sacrificial love, we find forgiveness, redemption, and the power to transform our lives. We are encouraged to extend that same love and kindness to others, recognizing the inherent value and worth of each person created in the image of God.

By reflecting on the sin of Yakumo Oomori, we are reminded of the importance of kindness, compassion, and treating others with respect and dignity. It urges us to consider the impact of our actions on both ourselves and those around us. By embracing kindness and empathy, we can build meaningful relationships and contribute to the well-being and flourishing of others, aligning with the teachings of love and compassion found throughout the Bible.

"Doing what one likes is the right of the strong." - Yakumo Oomori

September 8

Oh, give thanks to the Lord, for he is good; for his steadfast love endures forever! 1 Chronicles 16:34

Primera Espada

(Bleach)

In the anime series Bleach, Coyote Starrk is a character who initially appears as a solitary and melancholic individual. However, as the story unfolds, it becomes clear that he possesses a deep sense of gratitude and thankfulness for the companionship he finds in others, particularly his fellow Espada, Lilynette Gingerbuck.

1 Chronicles 16:34 prompts us to recognize the goodness of God and express gratitude for His unwavering love that lasts through all circumstances. By embracing a spirit of thankfulness, we acknowledge that God's love is constant and never-ending, regardless of our circumstances. This mindset of gratitude enables us to find joy and contentment in the relationships and blessings we have received, recognizing them as gifts from God.

Just as Coyote Starrk expresses thankfulness for the bonds he forms, we can express gratitude for the relationships we have with others and, ultimately, with God. We can recognize that these connections are gifts from God, intended to bring joy, support, and encouragement. By expressing gratitude, we shift our focus from our own struggles to the blessings we have received and the love that God pours out on us.

In emulating the thankfulness of Coyote Starrk, we cultivate a heart of gratitude. We acknowledge God's goodness, His enduring love, and the relationships He has blessed us with. This mindset of thankfulness helps us to find joy in the midst of challenges and to cultivate a deeper appreciation for the blessings in our lives.

"If you're weak, then you can gather in as large a group as you want. I want to become weak and if that's not possible, then I at least want to make friends that are as strong as me." - Coyote Starrk

September 9

Listen my beloved brothers, has not God chosen those who are poor in the world to be rich in faith and heirs of the kingdom which he has promised to those who love him? James 2:5

Phantom Thief Oracle

(Persona 5: The Animation)

In the series, Futaba Sakura is initially isolated and struggles with social interaction due to past traumas. However, as the story progresses, the protagonist and the other Phantom Thieves accept her wholeheartedly, embracing her unique qualities, and supporting her through her journey of healing. This acceptance allows Futaba to open up, form meaningful connections, and contribute her skills to the team.

The verse James 2:5 reminds us that God's love and acceptance extend beyond worldly standards and appearances. God doesn't judge individuals based on their societal status or outward appearances but looks at the heart and values faith and love for Him above all else. As believers, we are called to follow the example of Christ, who welcomed and embraced all people, regardless of their social standing or background.

Futaba's story reflects the transformative power of acceptance and how it aligns with God's character. When the protagonist and her friends extend love and compassion to Futaba, they emulate God's love in action. They recognize her inherent worth and potential, demonstrating that true acceptance goes beyond surface-level judgments.

By reflecting on Futaba's acceptance, we are reminded of our own responsibility as Christians to love and accept others unconditionally, looking beyond societal judgments and valuing individuals based on their faith and love for God. Just as God chooses the poor in the eyes of the world, we are called to extend grace and acceptance to those who may be overlooked or labelled by society, allowing them to experience the transformative power of God's love.

"You need to deal with the despair! It's bad to just ignore it!" - Futaba Sakura

September 10

But now you must put them all away: anger, wrath, malice, slander, and obscene talk from your mouth.
Colossians 3:8

White Album Assassin

(JoJo's Bizarre Adventure)

Ghiaccio is a character from the JoJo's Bizarre Adventure anime series. He is a member of the Passione assassination squad and possesses a Stand named White Album. His character embodies intense anger and rage, driven by a desire for vengeance and a lack of control over his emotions. His actions and words are often filled with malice and harmful intent.

Colossians 3:8 reminds us that anger, along with other negative emotions and behaviours, should not have a place in our lives. Instead, we are called to rid ourselves of these destructive tendencies and cultivate virtues that reflect the character of Christ. We are urged to replace them with qualities such as love, forgiveness, and kindness.

Ghiaccio's anger serves as a cautionary example, illustrating the harmful consequences of holding onto anger and allowing it to control our actions. It highlights the importance of seeking God's guidance in managing our emotions and responding to difficult situations with grace and self-control. Rather than allowing anger to lead us astray, we can seek God's help in overcoming our negative emotions. Through prayer, self-reflection, and the empowerment of the Holy Spirit, we can align our attitudes and actions with the teachings of Christ, bearing witness to His love and grace in the world.

The character of Ghiaccio from JoJo's Bizarre Adventure calls us to examine our own hearts and strive for a life free from destructive emotions and behaviours. It encourages us to embrace the transformative power of God's love, allowing His grace to shape our responses and relationships, and reflecting His character in all that we do.

"This is what resolve is! It is to carve out your destined path through the darkened wastes!" - Giorno Giovanna

September 11

So, God created man in his own image, in the image of God he created him; male and female he created them.
Genesis 1:27

Rainy Season Hero

(My Hero Academia)

Tsuyu Asui, also known as Froppy, is a character from the anime series My Hero Academia. She possesses a Quirk called Frog, which grants her frog-like abilities such as an extendable tongue, the ability to stick to walls, and enhanced jumping power. Her character is known for her calm and level-headed nature, as well as her strong sense of justice.

The verse Genesis 1:27 emphasizes the inherent value and worth of every individual, regardless of our outward appearances. We are all created in the image of God, which means we bear a reflection of His divine nature and possess inherent dignity. We are called to honour and respect the inherent dignity of all people, appreciating the diverse expressions of humanity as a reflection of God's handiwork.

The appearance of Tsuyu in the anime serves as a reminder of the incredible diversity within God's creation. Just as God created various animal species with unique characteristics, He also crafted human beings with a wide range of physical attributes. Tsuyu's frog-like features remind us of the imaginative and creative power of God, who designed every aspect of creation with intention and purpose.

Consider ing Tsuyu Asui's appearance from My Hero Academia reminds us to reflect on the beauty, diversity, and inherent worth of God's creation. It challenges us to redefine our understanding of beauty, appreciating the uniqueness of individuals and valuing them as reflections of God's image. Let us celebrate the variety of physical appearances and embrace the truth that we are fearfully and wonderfully made by our loving Creator.

"If we start another fight...if we break the law...then we're no better than the villains!" - Tsuyu Asui

September 12

Let another praise you, and not your own mouth; a stranger, and not your own lips. Proverbs 27:2

Jet-Black Wings

(The Disastrous life of Saiki K.)

In The Disastrous Life of Saiki K., Shun Kaido is known for his overconfident and self-centred attitude. He often brags about his looks, intelligence, and supposed popularity, displaying a sense of arrogance and superiority over others. He frequently tries to get involved in various situations to play the role of a hero, although his actions usually end up causing more problems than solving them.

Proverbs 27:2 advises against self-promotion and seeking praise for oneself. It encourages humility and modesty, suggesting that it is more appropriate for others to acknowledge and commend our qualities rather than boasting about them ourselves. The verse also reminds us that it is more appropriate and respectable to receive praise from others rather than boasting about one's own accomplishments.

Shun Kaido's tendency to constantly praise himself and seek validation from others serves as a reminder to let our actions and character speak for themselves rather than seeking self-glorification. Instead, we are called to serve others with humility, recognizing that any talents or qualities we possess are gifts from God. It is through genuine humility that we can reflect Christ's character and demonstrate selfless love for others.

Reflecting on Shun Kaido's attitude in the anime calls us as followers of Christ to cultivate humility, value the input of others, and seek the approval of God rather than constantly seeking self-praise or validation from others. It reminds us to place our focus on internal character rather than external recognition.

"I don't care about your past. What matters is who you are now and who you'll be in the future!" - Shun Kaidō

September 13

And I will lead the blind in a way that they do not know, in paths that they have not known I will guide them. I will turn the darkness before them into light, the rough places into level ground. These are the things I do, and I do not forsake them. Isaiah 42:16

Melon Lord

(Avatar: The Last Airbender)

Toph Beifong is a blind character from Avatar: The Last Airbender, who initially faced the challenge of navigating a world that relied heavily on sight. However, she adapted and developed her unique earth bending abilities, which allowed her to see the world in a different way. She relied on her heightened senses and her connection to the vibrations in the earth to perceive her surroundings and overcome obstacles.

In Isaiah 42:16, the prophet speaks of God's promise to guide the blind along unfamiliar paths and turn darkness into light. As Christians, we may often find ourselves in unfamiliar territories, facing challenges and uncertainties. However, we can take comfort in knowing that God promises to lead us, even when the path seems unclear. When we trust in God's guidance, He will be with us every step of the way.

Toph's story also showcases the theme of God's unwavering presence and support. Despite her initial struggles, Toph remains determined, courageous, and ultimately triumphs over various challenges. This mirrors the assurance in the verse that God will not forsake those He leads, ensuring they find their way and experience transformation in their lives.

The character arc of Toph Beifong reflects the transformative power of God's light in our lives. As we surrender our struggles and weaknesses to Him, He can illuminate our path, bring healing to our brokenness, and make the rough places smooth. We can be assured that through God's presence and grace, we can experience profound inner transformation.

"Sometimes life is like this tunnel. You can't always see the light at the end of the tunnel, but if you keep moving, you will come to a better place." - Iroh

September 14

No one can serve two masters, for either he will hate the one and love the other, or he will be devoted to the one and despise the other. You cannot serve God and money.
Matthew 6:24

5th Division Lieutenant

(Bleach)

Momo Hinamori from the Bleach anime series demonstrates a strong sense of commitment, particularly in her loyalty and dedication to her captain, Sōsuke Aizen. However, she becomes entangled in a master-servant relationship that leads her astray from the path of righteousness. Despite her genuine intentions, her commitment becomes misplaced and misdirected, blinding her to the truth of Aizen's deceit.

Matthew 6:24 emphasizes the importance of choosing one master to serve. It highlights the inherent conflict that arises when our allegiance is divided between different entities. The verse reminds us that we cannot simultaneously serve both God and worldly pursuits, such as money or power. We are called to wholeheartedly devote ourselves to God, allowing Him to be our ultimate master.

Momo's story highlights the importance of discernment and aligning our commitments with God's will. It reminds us that even well-intentioned commitments can lead us astray if they divert our focus from God's truth and righteousness. It serves as a reminder to regularly evaluate our allegiances and ensure they align with God's teachings and principles.

In light of this reflection on Momo Hinamori, we are encouraged to prioritize our commitment to God above all else. By seeking His guidance, immersing ourselves in His Word, and aligning our actions with His will, we can avoid the pitfalls of divided loyalties and experience the fullness of a committed relationship with our true and faithful Master.

"Fear is necessary for evolution. The fear that could be destroyed at any moment." - Sōsuke Aizen

September 15

For where two or three are gathered in my name, there am I among them. Matthew 18:20

Earth's Special Forces

(Dragon Ball)

In Dragon Ball anime series, the Z-Fighters, consisting of Goku, Vegeta, Piccolo, Gohan, and others, come together as a community of individuals with unique abilities and roles. Each member contributes their own strengths and skills to protect the Earth and defend against various threats. Despite their differences, they unite under a common purpose and work together for the greater good.

The verse Matthew 18:20 challenges us to prioritize gathering together as believers, whether it be in worship, fellowship, or prayer. This verse reminds us that when we come together in the name of Jesus, He is present among us, guiding, comforting, and empowering us for His purposes. We need to unite with other believers, recognizing that when we gather in the name of Jesus, His presence is with us.

The Z-Fighters exemplify the value of support and encouragement within a community. They lift each other up, provide guidance, and push one another to grow and improve. In our own Christian communities, we are called to similarly support and encourage one another, spurring each other on in faith and good works. As followers of Christ, we are called to form communities that reflect the unity and love of Christ. We are reminded that our faith is not meant to be lived in isolation but in fellowship with others.

The community of Z-Fighters from Dragon Ball inspires us to foster unity, collaboration, and support within our own Christian communities. We are called to value the power of gathering in Jesus' name, recognizing His presence and seeking His guidance as we navigate life's challenges. May we be encouraged to actively participate in a community of believers, experiencing the strength and transformation that come from gathering in the name of Jesus.

"Push through the pain. Giving up hurts more." - Vegeta

September 16

With man this is impossible, but with God all things are possible. Matthew 19:26

Jue Viole Grace

(Tower of God)

Baam's character exhibits immense courage throughout the Tower of God series. He confronts numerous trials, faces powerful adversaries, and navigates treacherous situations. Despite being a mere human, he continues to persevere and overcome obstacles with a tenacity that defies human limitations. His unwavering determination to protect his friends and seek the truth is truly inspiring.

Matthew 19:26 highlights the transformative nature of God's involvement in our lives, reminding us that we can find courage in understanding that nothing is beyond God's control. This verse encourages us to recognize that our own strength may fall short, but when we place our trust in God, there is no limit to what can be accomplished.

Baam's character in the anime reminds us of the importance of relying on community. Throughout his journey, he forges deep bonds of friendship, relying on the strength and support of others. This highlights the Christian value of unity and the understanding that we are not meant to face our trials alone. By surrounding himself with allies and drawing on their support, Baam exemplifies the idea that courage can be found in unity and the collective strength of a community.

When we reflect on Twenty-fifth Baam's character in the Tower of God anime series, we are reminded of the transformative power of faith and trust in God. His courage serves as an inspiration for believers to step out in faith, knowing that through God's guidance and intervention, the seemingly impossible can become possible. His story encourages us to confront challenges with confidence, relying on God's strength to overcome them and witnessing His miraculous works along the way.

"The heart moves where the heart wills." - Twenty-Fifth Baam

September 17

There is a way that seems right to a man, but its end is the way to death. Proverbs 14:12

Shadow Hokage

(Naruto)

In the Naruto series, Sasuke Uchiha makes several decisions driven by his desire for vengeance and the pursuit of power. He believes that these choices are justified and necessary to bring about justice for the destruction of his clan. However, his relentless pursuit of revenge leads him down a path of darkness, isolation, and ultimately, self-destruction.

The verse Proverbs 14:12 cautions us about the dangers of following our own perceptions of what is right without seeking guidance and wisdom from God. It reminds us that our human understanding may be flawed and that the choices we make based solely on our judgment can lead to negative consequences. We are called to seek guidance and wisdom from God in our decision-making. We are reminded that our own understanding may be limited and fallible.

Sasuke Uchiha's decision to seek vengeance and power in Naruto can be seen as an example of someone who falls into the trap of thinking that his path is justified and righteous. His desire for revenge blinds him to the potential consequences and the destructive nature of his actions. Sasuke Uchiha's story also highlights the need for forgiveness and reconciliation. While his path initially led him astray, he eventually realizes the error of his ways and seeks redemption. This serves as a powerful reminder of God's grace and the opportunity for transformation and restoration that comes through repentance and turning back to Him.

When examining Sasuke Uchiha's decisions in the anime, we are reminded of the importance of seeking God's wisdom, discernment, and grace in our own lives. It encourages us to approach decision-making with humility, recognizing our limitations and relying on God's guidance to navigate the complexities of life.

"The people that are the hardest to love are usually the ones who need it the most." - Sasuke Uchiha

September 18

For you were called to freedom, brothers. Only do not use your freedom as an opportunity for the flesh, but through love serve one another. Galatians 5:13

Colossus Titan

(Attack on Titan)

Armin's devotion in Attack on Titan is rooted in a deep sense of responsibility towards his friends, humanity, and the pursuit of freedom. Despite facing overwhelming challenges, he consistently chooses to use his abilities and knowledge for the benefit of others, rather than seeking personal gain or succumbing to his own fears and desires. He also demonstrates humility and selflessness by willingly taking on burdens and risks to protect and serve his comrades. He recognizes that true freedom is not about individual desires or selfish ambitions, but about using one's gifts and strengths to support and uplift others.

In Galatians 5:13, believers are encouraged to use their freedom wisely and serve one another in love. We are called to recognize the freedom we have been given through Christ's sacrifice and to use that freedom for the service of others. Like Armin, we should not allow our freedom to become an excuse for self-centred pursuits, but rather, we should humbly serve one another in love.

The unwavering devotion shown by Armin challenges us to examine our own lives as Christians. Despite overwhelming odds, he consistently chooses to put the needs of others before his own. Armin's selflessness reflects a deep understanding of the responsibility that comes with the freedom he possesses.

Armin Arlert's devotion in the Attack on Titan anime series showcases the transformative power of selfless service and the responsible use of freedom. As Christians, we are encouraged to follow Armin's example by using our freedom to serve others and demonstrate the love of Christ in our actions.

"A person who cannot sacrifice everything, cannot change anything." - Armin Arlert

September 19

A soft answer turns away wrath, but a harsh word stirs up anger. Proverbs 15:1

Todoroki Family

(My Hero Academia)

The Todoroki family from My Hero Academia consists of Endeavor, the father, and his four children: Toya Todoroki, Shoto Todoroki, Fuyumi Todoroki, and Natsuo Todoroki. The family dynamics in the Todoroki household are complex and strained, particularly due to Endeavor's abusive treatment of his wife and children. The scars of the past have created a toxic environment filled with anger, resentment, and a lack of understanding.

In Proverbs 15:1, we are reminded that responding with gentleness and compassion has the potential to turn away wrath. Healing and restoration can only begin with a humble and gentle approach. Just as God's love and mercy can transform hearts, the power of forgiveness and understanding can break the cycle of anger and resentment within the family. We are called to extend grace to those who have hurt us, even when it seems impossible.

The story of the Todoroki family serves as a reminder that true transformation requires personal growth and change. If Endeavor had adopted a more compassionate and understanding demeanour, it could have allowed for open communication and healing within the Todoroki family. A gentler approach from Endeavor might have encouraged his children to express their feelings and concerns, leading to a healthier family dynamic.

The Todoroki family prompts us to reflect on the power of forgiveness, reconciliation, and the transformative nature of love. It emphasizes the importance of responding with gentleness and understanding, rather than exacerbating anger through harsh words. By responding to conflicts with gentleness and empathy, we can foster an environment conducive to healing and restoration, mirroring the love and grace of our Lord Jesus Christ.

"If you're going to rely on words alone, then they better be incredibly powerful." - Shoto Todoroki

September 20

For you did not receive the spirit of slavery to fall back into fear, but you have received the Spirit of adoption as sons, by whom we cry, "Abba! Father!" Romans 8:15

White Demon

(Gintama)

Gintoki Sakata, the protagonist of the anime series Gintama, is known for his fearless and unconventional nature. He carries deep emotional scars and a sense of responsibility for the pain and suffering he and others have endured. However, he refuses to be controlled by fear and instead chooses to confront his fears head-on. Gintoki's fearlessness is not born out of recklessness but from a desire to protect and fight for what he believes in.

The apostle Paul reminds believers in Romans 8:15 that we have received the Spirit of adoption through our faith in Jesus Christ. This Spirit empowers and frees us from a spirit of fear and bondage. We can approach God as our loving Father, calling out to Him with familiarity and trust. We are set free from the chains of fear, doubt, and insecurity as we trust in God's love and sovereignty.

The fearlessness of Gintoki Sakata can encourage us to confront our own fears, doubts, and uncertainties with courage. Just as he faces formidable foes without flinching, we can approach the challenges in our lives with unwavering trust in God's strength and provision. His fearlessness serves as a reminder that we are not defined by our past but rather by our identity as children of God.

Gintoki Sakata's character in the anime reminds us that as believers, we have received the Spirit of adoption, freeing us from the spirit of fear and bondage. By embracing the Spirit of adoption and trusting in God's love and provision, we can face life's challenges with boldness, resilience, and unwavering faith in our Heavenly Father.

"Life is like a mountain - you can say you've reached the top, but only after climbing back down." - Gintoki Sakata

September 21

And Jesus said, "Father, forgive them, for they know not what they do." Luke 23:34

Psychic Duck

(Pokémon)

In the Pokémon series, Psyduck is often depicted as a Pokémon with constant headaches and anxiety. These conditions often lead Psyduck to behave erratically and cause unintended trouble for its trainer and others around it. Despite Psyduck's challenging behaviour, trainers show patience, understanding, and forgiveness towards it.

In Luke 23:34, while Jesus was being crucified, He expressed remarkable forgiveness towards those who were responsible for His crucifixion. He prayed to God asking him forgive them, for they do not know what they are doing. Even in the midst of immense physical and emotional suffering, Jesus chose forgiveness and demonstrated compassion towards His executioners.

Just as trainers forgive Psyduck's unintended consequences and understand that its actions are rooted in anxiety, Jesus forgave those who crucified Him, recognizing their ignorance of the full weight and impact of their actions. This connection emphasizes the transformative power of forgiveness. It encourages us to extend forgiveness to others, even when they have caused us pain or harm. Similar to how trainers patiently deal with Psyduck's difficulties, we are called to exhibit grace and understanding towards others, recognizing that they may not fully comprehend the consequences of their actions.

In contemplating the forgiveness of Psyduck in Pokémon, we are reminded of the immense love and grace of God. It challenges us to extend forgiveness to others, even when it may seem difficult or undeserved. Through forgiveness, we embody the transformative power of Christ's forgiveness, fostering healing, reconciliation, and the restoration of relationships as we strive to live out our faith.

"Everybody makes a wrong turn once in a while." - Ash Ketchum

September 22

And above all these put on love, which binds everything together in perfect harmony. Colossians 3:14

Lightning Fire Duo

(Black Clover)

In Black Clover, Magna Swing and Luck Voltia are both members of the Black Bulls, a group of misfit magic knights in the series. Despite their contrasting personalities and backgrounds, they develop a deep bond over time. Magna, a fiery and impulsive character, finds in Luck, a more aloof and unpredictable individual, someone who can match his energy and enthusiasm for battle. Meanwhile, Luck, who tends to keep his distance from others, appreciates Magna's straightforward and passionate nature.

The verse Colossians 3:14 emphasizes the importance of love as a unifying force, binding together various virtues and qualities. Our love for one another must foster a sense of unity and camaraderie, enabling us to work as a team and overcome obstacles. As followers of Christ, we are called to love one another and extend that love to our friendships.

Magna and Luck's friendship in the anime demonstrates the value of forgiveness and acceptance. Despite their differences and occasional disagreements, they remain committed to their friendship and do not hold grudges. Their friendship also serves as an example of how love can inspire personal growth. Just as Magna and Luck motivate and encourage each other to become stronger magic knights, we can uplift and support our friends in their own journeys of faith and personal development.

Through the friendship of Magna Swing and Luck Voltia in Black Clover, we see how their love for each other transcends their differences and unites them in a deep and meaningful way. Their friendship teaches us that when love becomes the guiding force in our relationships, it has the power to transform, unite, and bring forth the best in us.

"People live through their interactions with one another!"
- Luck Voltia

September 23

To put off your old self, which belongs to your former manner of life and is corrupt through deceitful desires, and to be renewed in the spirit of your minds, and to put on the new self, created after the likeness of God in true righteousness and holiness. Ephesians 4:22-24

Mister 255

(Silver Spoon)

In Silver Spoon, Yūgo Hachiken is a city boy who enrols in an agricultural high school in order to escape the pressures of his academic life. Through his school experiences, he undergoes significant personal growth and a transformation in his perspective on life and his own aspirations. He learns about hard work and the value of pursuing one's passion.

Ephesians 4:22-24 is a passage from the Bible that speaks to the process of personal transformation. It emphasizes the idea of leaving behind one's old self, with its destructive desires and behaviours, and embracing a new self that reflects righteousness and holiness. It speaks to the process of growth and transformation, wherein an individual sheds their former way of life and embraces a renewed mindset and a more virtuous existence.

The decision of Yūgo decision to attend an agricultural school and immerse himself in a completely different environment can be seen as putting off his old self. By engaging in hard work, overcoming challenges, and learning valuable life lessons, he gradually develops a new perspective and adopts a renewed mindset.

Yūgo's journey in Silver Spoon highlights the transformative power of personal growth. It emphasizes the importance of shedding old attitudes, beliefs, and behaviours, and embracing new ways of thinking and being. The underlying message is that growth and transformation can lead to a more fulfilling and virtuous life.

"I've had enough lessons over the past couple days to know that I can't make decisions based solely on my assumptions!" - Yūgo Hachiken

September 24

Blessed are the people to whom such blessings fall! Blessed are the people whose God is the Lord! Psalm 144:15

Solomon's Avatar

(Magi: The Labyrinth of Magic)

In the anime, Aladdin experiences moments of great joy and happiness throughout his journey. He discovers his magical abilities and forms strong friendships with Alibaba, Morgiana, and other characters. Throughout his journey, Aladdin develops a deep connection with the Rukh, a spiritual force, and embraces his role as a Magi. As he discovers his purpose and seeks to bring balance and justice to the world, he finds profound happiness.

The verse Psalm 144:15 encourages us to place God at the centre of our lives. It highlights that true happiness is found when God is the Lord of our lives. When we acknowledge and honour God as our ultimate authority, we are filled with a happiness that transcends worldly circumstances. As followers of Christ, we understand that true happiness is found when God is the centre of our lives.

Additionally, Aladdin's relationships with his friends, Alibaba, Morgiana, and others, demonstrate the importance of community and love. These connections exemplify the blessings that God provides when we seek Him. Aladdin's happiness is not just an individual experience but is intertwined with the joy that comes from experiencing the love and support of others, which is ultimately rooted in God's love for us.

Aladdin's happiness in the anime can be seen as a reflection of the joy that comes from experiencing the love and companionship God provides through meaningful relationships. His pursuit of righteousness and justice can inspire us to seek God's guidance in our own lives, leading to true and lasting happiness as we align ourselves with His divine plan.

"Don't you think that if you keep lying, eventually no one, not even yourself, will be able to believe your own words?"
- Aladdin

September 25

The soul of the sluggard craves and gets nothing, while the soul of the diligent is richly supplied. Proverbs 13:4

Honourable Disciplinarian

(Kaguya-Sama: Love is War)

In Kaguya-Sama: Love is War, Miyuki Shirogane is known for his dedication and commitment to his studies and various responsibilities as the student council president. He consistently puts in tremendous effort and works tirelessly to excel academically and fulfil his duties. His diligent nature leads to achievements, personal growth, and the admiration of others. He sets goals, works hard to attain them, and reaps the rewards of his efforts.

Proverbs 13:4 serves as a reminder that hard work is essential for fruitful outcomes and personal fulfilment. It highlights the contrast between the diligent, who are richly supplied with the results of their efforts, and the sluggard, who remains unsatisfied due to their lack of action. The verse suggests that individuals who excel in their work and display competence have the opportunity to serve before influential and respected figures.

Miyuki's character can inspire us to embrace diligence in our own lives, understanding that our actions and perseverance have the potential to bring about positive change and fruitful rewards. By cultivating a mindset of diligence and consistently putting in the necessary work, we can experience the satisfaction of achieving our goals and making progress in various areas of our lives.

Reflecting on the hard work of Miyuki Shirogane in the anime, we are reminded of the importance of diligence, both in our earthly pursuits and in our spiritual journey. Through our diligent efforts, we can honour God, fulfil His purposes, and experience the abundant blessings that flow from a soul committed to diligent work for His glory.

"Even though it's a single word, Love can have many meanings. Love for one's family. Love for one's friends. Love for those in one's care." - Miyuki Shirogane

September 26

You shall not bear false witness against your neighbour.
Exodus 20:16

Professional Liar

(Mob Psycho 100)

Reigen Arataka is a character from the anime series Mob Psycho 100, known for his charismatic personality and somewhat dubious honesty. While he often presents himself as a psychic expert, he lacks any real supernatural abilities and relies on deception to maintain his business. His habit of deceiving others for personal gain or manipulating situations brings harm to those around him.

In light of Exodus 20:16, we are reminded of the biblical commandment not to give false testimony against our neighbour. Honesty is a fundamental virtue that we are called to uphold in our lives, as it reflects God's nature and His desire for truth and integrity. As Christians, we are called to emulate Christ's example of truthfulness and love for others. We are urged to speak the truth in love, seeking to build up and edify those around us rather than tearing them down through falsehoods.

Reigen serves as a cautionary example of the consequences of dishonesty. His habit of deceiving others for personal gain or manipulating situations not only goes against the commandment but also brings harm to those around him. It is evident that his actions stem from selfish motives and a lack of regard for the well-being of others.

Reflecting on Reigen Arataka's character in the anime prompts us to examine our own lives and evaluate our commitment to honesty. It is important to remember that even when we fail in our pursuit of honesty, God's grace is available to us. Through repentance and reliance on His transforming power, we can grow in our commitment to truthfulness and strive to align our lives with His perfect standard.

"If you misuse a power that's all too great, you will only destroy yourself." - Reigen Arataka

September 27

And after you have suffered a little while, the God of all grace, who has called you to his eternal glory in Christ, will himself restore, confirm, strengthen, and establish you. 1 Peter 5:10

Marude Damena Ossan

(Gintama)

Taizou Hasegawa's character in Gintama often embodies a sense of hopelessness throughout the series. He faces constant failure, ridicule, and setbacks in his life, leading him to question his worth and purpose. This portrayal of hopelessness can resonate with our own experiences, as we too may have encountered moments of despair and a sense of being lost.

The verse 1 Peter 5:10 gives us a profound message of hope. It reminds us that the God of all grace, who called us to His eternal glory in Christ, will restore us after we have suffered for a little while. This verse acknowledges the reality of suffering and recognizes that we may experience seasons of hopelessness. However, it assures us that God is not indifferent to our pain and despair.

Just as Taizou Hasegawa goes through periods of despair in the anime series, we too can find solace in the understanding that our struggles can lead to a deeper dependence on God. Our hopelessness can become a catalyst for seeking God's grace and discovering the transformative power of His love.

The hopelessness depicted in Taizou Hasegawa's character can serve as a reminder that as Christians, we may encounter moments of despair. However, we are encouraged to embrace these seasons as opportunities for growth and to place our trust in God's restoration and grace. Even in the depths of hopelessness, we can find solace in the knowledge that God's plan is to lift us up, restore us, and establish us on a firm foundation of hope.

"Happiness depends on each person. If you think you 're happy, then you must be happy." - Gintoki Sakata.

September 28

Humble yourselves, therefore, under the mighty hand of God so that at the proper time he may exalt you. 1 Peter 5:6

Genius Witch

(Little Witch Academia)

Lotte Janssen's character in the Little Witch Academia anime embodies humility by willingly submitting herself to the authority and guidance of others. She recognizes that she has much to learn and doesn't let her ego get in the way of growth. She humbles herself under the authority of her mentors and embraces a teachable spirit, which allows her to develop her magical abilities and become a better witch.

In 1 Peter 5:6, we are encouraged to humble ourselves under God's mighty hand. This verse reminds us that true humility involves acknowledging our dependence on God and willingly submitting ourselves to His guidance and will. Lotte's humility reflects this principle as she trusts in the wisdom and guidance of her mentors and seeks to align herself with the higher purpose of her magical education. By humbling ourselves under God's authority, we position ourselves to receive His grace, wisdom, and blessings.

By humbling herself, Lotte opens herself up to God's guidance and blessings. She trusts in His timing and plans for her life, relying on His strength rather than her own. Lotte's humility enables her to grow in her magical abilities and personal development.

As we observe Lotte's humility in Little Witch Academia, we can be inspired to adopt a similar attitude in our own lives. By humbling ourselves before God, recognizing His sovereignty, and seeking His guidance, we position ourselves to receive His blessings and favour. Just as Lotte's humility leads to growth and fulfilment, our humility can lead us to experience the abundant life God has in store for us.

"You don't get the things you dream of; you get the things that you work for." - Ursula Callistis

September 29

Having the appearance of godliness, but denying its power. Avoid such people. 2 Timothy 3:5

Icy Marine Admiral

(One Piece)

Kuzan, also known as Aokiji, is a character from the One Piece series who initially appears as a Marine Admiral, upholding justice and enforcing the law. However, it is later revealed that he has a hidden agenda and acts hypocritically by aligning himself with corrupt individuals like Blackbeard and engaging in morally questionable actions. His rejection of genuine justice and his double standards highlight the hypocrisy in his character.

The verse 2 Timothy 3:5 speaks about individuals who maintain an appearance of religiousness or righteousness but reject the transformative power of God in their lives. It warns against associating with such people and encourages believers to distance themselves from their hypocrisy. It reminds believers to seek authenticity and to distance themselves from those who display such hypocrisy.

Kuzan's character embodies this hypocrisy as he initially presents himself as a defender of justice but later reveals his true intentions and questionable alliances. This serves as a cautionary tale about the importance of consistency between one's outward actions and inner character and the consequences of living a life of hypocrisy. We are called to live in integrity, allowing God's power to work within us and transform us into His image.

By reflecting on the hypocrisy of Kuzan in the One Piece anime, we are reminded to pursue a deep and genuine relationship with God, allowing His transformative power to work within us and manifest in our words and deeds. Let us strive to live out our faith with sincerity and authenticity, avoiding the pitfalls of hypocrisy and embracing the power of God's truth and love in our lives.

"The thing called "justice" changes its shape... Depending on where you stand." - Kuzan

September 30

Finally, all of you, have unity of mind, sympathy, brotherly love, a tender heart, and a humble mind.
1 Peter 3:8

Apostle of the Goddesses

(Seven Deadly Sins)

Elisabeth Liones is a fictional character from The Seven Deadly Sins, who serves as the third princess of the Kingdom of Liones. She is depicted as a caring and selfless character, always putting others before herself. Despite her noble upbringing, Elisabeth often challenges traditional societal norms and fights against injustice. Her journey involves numerous challenges and sacrifices, but she remains determined to protect her loved ones and the kingdom she holds dear.

1 Peter 3:8 serves as a reminder for Christians to treat one another with kindness and understanding, showing love and compassion in their interactions. It emphasizes the importance of unity and harmony within the community of believers. By following these virtues, believers can create an atmosphere of mutual support and encouragement.

Elizabeth Liones extends love to both friends and foes, showcasing a selfless love that seeks the well-being and restoration of others. Her love goes beyond personal feelings or preferences and extends to a genuine care for the needs of others.

The kindness of Elizabeth Liones, as depicted in The Seven Deadly Sins, serves as an inspiration for us to follow. By embracing like-mindedness, sympathy, love, compassion, and humility, we can foster a spirit of kindness and reflect the love of Christ to those around us. In doing so, we become vessels of God's grace and agents of transformation in a world in need of kindness and compassion.

"As long as you still breathe, you are afforded the opportunity to fight and protect those of your own choosing. And, as such, you'll have people to share your suffering, misery, and sorrow with." -Elizabeth Liones

October 1

We love because he first loved us. 1 John 4:19

Pirate Empress

(One Piece)

In the One Piece series, Boa Hancock's love for Luffy is deeply rooted in her past experiences. As a former slave and a victim of abuse, she had never experienced genuine love until she encountered Luffy. the unwavering determination, kindness, and selflessness of Monkey D. Luffy touched her heart and awakened her capacity to love.

The verse 1 John 4:19 reminds us that our ability to love is derived from God's love for us. We are recipients of God's unconditional love and grace, demonstrated through the sacrificial death and resurrection of Jesus Christ. It is through experiencing this divine love that our own capacity to love is awakened. Boa Hancock's journey parallels the Christian experience of encountering God's love and being transformed by it. Her initial self-centred infatuation with Luffy gradually gives way to a selfless, sacrificial love. This transformation reflects the work of God's love in our lives, where we move from self-centeredness to genuine care and compassion for others.

Boa Hancock's love for Luffy also demonstrates the power of love to heal past wounds. Having experienced abuse and trauma in her past, she carried a guarded and mistrustful heart. However, Luffy's love breaks through those barriers, bringing healing and restoration to her wounded soul. In a similar way, God's love has the power to heal our deepest wounds and restore us to wholeness.

As Christians, reflecting on Boa Hancock's love in the anime challenges us to examine our own capacity to love. It invites us to consider the transformative power of God's love in our lives and how it compels us to love others selflessly. It also reminds us that our ability to love is not self-generated but is a response to the love we have received from God.

"I'll tell you guys something good. Love is always like a hurricane!" - Boa Hancock

October 2

The earth is the Lord's and the fullness thereof, the world and those who dwell therein. Psalm 24:1

Wolf Girl

(Princess Mononoke)

San, also known as Princess Mononoke, is a fierce and independent character who serves as a bridge between the human and natural worlds. As a child raised by wolves, she sees herself as a guardian and protector of the forest and its inhabitants. She fights against human encroachment and strives to maintain the delicate balance between humanity and nature.

Psalm 24:1 reminds us that the earth and everything in it belong to the Lord. It affirms that God is the ultimate owner and caretaker of all creation. We are called to recognize the value and beauty of the natural world and actively protect and preserve it. This verse invites us to reflect on how we can contribute to the well-being of the earth, honouring God's ownership and our role as caretakers.

San's connection with the wolves and her affinity for nature demonstrate the interconnectedness of all living things. Just as she understands the interdependence of different elements within the forest, we are called to recognize the intricate web of life that God has designed. Every creature, every ecosystem, is part of God's grand creation and deserves our respect and care.

When contemplating the life of San from Princess Mononoke, we are prompted to reflect on our role as stewards of God's creation. We are reminded of the interconnectedness of all living things and the need to honour and protect the earth as a reflection of our reverence for God's ownership. San's dedication to preserving the forest challenges us to consider how we can actively care for the environment and embrace our responsibility to nurture and sustain God's creation for future generations.

"You cannot alter your fate. However, you can rise to meet it." - Hī-Sama

October 3

Keep your life free from love of money, and be content with what you have, for he has said, "I will never leave you nor forsake you." Hebrews 13:5

Young Master

(The Disastrous Life of Saiki K.)

Metori Saiko is a character known for her extreme materialism. She is constantly seeking material possessions and is driven by a desire for luxury and wealth. Her actions and decisions often revolve around obtaining and flaunting expensive items. This obsession with material wealth can be seen as a commentary on the superficiality and emptiness of a life cantered around material possessions. Saiko's character highlights the potential negative consequences of prioritizing materialism over more meaningful aspects of life.

In Hebrews 13:5, we are challenged to examine our own hearts and attitudes towards material possessions. It calls us to be content with what we have, recognizing that true satisfaction and security come from our relationship with God rather than the accumulation of worldly goods. In a world that constantly bombards us with messages of consumerism and the pursuit of more, it is essential to anchor our hearts in the unchanging faithfulness of God.

Despite Metori's materialistic nature, she is portrayed as a flawed character. Her obsession with material wealth is depicted in a comedic manner, highlighting the absurdity of placing so much importance on superficial things. Her character serves as a satirical commentary on the excesses and shallowness of the entertainment industry and consumer culture.

Metori Saiko's materialism in the anime serves as a reminder of the pitfalls of worldly desires and the emptiness they ultimately bring. It prompts us to examine our own lives and identify any areas where we may be pursuing material gain at the expense of our spiritual well-being. By embracing contentment and trusting in God's promises, we can resist the allure of materialism and live lives that reflect our dependence on Him.

"I hate attracting attention but I hate owing someone even more." - Kusuo Saiki

October 4

Blessed are those who mourn, for they shall be comforted.
Matthew 5:4

Leader of Sleeping Knights

(Sword Art Online)

Yuuki's character in the Sword Art Online anime series faces a challenging situation as she deals with a terminal illness. Despite knowing her fate, she remains determined and motivated to make the most of her remaining time, leaving a lasting impact on those around her. Her motivation stems from a deep sense of purpose and a desire to find joy and fulfilment despite the circumstances.

The verse from Matthew 5:4 speaks to those who mourn, acknowledging the presence of grief and sorrow in life. It assures that those who mourn will be comforted. It reminds us that, as believers, we are not left to navigate our grief alone. God offers His loving presence and promises to comfort us through the power of the Holy Spirit.

Yuuki's journey demonstrates the idea of finding comfort and solace in the face of challenging circumstances. Despite her illness, she forms deep bonds with others and creates lasting memories. Through her relationships and the impact, she has on others, Yuuki discovers a sense of comfort and fulfilment that surpasses the limitations of her physical condition.

By relating Yuuki Konno's motivation in the anime, we see the parallel between her ability to find comfort and the promise of comfort given to those who mourn in the biblical verse. It highlights the transformative power of finding purpose and meaningful connections even in the midst of challenging times. Yuuki's story encourages us to embrace the blessings that can arise from mourning and to seek comfort through genuine relationships and the pursuit of meaningful experiences.

"God would never put us through all this suffering if he didn't think we could bear it." - Yuuki Konno

October 5

Cast your burden on the Lord, and he will sustain you; he will never permit the righteous to be moved. Psalm 55:22

Quirkless Hero

(My Hero Academia)

In My Hero Academia, Izuku Midoriya faces various forms of pain, both physical and emotional, as he strives to become a hero. He carries the weight of his dreams, battles self-doubt, and confronts the harsh realities of a challenging world. His experiences mirror the struggles we encounter in our own lives as we navigate hardships, disappointments, and uncertainties.

Psalm 55:22 reminds us that we don't have to carry our burdens alone. We are invited to cast our cares upon the Lord, entrusting Him with our pain and anxieties. God is not distant or indifferent to our struggles; He promises to sustain us, providing the strength and support we need to endure and overcome. Through prayer, we can lay our burdens at His feet, seeking His guidance, comfort, and provision. We can draw upon the assurance that God is intimately involved in our lives, working all things together for our good, even in the midst of pain.

The pain that Izuku endures becomes a catalyst for growth and transformation. Similarly, our own pain can lead to spiritual maturity, deepened faith, and a greater reliance on God. As we cast our cares upon the Lord, we open ourselves to His sustaining grace and discover that our strength is not found in our own abilities but in His power working within us.

Izuku's experiences of pain in the anime invite us to reflect on the importance of surrendering our pain to God and finding comfort in His presence. It encourages us to trust in His faithfulness, knowing that He will sustain us through every trial and enable us to stand firm in our faith. Through our own journey of casting our cares upon the Lord, we can find hope, peace, and the strength to overcome the challenges that come our way.

"Giving help that's not asked for is what makes a true hero!" - Izuku Midoriya

October 6

Rejoice in hope, be patient in tribulation, be constant in prayer. Romans 12:12

Guardian of Q-City

(One-Punch Man)

Watchdog Man's character in One-Punch Man anime showcases a remarkable level of patience in the face of adversity and affliction. He remains committed to protecting his city and fulfilling his duty as a hero, even when faced with challenging situations. His patience is rooted in his unwavering hope and dedication to his mission.

The verse Romans 12:12 encourages believers to maintain a joyful disposition in the hope found in Christ. It urges us to exhibit patience in times of affliction, remaining steadfast and unwavering in our trust and reliance on God. It also emphasizes the importance of faithfulness in prayer, maintaining a constant connection with God throughout our journey.

Watchdog Man remains steadfast and resolute. He endures through difficult circumstances without losing sight of his purpose. In the same manner, we must cultivate patience in times of affliction, trusting in God's sovereignty and His ability to work all things for our good. Moreover, Watchdog Man's vigilance and dedication to his duty parallel the call for us to remain faithful in our communication with God. Through prayer, we establish a continuous connection with our Heavenly Father, seeking His guidance, strength, and comfort in every circumstance.

Just as Watchdog Man faithfully carries out his mission, we are called to persevere in our faith, remaining patient and trusting in God's plan even when faced with challenges. By embracing the patience of Watchdog Man, we can cultivate a resilient spirit, find joy in our hope, endure afflictions with patience, and maintain a faithful connection with God through prayer. Through this, we can navigate the difficulties of life and grow in our relationship with Him, knowing that He is working all things together for our good.

"I'll leave tomorrow's problem to tomorrow's me." - Saitama

October 7

The Lord is on my side; I will not fear. What can man do to me? Psalm 118:6

Mermaid Princess

(One Piece)

In the One Piece anime, Shirahoshi, the princess of the Ryugu Kingdom, faces significant peer pressure due to her unique abilities and position. Many characters in the series, particularly the antagonistic ones, attempt to manipulate and control her for their own gain. Similarly, in our own lives, we may encounter situations where peer pressure causes us to fear the opinions, judgments, or actions of others.

Psalm 118:6 encourages us to shift our focus from the opinions and actions of others to the eternal truth of God's love and guidance. The pressures and manipulations of others cannot ultimately harm us or determine our worth when we are firmly rooted in God's love and guidance. Therefore, we can confidently navigate peer pressure, knowing that God's opinion of us is what truly matters.

Like Shirahoshi, we may encounter fear and uncertainty as we face the pressures of the world. Yet, through faith, we can trust in the Lord's faithfulness, knowing that His presence empowers us to overcome any external influence. When we anchor ourselves in the truth of God's Word, we can approach peer pressure with a renewed perspective.

As we reflect on Shirahoshi's story in the anime, let us remember that we have been called to live counter-culturally as followers of Christ. By relying on God's strength, seeking His guidance, and remaining rooted in His Word, we can resist the pressures to conform and instead live lives that bring glory to Him. Let us find courage and confidence in the assurance that the Lord is on our side, enabling us to navigate peer pressure with grace, integrity, and unwavering faith.

"Stop counting only those things you have lost! What is gone, is gone! So, ask yourself this. What is there... that still remains to you?!" - Jinbei

October 8

Little children, you are from God and have overcome them, for he who is in you is greater than he who is in the world. 1 John 4:4

King of Chaos

(Seven Deadly Sins)

Arthur Pendragon from the Seven Deadly Sins possesses extraordinary power and is destined to become the future king of Britannia. His strength and abilities are often depicted as a force that can bring about great change and wield immense power. He faces numerous challenges and adversaries along his journey.

The verse 1 John 4:4 reassures us that the one who is in us, referring to the Holy Spirit, is greater than the one who is in the world, referring to the forces of evil and opposition we may encounter. It emphasizes that as God's children, we have overcome the world because of the power and presence of God within us. This verse reminds us that we are not alone in our battles but have the assurance that the greater power of God is at work in and through us. With this awareness, we can approach life with courage, knowing that we have already overcome through the power of Christ within us.

Just as Arthur draws upon his power as the future king to overcome his adversaries, we can draw upon the power of the Holy Spirit within us. This power enables us to face the challenges and temptations of the world with confidence and victory. We can rely on God's strength, guidance, and wisdom to navigate through any obstacles or struggles we may encounter.

The power of Arthur Pendragon from the Seven Deadly Sins anime series can remind us of the power that resides within us as children of God. It encourages us to tap into that power, walk in confidence, and use it for the glory of God. Let us embrace the power we have been given, knowing that we have already overcome through Christ who is in us.

"A human cease to be once he or she stops thinking." - Merlin

October 9

Let not the wise man boast in his wisdom, let not the mighty man boast in his might, let not the rich man boast in his riches, but let him who boasts boast in this, that he understands and knows me, that I am the Lord who practices steadfast love, justice, and righteousness in the earth. For in these things I delight, declares the Lord.
Jeremiah 9:23-24

Third Six Paths

(Naruto)

In the Naruto storyline, Nagato, who possessed immense power and intelligence, developed a belief system centred around his own wisdom and strength. He saw himself as superior to others and believed that his actions were necessary for the greater good. His pride led him to boast about his own abilities and the righteousness of his cause.

Jeremiah 9:23-24 reminds us that true boasting should not be in our own wisdom, strength, or riches. Instead, it calls us to boast in our understanding and knowledge of God's character. The verse emphasizes that God values qualities such as kindness, justice, and righteousness. We are called to acknowledge that our wisdom and strength are gifts from God. It is not in our intellectual prowess or physical power that we should boast, but rather in our understanding of God's character and our relationship with Him.

Nagato's pride blinded him to the importance of these divine attributes. He failed to recognize that true peace and justice come from aligning our actions with God's will and embodying His kindness and righteousness. His misguided belief in his own abilities led to destruction and suffering.

By relating Nagato's pride in the Naruto anime series, we are reminded of the need to redirect our focus from self-centred pride to a recognition of God's character and a pursuit of His values. True boasting lies in understanding and knowing God, and delighting in His kindness, justice, and righteousness.

"If you don't share someone's pain, you can never understand them." - Pain

October 10

The true light, which gives light to everyone, was coming into the world. He was in the world, and the world was made through him, yet the world did not know him. John 1:9-10

Kind-Hearted Duck

(Princess Tutu)

Ahiru, also known as Duck, from the anime Princess Tutu, can be seen as a saviour figure in the story. She is a humble duck who transforms into a human girl and becomes Princess Tutu, a magical ballerina with the power to restore lost emotions and bring hope to those around her. Despite her small size and ordinary appearance, Ahiru's selfless acts of kindness and unwavering belief in the power of love make her a symbol of salvation in the series.

In John 1:9-10, the verse speaks of the true light coming into the world. This light refers to Jesus Christ, who brings spiritual enlightenment, redemption, and salvation to humanity. Despite being the Creator of the world, Jesus was not recognized or fully understood by the people He came to save, much like how Ahiru's true nature as Princess Tutu is initially unknown to those around her.

Through Ahiru's role as a saviour figure in Princess Tutu, we are reminded of the universal nature of salvation. Just as her transformative abilities and acts of selflessness bring healing and restoration to the characters in Princess Tutu, Jesus, as the true light, brings spiritual illumination and redemption to all people. Both Ahiru and Jesus represent a source of hope, love, and salvation in their respective contexts.

By contemplating Ahiru as a saviour figure in the Princess Tutu anime series, we recognize the parallels between her character and the mission of Jesus. It emphasizes the transformative power of love, the hidden nature of salvation, and the universality of redemption. Ultimately, it inspires us to embrace our own calling as agents of God's light and love, spreading hope and restoration in the world around us.

"Stories aren't always guaranteed a happily ever after." - Drosselmeyer

October 11

if you pour yourself out for the hungry and satisfy the desire of the afflicted, then shall your light rise in the darkness and your gloom be as the noonday. Isaiah 58:10

Traitorous Caretaker

(The Promised Neverland)

In The Promised Neverland anime series, Isabella initially assumed the role of Mama at Grace Field House, where she raised children with the ulterior motive of eventually offering them as food to the demons. However, when a group of her children successfully escaped, Isabella experienced a profound change of heart. She made the decision to defy the demons while strategically pretending to comply with their instructions.

The verse Isaiah 58:10 emphasizes the transformative impact of selfless acts of service and compassion, urging believers to move beyond mere religious observance and rituals. It encourages active engagement in acts of love and justice. When we actively participate in acts of compassion and justice, our light rises in the darkness. This signifies that our actions not only have a transformative effect on those we help but also on ourselves. We become beacons of hope and agents of change in a world that is in desperate need of light and love.

Isabella's sacrifice aligns with the Christian faith, which emphasizes love, compassion, and selflessness. Her willingness to expend herself on behalf of the hungry and oppressed mirrors the sacrificial love of Jesus Christ. Just as Jesus laid down His life to redeem humanity, Isabella willingly sacrifices her own happiness and freedom to protect the children.

Reflecting on Isabella's sacrifice in the anime prompts us to consider the transformative power of Christ's love and the call for believers to extend compassion and justice to the oppressed. Her story encourages us to examine our own actions and contemplate how we can let the light in us rise and bring hope even in the darkest of circumstances.

"Life is just one big gamble. Believe in what you've decided. And no matter what results from it, keep going."
- Norman

October 12

See what kind of love the Father has given to us, that we should be called children of God; and so we are. The reason why the world does not know us is that it did not know him. 1 John 3:1

Pessimistic Mastermind

(My Teen Romantic Comedy SNAFU)

Hachiman Hikigaya, the protagonist of the anime series My Teen Romantic Comedy SNAFU, presents an intriguing character study when it comes to self-esteem and personal growth. Throughout the series, Hachiman displays a distinct lack of self-esteem, often distancing himself from others and adopting a cynical worldview.

1 John 3:1 reminds us of the remarkable love that God has lavished upon us. It reveals that we are not merely ordinary beings, but that God has called us His children. This truth is transformative and provides a solid foundation for our self-esteem. Through this verse, we are called to shift our perspective and find our self-worth in the incredible love that God has poured out on us.

The self-esteem Hachiman seeks is not found in conforming to societal expectations, trying to please others, or achieving worldly success. Instead, it is found in embracing our identity as children of God. We are loved unconditionally, regardless of our flaws, mistakes, or past experiences. This truth gives us a sense of belonging, purpose, and value.

As we reflect on Hachiman's journey, we are reminded of the importance of finding our self-esteem in our relationship with God. We can empathize with his struggles but also find hope and encouragement in the truth that we are beloved children of God. This realization allows us to navigate life's challenges with confidence, knowing that our worth is secure in the unchanging love of our Heavenly Father.

"Fake friends are like shadows. They follow you in the sun. But leave you in the dark." - Hachiman Hikigaya

October 13

Then desire when it has conceived gives birth to sin, and sin when it is fully grown brings forth death. James 1:15

Crimson Lotus Alchemist

(Fullmetal Alchemist: Brotherhood)

In Fullmetal Alchemist: Brotherhood, Solf J. Kimblee's sinfulness is depicted through his unyielding desire for power and destruction. He embodies the idea of unchecked ambition, willingly participating in acts of violence and seeking personal gain at the expense of others. His alchemical abilities, particularly his mastery of explosions, become tools for causing harm and sowing chaos. This reflects the notion of desire conceiving sin, as Kimblee's unbridled ambition leads him down a destructive path.

The verse James 1:15 emphasizes the progression of sin and its consequences, highlighting the importance of resisting temptation and avoiding sinful behaviour. It serves as a reminder of the insidious nature of sin and its destructive potential. It cautions against giving in to our sinful desires, knowing that they can lead us further away from God and towards spiritual and moral death.

Kimblee's pursuit of power, manipulation, and disregard for human life reflects the corrupting influence of sin. His initial desires, fuelled by his ambition and pleasure-seeking nature, give birth to sinful actions that cause harm and suffering. As he continues down this path, the consequences of his sins become more pronounced, culminating in death.

In the character of Solf J. Kimblee, we can learn valuable lessons about the dangers of unchecked desires and the devastating consequences of sinful actions. It serves as a reminder to examine our own hearts and motivations, ensuring that we align ourselves with God's teachings and resist the temptations that can lead us astray.

"What could be more beautiful than doing work that puts your soul at risk because that's what it means to be alive!"
- Solf J. Kimblee

October 14

I will give thanks to the Lord with my whole heart; I will recount all of your wonderful deeds. Psalm 9:1

Armoured Alchemist

(Fullmetal Alchemist: Brotherhood)

Alphonse Elric from the Fullmetal Alchemist: Brotherhood anime is a character who goes through significant challenges and hardships. Despite his difficult journey, Alphonse displays a sense of gratitude and thankfulness. He is grateful for the bond and support he shares with his older brother, Edward. Alphonse also acknowledges and appreciates the deep connection they have, as they rely on and trust each other throughout their journey.

In Psalm 9:1, the psalmist's commitment to giving thanks with all their heart reflects a deep sense of gratitude that surpasses mere superficial acknowledgment. It emphasizes the sincerity and depth of the praise offered to God. As followers of Christ, this verse reminds us to cultivate a genuine attitude of gratitude, recognizing that all good things come from God and expressing our thankfulness to Him in both words and actions.

Alphonse is thankful for the knowledge and wisdom he gains along the way. As he uncovers the mysteries of alchemy and encounters various people and cultures, he remains open-minded and appreciative of the lessons learned. He recognizes that each experience contributes to his growth and understanding of the world. He also demonstrates gratitude for the sacrifices made by others. Alphonse understands that he wouldn't have been able to progress without the assistance and kindness of those around him.

In the anime, Alphonse not only appreciates the specific acts of kindness he receives but also demonstrates an overall gratitude for the blessings and support he encounters in his life. It serves as a reminder to us of the importance of acknowledging and expressing gratitude for the goodness and provisions we receive, attributing them to the divine source of all blessings.

"Dedication is talent all on its own." - Alphonse Elric

October 15

For I am sure that neither death nor life, nor angels nor rulers, nor things present nor things to come, nor powers, nor height nor depth, nor anything else in all creation, will be able to separate us from the love of God in Christ Jesus our Lord. Romans 8:38-39

Dark Mousy

(D.N. Angel)

In the anime "D.N. Angel"Daisuke struggles with his dual role as the descendant of the Niwa family and as the host of the phantom thief Dark Mousy, which brings challenges to his life. He often feels isolated, misunderstood, and unable to fully accept himself. However, as the story unfolds, he encounters individuals who demonstrate unwavering love, understanding, and acceptance towards him.

Romans 8:38-39 serves as a reminder that there is nothing in all of creation that can separate us from the love of God. It is a declaration that affirms the unbreakable bond between God and His children. This verse assures us that His love is not conditional, dependent on our circumstances, or swayed by external influences. It remains constant and unwavering.

Daisuke's journey in seeking acceptance and understanding resonates with our own human experience. We, too, may struggle with our identity, battle against societal pressures, or face moments of doubt and insecurity. However, the truth is that God's love transcends all of these challenges. As Christians, we are called to extend this same acceptance and love to others, just as Daisuke receives it from those around him.

In the acceptance of Daisuke, we witness the power of unwavering love and support. We must trust in God's unfailing love, find security in His acceptance, and extend that same love and acceptance to those around us. We can walk alongside others in their own journeys of self-discovery and remind them that nothing can separate them from the love of God.

"That which is incomplete seeks completion... yet... that which is incomplete is no better than that which is complete. Do you understand?" - Argentine

October 16

But I say to you that everyone who is angry with his brother will be liable to judgment; whoever insults his brother will be liable to the council; and whoever says, 'You fool!' will be liable to the hell of fire. Matthew 5:22

Medical Ninja

(Naruto)

Sakura's anger in Naruto is often driven by her passionate nature and her desire to protect those she cares about. However, she occasionally struggles to manage her anger, leading to impulsive actions and heated exchanges. While she may not necessarily use derogatory language, her anger sometimes leads her to act impulsively or lash out in ways that can hurt those around her.

The verse Matthew 5:22 reminds us of the significance of addressing anger and reconciling relationships rather than holding onto bitterness or seeking to demean others. It invites us to consider the spiritual consequences of anger and calls us to be mindful of the impact our anger can have on our own hearts and the potential damage it can cause to our relationships.

The journey of Sakura can be viewed as an opportunity for growth and transformation. We can learn to channel our anger in a constructive manner. This involves developing self-control, seeking understanding, and choosing to respond with kindness and forgiveness rather than letting anger consume our actions.

Sakura's anger in the Naruto anime emphasizes the importance of seeking reconciliation, controlling our words and actions, and cultivating a spirit of love and understanding in our interactions with others. It offers a reminder that the path of discipleship involves continually striving to manage our emotions, resolve conflicts, and promote peace in our relationships, mirroring the example of Christ.

"The things that are most important aren't written in books. You have to learn them by experiencing them yourself." - Sakura Haruno

October 17

Char m is deceitful, and beauty is vain, but a woman who fears the Lord is to be praised. Proverbs 31:30

Iron Mace

(One Piece)

Alvida's appearance in the early stages of One Piece exemplifies the transient nature of physical beauty. Initially, she is depicted as a large and unattractive pirate captain, emphasizing that outward charm can be deceptive and misleading. However, as the story progresses, Alvida consumes the Sube Sube no Mi Devil Fruit, which dramatically changes her physical appearance.

Proverbs 31:30 cautions against placing excessive value on charm or outward attractiveness. It reminds us that charm alone can be deceptive, as it can mask the true character of an individual. We should be cautious not to be swayed solely by external appearances but instead look deeper into a person's heart and actions. Outer beauty, though often sought after and celebrated in our culture, is temporary and subject to change. It serves as a reminder that our focus should not be solely on maintaining external appearances but on cultivating qualities and virtues that endure beyond physical attractiveness.

Alvida's transformation highlights the transient nature of physical attractiveness. While she undergoes a significant change in her appearance, it does not alter the underlying truth that physical beauty is temporary. We need to place greater emphasis on qualities that endure beyond external appearances, such as wisdom, kindness, and a heart that fears the Lord.

The appearance of Alvida from the anime series One Piece can prompt us to examine our own hearts and attitudes toward beauty. It encourages us to seek true beauty that transcends the superficial, focusing on developing a character that aligns with God's values and brings honour to Him.

"Yesterday's ally can be tomorrow's enemy." - Alvida

October 18

For you equipped me with strength for the battle; you made those who rise against me sink under me. Psalm 18:39

Lord of Destruction

(Black Clover)

Yami Sukehiro is the captain of the Black Bulls, a squad of magical knights, and he approaches battles with unwavering confidence. He is known for his incredible combat skills and his unique magic called Dark Magic. He channels this magic and these skills to overcome powerful opponents, never backing down from a fight. Yami's attitude reflects his strong belief in his own abilities and his determination to defeat anyone who stands in his way.

Psalm 18:39 reminds us that our strength comes from God. The verse acknowledges that it is God who equips and empowers us for the battles we face in life. As believers in Christ, we can recognize that our strength does not come from our own abilities or resources but from the Lord who strengthens us.

Yami boldly confronts and triumphs over his enemies, encouraging us to confront and overcome the battles we encounter. While Yami's battles in the anime are physical, our battles as Christians are often spiritual in nature. We face opposition from the forces of darkness, such as sin, temptation, and spiritual attacks. Through our faith in Christ, we have the power to resist and subdue the forces that oppose us.

The attitude of Yami Sukehiro in Black Clover can be used as a metaphor for our own spiritual journey. By embracing biblical principles, we can find strength and courage in God, persevere through trials, and rely on His power to overcome the spiritual battles we face. Yami's unwavering determination can serve as a reminder of our own call to stand firm in our faith, relying on the strength and victory found in Christ.

"Protect whatever is precious to you. One day it'll lead you to protect something else." - Yami Sukehiro

October 19

Therefore, do not be anxious about tomorrow, for tomorrow will be anxious for itself. Sufficient for the day is its own trouble. Matthew 6:34

Passionate Adventurer

(Made in Abyss)

Throughout her perilous journey in the Abyss, Riko faces constant uncertainty, danger, and the fear of the unknown. She often finds herself in life-threatening situations and encounters numerous challenges that could easily overwhelm her with anxiety about the future. Riko's journey into the Abyss is a metaphor for our own earthly pilgrimage. Like Riko, we face challenges, uncertainties, and dangers along the way. The Abyss represents the trials and tribulations of life, the deep and dark places we must navigate.

The verse Matthew 6:34 reminds us that worrying about tomorrow does not change our circumstances, but it does steal our peace and joy in the present. As followers of Christ, we have the assurance that God is always with us, providing for our needs and guiding us through the trials we encounter.

Riko's circumstances teach us the importance of community and friendship. Along her journey, she forms deep bonds with her friends who offer support, encouragement, and help in times of need. In the same way, as believers, we are called to journey together, supporting and uplifting one another as we face the challenges of life.

The story of Riko in the anime series Made in Abyss reminds us that while we cannot control or predict what lies ahead, we can find peace and strength in our relationship with God. By entrusting our worries and anxieties to Him, we can live in the present moment, fully embracing the journey before us.

"You're saying as if a family can only be made with blood relations. I do not think that is the case. A compassionate heart is what makes people a family. Blood does not help much in that regard. Love. It's love." - Bondrewd

October 20

Now as the church submits to Christ, so also wives should submit in everything to their husbands. Ephesians 5:25

First Chevalier

(Blood+)

In the anime series Blood+, Hagi consistently demonstrates unwavering loyalty and dedication to Saya. He acts as her protector, guardian, and confidant, willingly making personal sacrifices and enduring physical and emotional pain to ensure her safety and happiness. Although Hagi and Saya are not married, Hagi exhibits sacrificial love towards Saya throughout their journey.

Ephesians 5:25 not only addresses husbands and wives but also carries a broader message of love and commitment within Christian relationships. This form of love goes beyond personal desires and interests, focusing on selfless giving and service for the beloved. We are prompted to evaluate our own commitments to those around us, encouraging us to exhibit sacrificial love and give of ourselves for the sake of others.

Hagi's character exemplifies selfless devotion and sacrificial love, as described in the scripture. His unwavering commitment to Saya parallels Christ's sacrificial love for the church. Hagi's willingness to lay down his life and make personal sacrifices for Saya's well-being mirrors the extent to which Christ gave Himself up for His followers. Just as Christ remains steadfast and faithful to the church, Hagi's commitment to Saya is marked by constancy, selflessness, and an enduring presence.

Reflecting on Hagi's commitment in Blood+ brings to light the powerful themes of sacrificial love and Christ-like devotion. His character serves as an inspiration for Christians to emulate his selflessness, reminding us of Christ's ultimate sacrifice and encouraging us to love and commit to others in a similar manner.

"There is no guarantee that your dreams are just good ones." - Hagi

October 21

And all who believed were together and had all things in common. And they were selling their possessions and belongings and distributing the proceeds to all, as any had need. And day by day, attending the temple together and breaking bread in their homes, they received their food with glad and generous hearts. Acts 2:44-46

Crime Organization

(Hunter x Hunter)

The Phantom Troupe, also known as the Spiders, is a group of notorious criminals in the anime series Hunter x Hunter. They are a close-knit community that operates with their own set of rules and values. Each member possesses unique talents and strengths, and through their interactions and collaboration, they push each other to improve and become stronger. While their intentions and actions may be questionable, they do gather together and operate as a collective force.

Th verses Acts 2:44-46 presents a beautiful picture of a community of believers who share everything in common, support one another, and show selflessness in meeting each other's needs. As followers of Christ, we are called to love our neighbours, seek justice, and promote the well-being of others.

The Phantom Troupe, as a criminal community, engages in unlawful activities that harm others and pursue personal gain. Their story in the anime serves as a reminder of the importance of using our communities and relationships for positive and righteous purposes.

While we may find certain aspects of the Phantom Troupe's camaraderie intriguing or captivating from a storytelling perspective, it is essential to distinguish between fiction and reality. We are called to embrace values of love, justice, and compassion, striving to build communities that reflect these principles and work towards the betterment of all.

"The legs do what the head says. But there will be times when the legs are more important than the head." - Chrollo Lucifer

October 22

And do not fear those who kill the body but cannot kill the soul. Rather fear him who can destroy both soul and body in hell. Matthew 10:28

Legendary Sucker

(Naruto)

Tsunade is a fan-favourite character in Naruto anime series, who's courage is derived from her conviction to protect and defend others, even at the risk of her own life. She understands the fleeting nature of the physical body and focuses on the deeper values and principles that drive her actions. Tsunade is willing to confront formidable adversaries and endure bodily harm because she values the well-being and safety of others above her own.

Matthew 10:28 encourages believers to prioritize the eternal well-being of their souls. This verse reminds us that genuine courage stems from placing our trust in God rather than fearing worldly threats. It calls us to adopt a perspective that extends beyond the physical realm and underscores the importance of standing firm in our faith, irrespective of the external dangers we may encounter.

Tsunade's courage serves as a reminder to prioritize the eternal well-being of others. Similar to how she selflessly risks her life to protect and serve, we are also called to act in love and selflessness, seeking the spiritual welfare of those around us. Our courage should be anchored in a desire to share the hope and truth of the Gospel, recognizing that our actions can have an everlasting impact on the destiny of others.

While we can appreciate the courage displayed by Tsunade in the Naruto anime series, our ultimate source of courage and strength comes from our faith in Jesus Christ and the indwelling of the Holy Spirit. Through God's power, we can confront any challenge with courage, knowing that our souls are secure in His hands.

"People become stronger because they have things they cannot forget. That's what you call growth." - Tsunade

October 23

For whoever would save his life will lose it, but whoever loses his life for my sake and the gospel's will save it. Mark 8:35

Math Prodigy

(The Promised Neverland)

In the anime, Norman faces a critical choice where he must decide between his own personal safety and the well-being of his friends. He understands the dire circumstances they are in and the potential danger they face if he doesn't take action. In a selfless act of love and sacrifice, Norman chooses to put his friends' lives above his own and devises a plan that requires him to give up his freedom and possibly even his life.

In the verse Mark 8:35, Jesus teaches his disciples that those who seek to save their lives and prioritize their own interests above everything else will ultimately lose the true essence of life. However, those who are willing to lose their lives for the sake of Jesus and the gospel will find true and abundant life.

Norman recognizes that by sacrificing himself and risking everything for the well-being of others, he can potentially save his friends and secure a better future for them. His act of selflessness aligns with the teachings of Jesus, emphasizing the importance of giving up one's own desires, ambitions, and even physical safety for a higher cause. Just as Norman willingly prepared to lay down his life for his friends, Jesus gave his life for the redemption and salvation of all humanity.

Norman's decision from The Promised Neverland prompts us to examine our own willingness to lay down our lives, ambitions, and desires for the sake of others and the gospel. His example reminds us of the profound impact that selfless acts of love and sacrifice can have, and it inspires us to follow Jesus' teachings and embrace a life of sacrificial love for the greater good.

"Kindness alone can't win in this world." - Norman

October 24

I have fought the good fight, I have finished the race, I have kept the faith. 2 Timothy 4:7

Demon Cyborg

(One-Punch Man)

Genos, a prominent character from the anime series One Punch Man, is a cyborg with a deep sense of devotion and a strong desire to become a hero. He consistently exhibits relentless dedication to his mission of becoming a hero and protecting others. He engages in countless battles and challenges, demonstrating his commitment to the fight against evil.

The verse 2 Timothy 4:7 emphasizes the importance of engaging in the good fight and remaining faithful to one's beliefs and convictions until the end. It encourages believers to persevere and stay devoted to their faith and purpose, regardless of the obstacles they encounter. Genos embodies this spirit of perseverance and unwavering commitment as he fights for justice and remains resolute in his mission.

Genos' dedication reflects the idea of finishing the race. In the Christian journey, we are called to persevere until the end, remaining faithful to God's calling and purpose for our lives. Genos' tireless pursuit of becoming a hero and his continuous efforts to improve himself remind us of the importance of pressing on, even in the face of adversity, and never giving up on our pursuit of righteousness. Despite numerous setbacks and challenges, Genos remains steadfast in his mission, never losing sight of his purpose. Similarly, as followers of Christ, we are called to keep our faith firm, holding onto the truth of God's Word and trusting in His promises, even in the midst of trials and uncertainties.

The dedication of Genos from the anime One Punch Man serves as a reminder and encouragement for Christians to embrace a similar level of devotion in their own spiritual journey. May we strive to fight the good fight, finish the race, and keep the faith, just as Genos exemplifies, all for the glory of God.

"Even the most powerful weapon would be meaningless if it's wielder is weak." - Genos

October 25

Behold, children are a heritage from the Lord, the fruit of the womb a reward. Psalm 127:3

Uzumaki Family

(Boruto)

In Boruto, Naruto and Hinata Uzumaki prioritize their children and recognize them as precious blessings. They provide love, guidance, and support to their children, Boruto and Himawari, demonstrating the significance they place on their roles as parents. Together, they create a loving and supportive environment for their children to grow and thrive.

Psalm 127:3 emphasizes the value and blessing of children. It acknowledges that children are a gift from God, described as a heritage and a reward. This verse highlights the special role and significance of children in the lives of their parents and in society as a whole. It reminds us to seek the Lord's guidance, believing that our family is a reward from Him.

The Uzumaki family's journey reflects the joys and challenges that come with raising children. They navigate the complexities of parenting while instilling important values and life lessons in their children. Through their interactions, we witness their commitment to nurturing their children's growth, character, and spiritual development, which aligns with the idea of children being a heritage from the Lord. Similarly, our parents love us deeply, and they are always there to guide us, protect us, and help us grow. By relating to the Uzumaki family, we recognize the preciousness of children and the responsibility parents have in raising them. It encourages us to be thankful for our parents and to cherish the children in our lives, striving to provide them with love, guidance, and spiritual nurturing.

The Uzumaki family's example reminds us of the importance of stewarding the next generation with care and devotion, recognizing that they are indeed a heritage and reward from the Lord. Let us be grateful for the gift of family and strive to honour God by nurturing and supporting one another in love, just as the Uzumaki family does.

"Failing doesn't give you a reason to give up, as long as you believe." - Naruto Uzumaki

October 26

In God I trust; I shall not be afraid. What can man do to me? Psalm 56:11

Grape Juice Hero

(My Hero Academia)

Minoru Mineta is a character from the anime series My Hero Academia. He is a student at U.A. High School, a prestigious school for aspiring heroes. Minoru possesses the Quirk called Pop Off, which allows him to pluck sticky balls from his head and throw them as a means of immobilizing opponents or creating traps. He faces fears associated with failure, disappointing others, or not living up to expectations. Additionally, the pressures and dangers inherent in the world of heroes also evoke fear in him.

The verse Psalm 56:11 reminds us of the power of trust in God. When we place our trust in Him, fear loses its hold on us. It is in God that we find our ultimate security and refuge. The verse also encourages us to shift our focus from our own limitations to the limitless power of God. By trusting in God, we can find the strength to overcome our fears and confront any obstacles that come our way.

Despite his quirks and flaws, Minoru Mineta is a capable student who aims to become a respected hero. He participates in various training exercises and battles alongside his classmates, strategically utilizing his Quirk to contribute to the team's success. Over time, he learns to be resourceful, showcasing his growth as a hero-in-training.

As Christians, we can apply the same reflection to our own lives. Like Minoru, we face fears and uncertainties, but through faith in God, we can find courage and strength. We are reminded to trust in God's unwavering presence and His ability to overcome any obstacle. By anchoring ourselves in Him, we can move forward with confidence, knowing that we are never alone and that His plans for us are ultimately for our good.

"Being a hero doesn't make you cool... they're heroes because they're cool!" - Minoru Mineta

October 27

For this my son was dead, and is alive again; he was lost, and is found.' And they began to celebrate. Luke 15:20-24

Fourth Kazekage

(Naruto)

In the Naruto anime series, the concept of forgiveness is explored through the character Rasa, who is the father of Gaara. Rasa's initial actions in the series were driven by fear and a desire for power, leading him to orchestrate a plot to kill Gaara in order to extract and control a powerful entity within him, the One-Tail. However, later in the series, Rasa comes to regret his actions and seeks forgiveness from Gaara.

Luke 15:24 is a verse from the parable of the prodigal son, where a son squanders his inheritance and ends up destitute. Realizing the error of his ways, he returns to his father, hoping to be taken back even as a servant. However, the father's reaction is one of overwhelming love, forgiveness, and celebration. The father not only welcomes his son back but also reinstates him as his beloved child.

Similarly, Rasa, after realizing the harm he has caused his son Gaara and the pain he has inflicted upon him, seeks forgiveness. In the story, Gaara initially struggles with forgiving his father, much like the prodigal son who feels unworthy. However, as the story progresses, Gaara learns to forgive and reconcile with his father, ultimately embracing him as family.

The narrative of Rasa in the Naruto anime series emphasizes the power of forgiveness, the ability to let go of past mistakes and reconcile broken relationships. It portrays the mercy, grace, and compassion that can be extended to those who acknowledge their mistakes and seek forgiveness, emphasizing the redemptive power of forgiveness.

"Just because somebody is important to you, it doesn't necessarily mean that they're a good person. Even if you recognize that they're evil, people just can't win against their loneliness." - Gaara

October 28

Then Jonathan made a covenant with David, because he loved him as his own soul. 1 Samuel 18:3

Sworn Brothers

(That Time I Got Reincarnated as A Slime)

In the anime, Rimuru, a slime with unique powers, encounters Veldora, a powerful dragon who has been sealed away. Despite their differences in form and abilities, they develop an unbreakable friendship based on mutual trust, loyalty, and love. They form a special bond and make a covenant with each other, vowing to support and protect one another.

The verse 1 Samuel 18:3 describes the friendship between Jonathan and David in the Bible. Jonathan, the son of King Saul, forms a covenant with David, who would later become the celebrated King David. Jonathan's love for David is so profound that he considers David's well-being as important as his own. Their friendship is characterized by an unwavering commitment to each other's well-being and a willingness to sacrifice for one another.

Rimuru and Veldora's friendship demonstrates profound love and acceptance. Rimuru accepts Veldora unconditionally, valuing him as a cherished friend despite his intimidating appearance and past actions. This echoes the selfless love that Jonathan showed toward David. Rimuru and Veldora form a bond that is unyielding, supporting each other through trials and becoming pillars of strength in each other's lives.

The friendship of Rimuru and Veldora in the anime calls us to reflect on the biblical principles of love, acceptance, loyalty, self-sacrifice, and covenantal relationships that can be found within their bond. By examining their friendship through a Christian lens, we can appreciate the positive virtues and values depicted in their relationship and apply them to our own lives and friendships in a way that aligns with biblical teachings.

"Ideals without power to back them up are just idle daydreams and power without ideals is just empty." - Rimuru Tempest

October 29

He heals the broken hearted and binds up their wounds.
Psalm 147:3

NEET Woman

(Recovery of an MMO Junkie)

In the anime, Moriko is depicted as someone who struggles with her sense of identity, loneliness, and a lack of fulfilment in her daily life. Through her immersion in the virtual world and her interactions with other players, she begins to find solace, companionship, and a renewed sense of purpose. As she connects with others and opens herself up to new experiences, she starts to heal from her emotional wounds and grow as an individual.

Psalm 147:3 is a verse that speaks to God's ability to heal the broken hearted and mend their wounds. It reminds us that God's love and grace have the power to bring healing and restoration to our lives, even in the midst of pain and brokenness. The verse reminds us that God is the ultimate healer who can mend our brokenness and lead us on a path of growth, fulfilment, and purpose.

Just as Moriko experiences a transformation and growth through her journey, we too can find healing and wholeness. Her growth and recovery highlight the importance of finding support, connection, and understanding in our relationships with others, as well as in our spiritual journey. God's healing touch can mend our brokenness and help us grow into the people He has created us to be.

Moriko's story in the anime reminds us that God is compassionate and caring, ready to bind up our wounds and bring us to a place of healing and wholeness. As she finds healing and growth through her virtual experiences, it serves as a reminder that God can use various avenues to bring healing and growth into our lives. Her journey of growth and self-discovery points us to the transformative power of God's love and grace.

"I know there's no way my daydreaming is in line with reality, but... isn't it okay for me to dream just a little?" - Yuuta Sakurai

October 30

So also, you have sorrow now, but I will see you again, and your hearts will rejoice, and no one will take your joy from you. John 16:22

Night Raid Assassin

(Akame Ga Kill!)

In the anime Akame ga Kill, Leone is a strong, charismatic, and fiercely loyal member of the assassin group known as Night Raid. She exudes a sense of joy and happiness that shines through her carefree and spirited personality. Despite the dark and violent world, she inhabits, Leone manages to find moments of happiness and brings a lightness to the lives of those around her.

The verse John 16:22 speaks of the temporary nature of sorrow and the promise of lasting joy that comes from being reunited with Jesus Christ. Furthermore, the verse reminds us that our sorrows are not permanent. Jesus promises to return and bring ultimate joy and fulfilment. This points us to the hope we have as Christians, knowing that our present sufferings are temporary and that eternal joy awaits us in the presence of God.

Leone's happiness can be seen as a reflection of this biblical truth. Despite the difficult circumstances she faces, she holds on to hope and finds joy in moments of camaraderie and friendship. Her happiness is not dependent on her external circumstances but is rooted in her resilience and the relationships she forms with her comrades.

The happiness of Leone in Akame ga Kill can be seen as a reflection of the enduring joy that comes from a relationship with Christ. Her happiness serves as a reminder that even in the midst of darkness, we can find moments of joy and glimpses of the greater joy to come. It encourages us to seek happiness not solely in our circumstances but in our relationship with Christ and the hope of His return. It also inspires us to find reasons to rejoice in every situation and to trust in the promise of a joy that cannot be taken away.

"If we quit now, then all the dead would have died for nothing." - Leone

October 31

For while bodily training is of some value, godliness is of value in every way, as it holds promise for the present life and also for the life to come. 1 Timothy 4:8

World's Strongest Boy

(Baki)

The character Baki Hanma from the anime Baki is known for his relentless dedication and hard work in his pursuit of becoming the strongest martial artist. He puts his heart and soul into his training, striving to become the best he can be. Baki's dedication is not merely for personal gain or recognition but is driven by a desire to honour his own potential and abilities, pushing himself to his limits.

2 Timothy 2:15 encourages believers to approach their work and endeavours with a similar mindset of diligence, integrity, and competence. It reminds us that we are called to be diligent workers who handle the truth with accuracy and integrity. Just as Baki tirelessly trains to master his martial arts skills, we are called to diligently study and apply the word of God, correctly handling its truths and principles in our lives.

Baki's dedication can inspire us to channel our own diligence and perseverance toward growing in godliness. It reminds us that just as Baki pushes his physical limits to attain greatness, we should strive to develop virtues and characteristics that reflect Christ. While physical training can contribute to our well-being and accomplishments, it is the pursuit of godliness that carries eternal significance.

The hard work of Baki in the anime serves as a reminder to invest not only in physical training but also in cultivating a deep relationship with God, nurturing our spiritual lives, and aligning our actions and aspirations with His will. Through Baki's example, we are encouraged to seek a balanced approach to life, where our pursuit of physical excellence is integrated with our pursuit of godliness, ensuring that we honour God in all that we do.

"Not feeling free unless you're the freest person in the world. How unfree." - Baki Hanma

November 1

Let what you say be simply 'Yes' or 'No'; anything more than this comes from evil. Matthew 5:37

Tough-Talking Petite

(Kaguya-Sama: Love is War)

Miko is a character from Kaguya-Sama: Love is War known for her straightforwardness and unwavering commitment to speaking the truth. She does not shy away from expressing her opinions, even when they may be unpopular or uncomfortable. Miko's words hold weight and sincerity, reflecting her desire to be genuine and transparent.

The verse from Matthew 5:37 in Jesus' Sermon on the Mount cautions against going beyond simple honesty, as anything more can be attributed to the evil one. It urges individuals to refrain from deceit, manipulation, and dishonesty in their communication. This verse also encourages people to be truthful and straightforward in their communication, emphasizing the value of keeping one's word and avoiding false promises or misleading statements. When we let our "Yes"truly mean "Yes "and our "No"mean "No,"we demonstrate integrity and reliability in our words.

However, it is essential to note that while Miko's honesty is admirable, it is also important to exercise wisdom and love in our communication. As followers of Christ, we should strive not only to be honest but also to speak the truth with grace and kindness, considering the impact of our words on others.

Miko's character in the anime serves as a reminder of the value of honesty in our Christian walk. It encourages us to examine our own words and actions, seeking to align them with the teachings of Christ. By doing so, we can cultivate a spirit of integrity, reflecting God's truth in our interactions with others and ultimately bringing glory to Him.

"It's not good to be excessively afraid of physical contact with other people. I guess that's the dark side of modern society." - Kaguya Shinomiya

November 2

But I will hope continually and will praise you yet more and more. Psalm 71:14

Kumogakure Shinobi

(Naruto)

Omoi is a character from the Naruto series known for his serious and pragmatic personality. He is often depicted as lacking confidence in his abilities but strives to become stronger and protect those dear to him. Despite his doubts, he has a strong sense of duty and is fiercely loyal to his friends and village. Omoi is known for his cautious nature, carefully analysing situations before taking action.

Psalm 71:14 encourages us to maintain continuous and unwavering hope. As Christians, we are called to place our hope in God, even when faced with trials and uncertainties. The psalmist's commitment to praising God yet more and more highlights the transformative power of hope. In the Christian journey, hope fuels our spiritual growth, motivating us to praise God and seek His presence in all aspects of our lives.

Omoi's example reminds us that hope is a choice, a decision to anchor our trust in the faithfulness of God, knowing that He is with us in every situation. His story resonates with the Christian understanding that hope is not passive but active. It propels us to persevere, strive for righteousness, and trust in God's sovereign plan, even when the path is difficult. As we align our hope with God's purposes, we find strength, encouragement, and the assurance that He is working all things together for our good.

The story of Omoi in Naruto reflects themes of self-discovery, perseverance, and the power of loyalty. Despite his initial doubts, he finds hope and strength through unwavering loyalty to his friends and village. Omoi's hope reminds us that true hope is rooted in our relationship with God. It calls us to hold onto hope, praise Him in all circumstances, and trust that He is leading us towards a future filled with His goodness and love.

"Hard work is worthless for those that don't believe in themselves." - Uzumaki Naruto

November 3

All these things my hand has made, and so all these things came to be, declares the Lord. But this is the one to whom I will look: he who is humble and contrite in spirit and trembles at my word. Isaiah 66:2

Witch of Frost

(Re: Zero)

Emilia's character in Re: Zero anime consistently displays a humble and contrite spirit. Despite being a candidate for the royal throne with considerable power, she approaches situations with humility, acknowledging her own limitations and seeking guidance from others. Emilia's humility is evident in her interactions with people from different backgrounds, treating them with respect and kindness.

Isaiah 66:2 describes that God looks favourably upon those who are humble and contrite in spirit. It serves as a reminder that humility and a contrite spirit are qualities that God looks for in His followers. True greatness comes from a humble and contrite heart that seeks wisdom and guidance from God.

Emilia embodies these qualities as she recognizes her weaknesses, learns from her mistakes, and strives to become a better person. She trembles at the weight of her responsibilities and shows reverence for the guidance and teachings of others. She values the wisdom and guidance of others, seeking to understand different perspectives and learn from the experiences of those around her. Through her humility, Emilia becomes a source of inspiration and encouragement for others, embodying the qualities that God values.

Emilia's character in Re: Zero reflects the transformative power of humility and highlights the importance of being receptive to divine teachings and guidance. Her humility invites us to cultivate a humble and contrite spirit before God. It is in this humility that we can find favour in His eyes and experience the transformative power of His love and grace.

"A million sorry's is not equal to 1 thank you." - Emilia

November 4

And the Lord said: "Because this people draw near with their mouth and honor me with their lips, while their hearts are far from me, and their fear of me is a commandment taught by men. Isaiah 29:13

Spider Demon

(Demon Slayer)

In Demon Slayer, Rui's story takes a tragic turn due to Muzan's manipulation, causing him to harm both Demon Slayers and other demons. After he kills his parents, who tried to stop him from becoming a demon, Rui tries to create a family of spider demons. However, his way of doing so is harsh, involving lies, manipulation, and death. Although he wants a family, Rui doesn't treat them with care and instead chooses to get rid of anyone who disagrees with him.

Isaiah 29:13 exposes the peril of merely going through religious motions without wholeheartedly surrendering ourselves to God. It reminds us of the importance of aligning our inner convictions and intentions with our outward expressions of faith. This verse challenges us to examine our lives and ensure that our worship of God is driven by genuine desire, not empty rituals or human-imposed regulations.

Rui's hypocrisy serves as a catalyst for cultivating true justice, compassion, and empathy within us. It compels us to reflect on our own actions and motivations, ensuring that we do not become hypocrites who merely proclaim righteousness without living it out. Instead, we are called to sincerely pursue justice, demonstrate mercy, and humbly walk with God.

The example of Rui's hypocrisy warns against superficial religiosity and urges us to pursue an authentic, wholehearted relationship with God, where our inner devotion aligns harmoniously with our outward expressions of faith. By doing so, we can strive to live lives that genuinely reflect the transformative power of Christ's love and bring honor to His name.

"If you can do one thing, hone it to perfection. Hone it to the utmost limit." - Jigoro Kuwajima

November 5

In all things I have shown you that by working hard in this way we must help the weak and remember the words of the Lord Jesus, how he himself said, 'It is more blessed to give than to receive.' Acts 20:35

Fire Mage Salamander

(Fairy Tail)

Natsu Dragneel from Fairy Tail consistently strives to do what is right and just, fighting against injustice and standing up for the weak. He also demonstrates a deep sense of mercy, often giving second chances to those who have made mistakes or wronged him. Moreover, Natsu remains humble despite his tremendous power and abilities, always valuing his friends and treating them with kindness and respect.

The verse Acts 20:35 encourages a mindset of selflessness, generosity, and service towards others. It highlights the idea that true fulfilment and blessing come from self-sacrifice and acts of kindness. By prioritizing the well-being of others, particularly the vulnerable and less fortunate, we reflect the teachings of Jesus and experience the joy that comes from giving.

In Natsu's selfless actions, we see the power of sacrificial love and the impact it can have on those around him. His unwavering loyalty and support for his friends illustrate the biblical principle of bearing one another's burdens and uplifting each other. Natsu's kindness extends beyond mere words and is demonstrated through tangible acts of compassion, mirroring the love of Christ in practical ways.

The kindness of Natsu in the Fairy Tail anime series reflects the divine love and compassion that God calls us to emulate. As we witness his acts of kindness in the Fairy Tail anime, we can be inspired to cultivate a similar spirit of generosity, seeking opportunities to bless others and make a positive difference in their lives.

"The minute you think of giving up, think of the reason why you held on so long." - Natsu Dragneel

November 6

Many waters cannot quench love, neither can floods drown it. If a man offered for love all the wealth of his house, he would be utterly despised. Song of Solomon 8:7

Devil Hunter

(Chainsaw Man)

Himeno, a Devil Hunter in the Chainsaw Man series, develops romantic feelings for her partner Aki Hayakawa. They work together to defeat the Gun Devil and become close friends. Himeno loves Aki, but he doesn't clearly express his feelings in return. She sacrifices herself to save Aki, leading to her death.

Song of Solomon 8:7 highlights the enduring and powerful nature of love. It suggests that love is an unstoppable force that cannot be extinguished by external circumstances, symbolized by the metaphor of "many waters" or "rivers" being unable to quench it. It further emphasizes that love holds greater value than material wealth, as even the offer of all the riches in one's possession would be disregarded in comparison to love. This verse can be understood as a reminder of the transformative power of love in human relationships, emphasizing its importance and priceless nature.

Despite the dangers and chaos surrounding them, Himeno's love for Aki remains steadfast and unwavering. Her love for Aki is not motivated by wealth, power, or superficial desires. Instead, her love is genuine and selfless. It demonstrates that her love for him goes beyond any materialistic considerations. Even if she were offered all the wealth in the world, she would still choose her love for Aki.

When contemplating Himeno's love for Aki in Chainsaw Man, we can find inspiration to cultivate enduring, selfless, and resilient love in our own lives. It encourages us to view love as a gift from God, to be cherished and nurtured, and to recognize its power to transform lives and relationships.

"It must be nice having someone care enough to cry over you." - Himeno

November 7

Thus says the Lord God to these bones: Behold, I will cause breath to enter you, and you shall live. Ezekiel 37:5

Pokémon of Life

(Pokémon)

Xerneas, known as the Pokémon of Life, embodies the concept of rejuvenation and restoration. With its unique ability to share life energy, it revitalizes the environment and heals those in need. This Fairy-type Legendary Pokémon represents a force of renewal, bringing life and balance to the world it inhabits.

In the verse Ezekiel 37:5, we encounter a vision where God instructs the prophet Ezekiel to speak to a valley filled with dry bones. As Ezekiel prophesies, God breathes His life-giving breath into the bones, causing them to come alive and form a vast army. This verse serves as a reminder of God's power to breathe life into seemingly hopeless situations.

Xerneas also reminds us of our role as stewards of creation. It prompts us to recognize the importance of preserving and nurturing the natural world, which reflects God's creative and life-giving nature. Through its ability to heal and revitalize, Xerneas teaches us to cherish and care for the environment, partnering with God in the ongoing work of renewal. Its radiant and majestic presence echoes the awe-inspiring nature of God's power and glory. It inspires us to marvel at His ability to bring forth life and witness His hand at work in the world around us.

Just as Xerneas stands as a symbol of life, we are invited to witness and celebrate God's life-giving work in our own lives and in the world. Xerneas, the Pokémon of Life, illuminates the themes of restoration, renewal, and the power of God's life-giving breath. It encourages us to have faith in His ability to breathe new life into every aspect of our existence, to faithfully steward His creation, and to marvel at His awe-inspiring work of renewal and transformation.

"I see now that the circumstances of one's birth are irrelevant. It is what you do with the gift of life that determines who you are." - Mewtwo

November 8

Be not afraid when a man becomes rich, when the glory of his house increases. For when he dies, he will carry nothing away; his glory will not go down after him. Psalm 49:16-17

Flamboyant Tono

(Ouran High School Host Club)

Tamaki Suoh, a charismatic and flamboyant character from Ouran High School Host Club, is known for his love of luxury and extravagant experiences. While he may not explicitly be materialistic, he thoroughly enjoys the finer things in life and embraces a lavish lifestyle. Tamaki's role as the link that brings the Host Club together and connects them to their dreams showcases his influence and status within the group.

The message conveyed in Psalm 49:16-17 warns against placing our trust and confidence solely in worldly riches. It reminds us that material possessions are temporary and cannot accompany us beyond death. This passage emphasizes the need to prioritize matters of eternal significance over earthly wealth.

Throughout the series, Tamaki undergoes personal growth and learns important life lessons. Through his interactions with others and the relationships he develops, he comes to understand that true value lies not in material wealth, but in genuine connections and emotional bonds. This transformation aligns with the message of Psalm 49:16-17, urging us to seek and cherish things that hold lasting significance beyond material possessions.

Tamaki's journey serves as a reminder for us to examine our own attitudes towards material wealth and social status. It prompts us to consider the temporary nature of material possessions and encourages us to align our values with those of God's kingdom. His growth and transformation also provide a valuable lesson about finding true value in genuine connections and emotional depth. By aligning our values with those of God's kingdom, we can navigate our own lives with a focus on lasting significance and selfless acts of love.

"To just be yourself... I believe that's what true strength really is." - Tamaki Suoh

November 9

In the same way, let your light shine before others, so that they may see your good works and give glory to your Father who is in heaven. Matthew 5:16

Princess Serenity

(Sailor Moon)

Usagi Tsukino, the main character in Sailor Moon, is a teenage girl who transforms into the powerful warrior Sailor Moon to protect the world from evil forces. While initially portrayed as a carefree and somewhat clumsy girl, Usagi's motivation grows as she embraces her role as a guardian and fights for justice and love. She consistently uses her powers and abilities to fight against evil and stand up for justice. She strives to be a source of light and hope in the lives of those around her.

Matthew 5:16 encourages us to let our own light shine before others through our good deeds and actions. The verse reminds us that our actions have the power to impact others and bring glory to God. It encourages us to live a life that reflects God's love and goodness, inspiring and uplifting those around us.

Usagi's motivation in Sailor Moon serves as a reminder that we, too, are called to be beacons of light in a world that often feels overwhelmed by darkness. Through our words, actions, and attitudes, we can bring hope, love, and healing to those around us. By living out the values of the Kingdom of God, we can inspire others to seek truth, experience transformation, and ultimately give glory to God.

When we reflect on Usagi Tsukino's motivation in Sailor Moon, we are reminded of our own calling as Christians to be lights in the world. Just as Usagi's actions shine a light of hope and love, we are encouraged to let our light shine before others, illuminating the way to God and bringing glory to His name through our deeds of love, kindness, and compassion.

"No matter how much you change, please don't forget the people who care for you." - Usagi Tsukino

November 10

Surely, he has borne our griefs and carried our sorrows; yet we esteemed him stricken, smitten by God, and afflicted. Isaiah 53:4

Amorphous Narehate

(Made In Abyss)

Mitty was once a friendly and vibrant little girl in the Made in Abyss anime who quickly became Nanachi's friend. However, during an experiment involving her and Nanachi, she could no longer fight the curse's power, and her human form, along with her intelligence, vanished. The once brave and kind little girl became a Narehate who is unable to speak or walk. The pain she experiences is both physical and emotional, serving as a powerful representation of the depth of suffering that can be experienced in life.

The verse Isaiah 53:4 points to the person of Jesus Christ, who willingly took upon Himself the pain, grief, and suffering of humanity. Through His death on the cross, Jesus carried the weight of our sorrows and bore our afflictions. This verse provides comfort and hope, knowing that God is present with us in our pain. He empathizes with our suffering and offers us His love, comfort, and healing.

Mitty's pain also serves as a reminder of the brokenness of our world. It highlights the reality of human suffering and the depths of anguish that can be experienced. In the face of profound pain, we are reminded of the need for compassion towards those who are hurting. We are called to walk alongside the suffering, offering support, comfort, and the love of Christ.

Through Mitty's story in Made in Abyss, we are reminded that even in the midst of the darkest pain, there is hope. The suffering servant, Jesus Christ, is intimately familiar with our pain and invites us to bring our burdens to Him. He is the source of comfort, healing, and restoration for all who turn to Him.

"Dreams are stronger than poison and seize more firmly than disease, once captured one cannot escape." - Narrator

November 11

Desire without knowledge is not good, and whoever makes haste with his feet misses his way. Proverbs 19:2

Sy-on Boy

(Spy x Family)

Damian Desmond, from Spy x Family, has high expectations for himself because his older brother is very successful. He takes great pride in his achievements and expects everyone to treat him with respect because of his wealthy family. However, Anya's constant annoyances and attempts to get his attention irritate him. Damian becomes angry with Anya because she interrupts his path to success.

Proverbs 19:2 teaches us that impatience is associated with folly. When we allow impatience to drive our actions, we are more likely to make mistakes, overlook important details, and miss out on valuable opportunities for growth and learning. Instead, the verse encourages us to cultivate patience, recognizing that it is a virtue linked to understanding. Patience allows us to wait for the right timing, seek God's will, and make informed decisions.

By reflecting on Damian's impatience, we are reminded of the need to exercise discernment and seek wisdom before making decisions. It encourages us to pause, gather information, seek counsel, and patiently wait for the right timing. Impatience can lead us astray, but when we approach situations with wisdom and understanding, we align ourselves with God's plan and purpose.

In reflecting on Damian's impatience, we can examine our own lives and areas where impatience may hinder our spiritual growth. We can strive to cultivate patience, relying on God's guidance and trusting in His perfect timing. By doing so, we align ourselves with God's wisdom and are more likely to make choices that align with His purposes and bring about positive outcomes.

"It's not so easy to get things right with favourable conditions." - Loid Forger

November 12

Blessed is the man who walks not in the counsel of the wicked, nor stands in the way of sinners, nor sits in the seat of scoffers; but his delight is in the law of the Lord, and on his law, he meditates day and night. Psalm 1:1-2

Compulsive Gambler

(Kakegurui)

In the anime series Kakegurui, Yumeko Jabami faces intense peer pressure within the school's gambling system, where students are driven by obsession and the desire for power. She is constantly tempted to conform to the destructive patterns and mindset of the gambling world in order to gain acceptance or exert dominance. Despite being at a disadvantage when others resort to cheating, Yumeko refuses to give in or concede.

The verses in Psalm 1:1-2 remind us of the importance of our choices and associations. As Christians, we are called to be discerning and intentional about the company we keep. The pressures of peer influence can lead us away from God's path, compromise our values, and hinder our spiritual growth. However, these verses teach us that true blessings come from separating ourselves from the influence of the wicked, sinners, and mockers.

Yumeko's journey serves as a reminder that when we resist the peer pressure to conform to the ways of the world, we position ourselves for God's blessings. By delighting in God's law and meditating on it day and night, we gain wisdom and guidance to navigate through difficult situations. Through the power of God's Word, we can resist peer pressure, stand firm in our faith, and pursue a path that leads to true blessings and spiritual growth.

By relating Yumeko's experience in the Kakegurui anime series, we are reminded of the blessings that come from resisting peer pressure and choosing to align ourselves with God's truth. It encourages us to find joy in studying and applying God's Word, allowing it to guide our decisions and actions even when faced with challenging circumstances.

"To make your ambitions come true, you have to take risks." - Yumeko Jabami

November 13

To whom then will you compare me, that I should be like him? says the Holy One. Isaiah 40:25

Mother of Chakra

(Naruto)

In the Naruto series, Kaguya possesses immense power and is revered as the mother of chakra and an entity of unparalleled strength. Her abilities and position make her a dominant and awe-inspiring force within the story. Also known as the Rabbit Goddess, she stands as one of the most formidable antagonists in the Naruto franchise and is widely regarded as one of the most powerful female characters in the realm of anime.

Isaiah 40:25 serves as a humbling reminder that no matter how captivating these powers may be, they are merely a reflection of the boundless power of the Holy One. It invites us to shift our focus from earthly powers to the incomparable greatness of God. By keeping our perspective grounded in the supremacy of God, we cultivate a healthy understanding of our place as finite beings. It encourages us to worship and rely on God alone, acknowledging His unmatched power and seeking His guidance and strength in our lives.

Reflecting on the power of Kaguya can lead us to contemplate the limitations of human strength and achievements. Despite the remarkable abilities portrayed in the anime, they are still creations of the human imagination. In comparison, the power and authority of God are infinitely greater and beyond any human or fictional character.

Kaguya's power in the anime leads us to acknowledge and appreciate the creative imagination behind fictional characters while reminding us of the ultimate greatness and incomparability of God. It encourages us to place our trust and awe in the one true God, recognizing His authority and seeking a deeper relationship with Him.

"The moment people come to know love, they run the risk of carrying hate." - Obito Uchiha

November 14

Who alone has immortality, who dwells in unapproachable light, whom no one has ever seen or can see. To him be honor and eternal dominion. Amen. 1 Timothy 6:16

Symbol of Evil

(My Hero Academia)

The character All for One from My Hero Academia embodies the destructive nature of pride and the pursuit of power at all costs. His relentless desire for control and dominance reflects the fallen nature of humanity, driven by selfish ambitions and a disregard for the well-being of others. All For One's actions serve as a cautionary tale, reminding us of the dangers of unchecked pride and the consequences it can bring.

The verse 1 Timothy 6:16 reminds us of the infinite and transcendent nature of God. He alone possesses immortality and resides in a light that is beyond our reach. This verse directs our attention to the supremacy and majesty of God, highlighting the stark contrast between His eternal dominion and the fleeting nature of human power.

The pride of All for One can lead us to introspection and self-examination, inviting us to lay down our own desires for control and acknowledge our need for God's grace and guidance. It teaches us the importance of humility, recognizing that our strength and worth come from our relationship with God, rather than our own achievements or abilities. It serves as a reminder that true fulfilment and lasting significance are found in surrendering our pride and submitting to God's authority.

By embracing the truths found in All for One's character, we can cultivate a spirit of humility and surrender, allowing God to work in and through us. This encourages us to seek God and humbly serve others rather than seeking our own exaltation. In doing so, we align ourselves with the greater purpose and plan that God has for our lives, experiencing the true fulfilment and joy that come from walking in humble obedience to Him.

"The most inflated egos are often the most fragile." - All Might

November 15

He sent from on high, he took me; he drew me out of many waters. Psalm 18:16

Red-Haired Emperor

(One Piece)

In One Piece, Shanks plays a significant role in Luffy's life as a mentor and protector. He rescues Luffy from a dire situation and becomes a mentor, guiding him on his journey to become the Pirate King. His presence and influence serve as a turning point in Luffy's life, drawing him out of hopelessness, instilling purpose, and inspiring him to pursue his dreams and overcome challenges.

Psalm 18:16 is a poetic expression of the psalmist's gratitude and praise to God for rescuing them from a place of trouble or distress. The imagery of God reaching down from above and taking hold of the psalmist portrays a powerful and personal act of deliverance. The phrase "many waters"symbolizes a difficult and overwhelming situation that the psalmist was facing. It signifies a state of distress where one feels overwhelmed and in need of rescue.

While Shanks may not possess the divine attributes of salvation found in Jesus Christ, his role as a guiding and protective presence in Luffy's life can symbolize the way God works through people to lead us out of despair and into a life filled with purpose and adventure. Shanks, as a saviour figure in the anime, is a testament to how God uses people in our lives to bring us hope, guidance, and support.

Reflecting on Shanks' character can remind us of the profound impact individuals can have on our lives, leading us out of challenging circumstances and inspiring us to embrace our calling. It encourages us to recognize God's providential work through people and to be grateful for those who have played a role in our spiritual and personal growth. Ultimately, our hope and salvation rest in Jesus Christ, who offers us deliverance and eternal life.

"By experiencing both, victory and defeat, running away and shedding tears, a man will become a man. It's okay to cry, but you have to move on." - Shanks

November 16

Whoever finds his life will lose it, and whoever loses his life for my sake will find it. Matthew 10:39

God of Death

(Death Note)

In the anime Death Note, Rem is a Shinigami who gives Misa Amane a powerful tool called the Death Note. As Rem grows fond of Misa, she becomes protective of her and is manipulated by Light, who uses their relationship to his advantage. Eventually, Light convinces Rem to write the names of important people in the Death Note, knowing that doing so would result in Rem's own death. Rem willingly sacrifices herself because her love for Misa is more important to her than her own life.

The verse Matthew 10:39 calls believers to place Jesus at the centre of their lives and willingly let go of their own selfish desires and pursuits. It challenges individuals to prioritize the values and teachings of Christ above personal comfort, worldly gain, and self-centred ambitions. By giving up their lives in this way, believers can experience a deeper and more meaningful existence in union with God. Those who are willing to give up their lives, in a metaphorical sense, for the sake of Jesus and His kingdom will find true and everlasting life.

Rem's sacrifice prompts us to consider the depths of love and selflessness. It challenges us to evaluate our own lives and question whether we are willing to let go of personal desires and comforts for the sake of others and for the sake of our faith. It invites us to live a life of sacrificial love, following in the footsteps of Christ, who gave everything for us.

The sacrifice of Rem in the anime Death Note serves as a reminder that true life is found in selfless acts of love and service, even when they require personal sacrifice. It encourages us to seek a life that is not driven by self-preservation but by a deep desire to love and serve others, ultimately finding the abundant life that Christ promises.

"In this world, there are very few people who actually trust each other." - Light Yagami

November 17

God is our refuge and strength, a very present help in trouble. Psalm 46:1

Reliable Digi Destined

(Digimon)

Joe Kido is a character from the Digimon anime series who initially struggles with self-esteem and self-confidence. He lacks confidence in himself and frequently questions his worthiness to be a part of the team. As the series progresses, Joe's character evolves. He begins to embrace his role as a Digi Destined and discovers his own unique strengths and qualities, both in his friendships with his fellow Digi Destined and within himself.

Psalm 46:1 is a verse often interpreted as an assurance of God's constant presence and support in times of difficulty. It emphasizes that God is a reliable source of refuge and strength, offering assistance and protection when we face troubles and challenges in life. The verse conveys the idea that we can find solace, comfort, and strength by seeking God's presence and relying on His help in times of need. It serves as a reminder of God's faithfulness and His willingness to provide aid and support to those who turn to Him.

The transformation of Joe's self-esteem reflects the transformative power of God's love. Just as he evolves from self-doubt to confidence, we too can experience a shift in our self-perception when we embrace God's unwavering love for us. It is through this understanding that we can find true and lasting self-esteem, rooted in our identity as children of God.

When reflecting on Joe Kido's self-esteem journey in the Digimon anime, we are reminded of the invitation to seek refuge and strength in God. His growth serves as a reminder that our self-esteem can be rooted in the knowledge of God's unwavering love and support. As we navigate our own journeys, may we find the confidence to embrace our unique gifts and trust in God's ever-present help, just as Joe did.

"I swore I would never let anyone see me cry. But really, all I ever wanted to do was cry." - Yamato Ishida

November 18

What comes out of a person is what defiles him. For from within, out of the heart of man, come evil thoughts, sexual immorality, theft, murder, adultery, coveting, wickedness, deceit, sensuality, envy, slander, pride, foolishness. All these evil things come from within, and they defile a person."Mark 7:20-23

Anarchistic Art Teacher

(Psycho-Pass)

Shōgo Makishima from the anime series Psycho-Pass serves as one of the primary antagonists in the show. He is a highly intelligent and charismatic individual who possesses a deep disdain for the technological surveillance society in which the series is set. He manipulates others and incites acts of violence to challenge the established order and expose what he perceives as the flaws of the society in which he lives.

The verses in Mark 7:20-23 teach us the importance of addressing the root causes of sin rather than merely focusing on external actions. They remind us that true transformation occurs when our hearts are transformed by the power of God's love and grace. It is through repentance that we can experience freedom from the bondage of sin.

The rebellion of Makishima against the established order and his disregard for the value of human life can be seen as a distortion of God's intended order and the sanctity of life. Christianity emphasizes the importance of living in harmony with God's principles and valuing the well-being and dignity of every individual.

While Shōgo Makishima's character may serve as a thought-provoking exploration of various themes and moral dilemmas in the context of the Psycho-Pass anime, from a Christian perspective, his actions and worldview stand as a cautionary reminder of the potential consequences of prioritizing personal desires above ethical principles and the common good.

"When a man faces fear, his soul is tested. What he was born to seek... what he was born to achieve... his true nature will become clear." - Shōgo Makishima

November 19

Enter his gates with thanksgiving, and his courts with praise! Give thanks to him; bless his name! Psalm 100:4

Rewind Quirk User

(My Hero Academia)

Eri from My Hero Academia endured immense suffering at the hands of Overhaul, leaving her traumatized and fearful. With Midoriya's help, she was rescued and slowly began to heal. The U.A Festival played a significant role in restoring her hope and reminding her of the goodness in society. Eri's life was saved, and she manages to maintain a grateful heart amidst her challenging circumstances.

Psalm 100:4 calls believers to approach God's presence with thanksgiving and praise. It urges us to enter His gates, symbolizing His dwelling place, with hearts overflowing with gratitude. It emphasizes that thanksgiving is not merely an emotion but an intentional act of recognizing God's goodness, faithfulness, and provision in our lives.

Eri's gratitude resonates with this message as she appreciates the love, care, and support shown to her by others. Her thankfulness extends beyond the surface level and reflects a deeper understanding of the blessings she has received, attributing them to God's grace and providence. Her thankfulness invites us to reflect on our own lives and consider the ways in which we can cultivate a spirit of gratitude. It encourages us to shift our focus from what may be lacking or challenging to the countless blessings bestowed upon us by God.

As we contemplate Eri's thankfulness in My Hero Academia, we are called to emulate her grateful heart. We are encouraged to approach God with hearts filled with thanksgiving and praise, recognizing His goodness and faithfulness in our lives. Through the practice of thankfulness, we can experience a transformative shift in our perspective, deepening our relationship with God, and finding joy in His abundant blessings.

"I smile to show the pressure of heroes and to trick the fear inside of me." - All Might

November 20

For my thoughts are not your thoughts, neither are your ways my ways, declares the Lord. For as the heavens are higher than the earth, so are my ways higher than your ways and my thoughts than your thoughts. Isaiah 55:8-9

Lagann Pilot

(Gurren Lagann)

In the Gurren Lagann anime series, Simon is a hardworking digger in Jiha village who lacks confidence in his abilities. His mentor and "big bro,"Kamina, admires his work ethic and motivates him. However, when Kamina dies, Simon feels lost. With the support of Team Dai-Gurren and Nia, he discovers his own strength and learns to value himself.

The verse Isaiah 55:8-9 reminds believers that God's thoughts and ways are beyond human understanding. It encourages them to trust in God's wisdom and guidance, even when they cannot fully comprehend His plans. It emphasizes that God's perspective and ways are infinitely higher and more perfect than our own.

Simon's journey of acceptance involves letting go of his own limited understanding and trusting in a higher power. This mirrors the Christian call to surrender our own will and trust in God's plan for our lives. We are invited to embrace humility, acknowledging that God's wisdom surpasses our own and that He sees the bigger picture that we cannot fully grasp.

By reflecting on Simon's life in the anime series, we are reminded of the importance of faith and trust in our relationship with God. It encourages us to approach our own uncertainties and challenges with a humble and open heart, knowing that God's ways are ultimately for our good. Just as Simon found his worth and purpose by surrendering to the greater plan at work, we too can find acceptance and peace in trusting in God's higher wisdom and embracing His loving guidance.

"I don't want fear for a future, that may not even come, to stop me from acting today." - Simon

November 21

Whoever is slow to anger is better than the mighty, and he who rules his spirit than he who takes a city.
Proverbs 16:32

Tornado of Terror

(One-Punch Man)

Tatsumaki is a powerful character from the One-Punch Man anime, known for her tendency to be arrogant and violent. She possesses the ability to cause massive destruction and has shown aggression towards others, even going as far as stabbing someone for amusement while under the influence. Despite her flaws, some find her cute. However, it is important to remember that her actions can be dangerous and harmful.

Proverbs 16:32 teaches us that it is better to possess patience and self-control than to be a conqueror in battle. It emphasizes the value of inner strength and the ability to govern our emotions. This verse reminds us that true strength lies not in physical dominance but in the ability to restrain our anger and respond with wisdom and grace. From a Christian perspective, anger is not inherently wrong. However, the danger lies in allowing anger to control us and lead us into destructive actions.

Tatsumaki's struggle with anger serves as a reminder to examine our own hearts. We should reflect on how we handle anger, ensuring that we do not allow it to dictate our actions and harm others. Instead, we should seek the guidance of the Holy Spirit in developing patience and self-control.

By relating Tatsumaki's anger in the anime, we are reminded of the importance of self-control and patience in managing our emotions. It challenges us to consider the consequences of our actions and to seek peaceful resolutions rather than resorting to aggression. Through the guidance of the Holy Spirit, we can develop the self-discipline needed to control our anger, respond with wisdom, and contribute to a more harmonious and compassionate world.

"When the time comes, don't go expecting someone to come save you." - Tatsumaki

November 22

That their hearts may be encouraged, being knit together in love, to reach all the riches of full assurance of understanding and the knowledge of God's mystery, which is Christ, in whom are hidden all the treasures of wisdom and knowledge. Colossians 2:2-3

Copy Ninja

(Naruto)

In the Naruto series, Kakashi is known for his intelligence, tactical expertise, and deep understanding of ninjutsu. He is a skilled mentor who imparts his knowledge to his students, guiding them towards their full potential. He is known for his distinctive appearance, particularly his face being mostly covered by a mask and his one visible eye. Behind his mask lies a vast wealth of experiences, skills, and wisdom. This visual element represents the idea that there is more to Kakashi than meets the eye.

The verse Colossians 2:2-3 encourages believers to seek a complete understanding and knowledge of God. In the same way, the verse invites us to seek the fullness of understanding through Christ. It reminds us that in Christ, we can discover the hidden treasures of wisdom and knowledge that bring us closer to God. We are called to seek a similar hunger for understanding, not only in worldly matters but especially in our relationship with God.

Kakashi's masked appearance reminds us that people often carry hidden depths and complexities beyond what is immediately visible. Just as his true character and wisdom are gradually revealed through his actions and teachings, we are encouraged to approach others with patience, grace, and a desire to uncover their unique qualities.

By relating Kakashi's appearance in the anime, we are reminded of the importance of seeking a deeper understanding of God's mysteries and wisdom. It encourages us to go beyond surface-level knowledge and to continually explore the depths of our faith, allowing Christ to reveal His hidden treasures of wisdom and knowledge in our lives.

"In society, the ones without many abilities tend to complain more." - Kakashi Hatake

November 23

He made my feet like the feet of a deer and set me secure on the heights. Psalm 18:33

Wing Hero

(My Hero Academia)

In the anime series My Hero Academia, Hawks is known for his confident and assertive attitude. He possesses a strong sense of responsibility and is always ready to take action to protect others. He is a skilled hero who uses his wings and agility to navigate challenges and maintain a vigilant watch over society. He embodies the idea of using his abilities and strengths to serve and bring safety to others.

Psalm 18:33 highlights the idea that when we rely on God, He grants us the abilities and qualities needed to rise above difficult circumstances. It serves as a reminder that with God's guidance and support, we can navigate through life's obstacles with confidence and reach new levels of growth and achievement. Moreover, the image of standing on the heights suggests that God enables us to rise above adversity and gain a broader perspective. It signifies the spiritual and emotional strength He provides, enabling us to face trials with courage and overcome them victoriously.

Like hawks, we can develop confidence in our abilities and approach situations with determination and steadfastness. Just as Hawks uses his skills to safeguard others, we are called to use our God-given talents to serve and protect those around us.

By relating the attitude of Hawks in My Hero Academia, we are reminded of the unwavering support and empowerment we receive from God. It encourages us to embrace qualities of resilience, confidence, and dedication, knowing that God will guide our steps and help us navigate life's challenges. With His help, we can soar to new heights and make a positive impact in the lives of others.

"If you've got wings, you should stretch them out and fly. There's no need for you to be confined to the ground." - Hawks

November 24

So we do not lose heart. Though our outer self is wasting away, our inner self is being renewed day by day. For this light momentary affliction is preparing for us an eternal weight of glory beyond all comparison, as we look not to the things that are seen but to the things that are unseen. For the things that are seen are transient, but the things that are unseen are eternal. 2 Corinthians 4:16-18

Demon Girl

(Demon Slayer)

Nezuko's journey as a demon turned protector mirrors the spiritual journey of a believer. In her outward appearance as a demon, she represents the brokenness and fallen nature of humanity. Yet, inwardly, she experiences a renewal of spirit, showing that God's transformative work happens from within, despite our outward circumstances.

The passage, 2 Corinthians 4:16-18, reflects on the challenges and trials faced by believers in their earthly lives. It encourages them to maintain hope and perseverance despite the hardships they may encounter. As followers of Christ, we are called to stand against the forces of darkness and bring light into the world.

Nezuko's determination to fix her eyes not on what is seen but on what is unseen exemplifies the Christian call to focus on the eternal values and truths found in God's Word. Her unwavering commitment to love, justice, and self-sacrifice encourages us to prioritize these virtues in our own lives, even when faced with challenging circumstances.

The journey of Nezuko in the Demon Slayer anime reminds us that God's transformative power can work through even the most unexpected individuals. Her story encourages us to persevere, trust in God's renewing work within us, and fix our eyes on the eternal, transcendent truths that guide our lives as followers of Christ.

"It's no one's fault. Things don't go exactly the way we want them to. We're only human." - Nezuko Kamado

November 25

Therefore, since we are surrounded by so great a cloud of witnesses, let us also lay aside every weight, and sin which clings so closely, and let us run with endurance the race that is set before us, looking to Jesus, the founder and perfecter of our faith, who for the joy that was set before him endured the cross, despising the shame, and is seated at the right hand of the throne of God. Hebrews 12:1-2

Volleyball Club Alumnus

(Haikyu!!)

In the Haikyu anime series, Keishin Ukai helps his players overcome their personal obstacles and develop their skills. He guides his team through various challenges, emphasizing the importance of staying focused on their goals and working together as a cohesive unit.

Hebrews 12:1-2 encourages believers to persevere in their faith, throwing off anything that hinders their relationship with God. We are also called to fix our eyes on Jesus, the pioneer and perfecter of our faith. The verse further points to the spiritual growth that comes through perseverance and fixing our eyes on Jesus. Our commitment to Christ leads to spiritual growth as we learn to walk in His ways, grow in character, and become more like Him.

Keishin Ukai exemplifies perseverance as he guides and supports his team through the challenges of volleyball. His commitment to coaching his team is driven by a clear vision and goal: to help his players reach their full potential. He understands the importance of staying focused on the task at hand and working together as a team. He also invests in their lives, teaches them valuable life lessons, and encourages them to become better individuals.

The commitment of Keishin Ukai from the Haikyu anime invites us to embrace perseverance, focus, and spiritual growth in our Christian journey. Just as his dedication inspires his team, may our commitment inspire those around us and bring glory to God.

"There's only one thing to do in order to win. Practice practice practice. Even if you're puking your guts out, pick up the ball and continue." - Keishin Ukai

November 26

What do you think? If a man has a hundred sheep, and one of them has gone astray, does he not leave the ninety-nine on the mountains and go in search of the one that went astray? And if he finds it, truly, I say to you, he rejoices over it more than over the ninety-nine that never went astray. So, it is not the will of my Father who is in heaven that one of these little ones should perish. Matthew 18:12-14

Team Rocket

(Pokémon)

In the Pokémon anime series, Team Rocket consists of Jessie, James, and Meowth, who often find themselves straying from the path of righteousness as they pursue their goal of capturing Pikachu. They engage in schemes and mischievous acts in their attempts to achieve their selfish ambitions.

Matthew 18:12-14 presents the parable of the lost sheep, where a shepherd leaves the ninety-nine to search for the one that has gone astray. This parable reveals God's deep love and concern for every lost soul, emphasizing the lengths He would go to bring them back into the fold. In relation to Team Rocket, this parable reminds us that no one is beyond the reach of God's grace and redemption. It encourages us to view them with compassion, recognizing that even those who have strayed can find forgiveness and transformation.

We can see glimpses of goodness and humanity within Team Rocket. Despite their misdeeds, they display moments of compassion, loyalty, and even selflessness. This reminds us that even in the most unlikely places, God's image can be found in every person.

Team Rocket's journey becomes a powerful illustration of the redemptive nature of God's grace. Their potential for change and growth serves as a reminder that no one is beyond the reach of God's transforming hand. It encourages us to see the value in every individual and to actively participate in the restoration and reconciliation of those who have lost their way.

"There's no sense in going out of your way to get somebody to like you." - Ash Ketchum

November 27

The Lord is my helper; I will not fear; what can man do to me? Hebrews 13:6

Ice Queen

(Fullmetal Alchemist: Brotherhood)

Olivier Mira Armstrong demonstrates incredible courage and strength throughout the series. As a military leader, she faces numerous challenges and dangers, yet she remains steadfast and unwavering in her resolve. She is unafraid to stand up against injustice, fight for what she believes in, and protect those under her command. Olivier's courage is rooted in her deep sense of duty and her commitment to justice and honor.

Hebrews 13:6 reminds believers that they can approach life with confidence, knowing that the Lord is their helper. It reassures us that we need not be afraid of human adversaries or circumstances, for God is with us. This verse encourages us to rely on God's assistance, understanding that mere mortals hold no ultimate power over us when we have the Almighty on our side.

Olivier's example challenges us to trust in God's provision and guidance. Just as she fearlessly confronts her enemies, we are called to confront the challenges that come our way, knowing that we have the ultimate Helper in our corner. Our faith empowers us to stand firm in the face of adversity, to persevere through difficulties, and to embrace a courageous mindset that reflects our trust in God.

Let us draw strength from Olivier Mira Armstrong's courage and approach life with confidence, unafraid of what mere mortals can do to us because we have the Lord as our helper. In our own journeys, let us display the same unwavering courage, rooted in faith, and boldly proclaim that our trust is in God alone.

"However little strength I'm capable of, I'll do everything humanly possible to protect the people I love, and in turn, they will protect the ones they love. It seems like the least we tiny humans can do for each other." - Roy Mustang

November 28

Come now, you who say, "Today or tomorrow we will go into such and such a town and spend a year there and trade and make a profit"yet you do not know what tomorrow will bring. What is your life? For you are a mist that appears for a little time and then vanishes. James 4:13-14

Legendary Snake Sannin

(Naruto)

Orochimaru, a former villain in the Naruto anime, faced severe consequences for his actions. He attacked the Leaf Village, which led to the death of the Third Hokage and the loss of both his arms. As a punishment, his former teacher cut off his remaining arm. This meant Orochimaru could no longer use powerful jutsu or perform ninjutsu with hand seals. Despite these setbacks, he remained a cunning and intelligent individual.

James 4:13-14 reminds us that our lives are uncertain and transient. It challenges us to recognize the brevity and fragility of our existence, reminding us that our lives are like a fleeting mist that appears for a brief moment and then dissipates. The verse calls us to embrace humility and surrender our plans to God, acknowledging that He alone holds the ultimate authority over our lives.

Orochimaru sought power through manipulating others but was ultimately betrayed. His misguided pursuit of power reminds us of the inherent dangers of seeking ultimate control and gratification in this temporary world. It highlights the importance of surrendering our plans to God and aligning ourselves with His divine will.

The decision of Orochimaru in the Naruto anime serves as a cautionary tale, reminding us of the dangers of selfish ambition and the importance of embracing the fleeting nature of our lives. It prompts us to prioritize our relationship with God and seek His guidance, recognizing that true fulfilment and purpose come from aligning ourselves with His will.

"It's human nature to not realize the true value of something until it's lost." - Orochimaru

November 29

Rendering service with a good will as to the Lord and not to man. Ephesians 6:7

Katana Hero

(The Rising of The Shield Hero)

In the anime series The Rising of the Shield Hero, Raphtalia is incredibly loyal to Naofumi because he rescued her from a terrible situation and treated her with kindness and respect. Even though he technically bought her as a slave, he never treated her like one and made it clear that she was free to leave if she wanted to. But Raphtalia chooses to stay by his side because of the way he has shown her care. She becomes his trusted companion and fights alongside him, believing in his innocence even when others accuse him. Her loyalty is one of the reasons why people find her so charming.

In Ephesians 6:7, believers are called to serve wholeheartedly, as if serving the Lord Himself. As Christians, we are reminded that our service to others is not just a task to be completed but an act of worship. It is an opportunity to embody the love and grace of Christ, bringing healing and restoration to those who have been broken and marginalized.

Raphtalia's devotion sees her service to Naofumi as an opportunity to express her love and gratitude. Her commitment goes beyond mere duty, transcending societal norms and expectations. Her dedication to Naofumi, despite the accusations and challenges they face, reminds us of the importance of standing by those we care about. Just as Raphtalia believes in Naofumi's innocence, we are called to support our loved ones, even in the face of adversity. This reflects the unconditional love and loyalty that Christ shows towards His followers.

Raphtalia's devotion in the anime serves as a powerful reminder of the transformative power of love and the call for believers to serve wholeheartedly. Through her example, we are inspired to embrace opportunities for service, display loyalty in relationships, and reflect the love of Christ in our interactions with others.

"What kind of knight neglects the people he's meant to defend?" - Raphtalia

November 30

Their feet run to evil, and they are swift to shed innocent blood; their thoughts are thoughts of iniquity; desolation and destruction are in their highways. Isaiah 59:7

Zoldyck Family

(Hunter x Hunter)

The Zoldyck Family is a group of dangerous assassins and killers, including members like Killua, Illumi, Zeno, Silva, Kalluto, Milluki, Kikyo, and Alluka. They have a strict rule that forbids hurting each other, or else there are consequences. Killua, who was trained as an assassin from a young age, possesses exceptional skills. Despite their violent profession, the family values their bond and imposes punishments for those who break the rule.

The verse Isaiah 59:7 challenges us to consider our own lives and the ways in which we may be tempted to engage in similar behaviour. It calls us to examine the thoughts and intentions of our hearts, ensuring that they are aligned with God's will and rooted in love, justice, and compassion. This verse also highlights the importance of seeking forgiveness and restoration through Christ. It reminds us that even those who have been caught up in a cycle of darkness and violence can find redemption and a new path through God's grace and mercy.

The Zoldyck family's pursuit of power, their willingness to engage in violence, and their manipulative tendencies all reflect the brokenness and darkness of the human condition. Their actions remind us of the pervasiveness of sin in the world and the need for redemption and transformation.

In reflecting on the Zoldyck family from Hunter x Hunter, we are reminded of the brokenness of the world and the constant need for God's transformative power. It prompts us to extend grace and compassion to those who are trapped in destructive patterns while also encouraging us to strive for righteousness and actively work towards bringing about positive change in the world around us.

"It takes a mere second for treasure to turn to trash." - Hisoka Morow

December 1

Be strong; fear not! Behold, your God will come with vengeance, with the recompense of God. He will come and save you. Isaiah 35:4

Sniper King

(One Piece)

Usopp from One Piece is a character who often panics and complains about the situations he faces. Unlike his crewmates who have special powers, he relies on his skills as a marksman and his weapons. He is also known for his contradictory nature. He is incredibly cowardly and avoids conflict, yet he loves taking credit for the group's victories and exaggerates his role in their success. However, as he faces his fears and embraces his role in the crew, he grows in courage and becomes an integral part of their adventures.

Isaiah 35:4 reassures those with fearful hearts to be strong and not to fear. It reminds us that our God will come with vengeance and divine retribution to save us. This verse speaks to the nature of God, who is powerful, just, and faithful. It reminds us that we are not alone in our fears and that God is present with us, ready to intervene and bring deliverance.

Usopp's growth and transformation throughout the series remind us of the transformative power of God's presence in our lives. As Usopp faces his fears head-on and relies on his inner strength, he becomes an inspiration to others. Similarly, when we confront our fears with faith, relying on God's strength and guidance, we can experience personal growth and become a source of encouragement to those around us.

By connecting Usopp's character development in the anime, we see the message of courage and faith in God's deliverance. It reminds us that even in moments of fear, we can find strength and hope by trusting in God's intervention. Just as Usopp learns to be brave and rise above his fears, we too can find the courage to face our own challenges, knowing that God is with us and will ultimately bring salvation and justice.

"Man, or child, strong or weak, none of that matter once you are out at sea." - Usopp

December 2

Beloved, never avenge yourselves, but leave it to the wrath of God, for it is written, "Vengeance is mine, I will repay, says the Lord." Romans 12:19

Goddess of War

(Noragami)

In the anime Noragami, Bishamonten is one of the Seven Gods of Fortune, known as the god of combat and wealth. She leads a group of divine spirits called Shinki. Initially, she deeply resents the main character, Yato, due to a tragic incident in their past. She blames him for the death of her regalia, which are spirits serving as weapons and partners to gods. This fuels her desire for revenge. However, as the story unfolds, Bishamonten undergoes character development and starts questioning her anger. Through her interactions with Yato and others, she learns the importance of forgiveness.

The verse Romans 12:19 reminds us that vengeance belongs to God alone. As Christians, we are called to surrender our desire for revenge and trust in God's ultimate justice. Jesus taught us to forgive others, even our enemies, and release the burden of judgment and condemnation. This verse encourages us to resist seeking personal revenge and instead rely on God's justice and mercy.

Bishamonten's journey portrays a transformation from anger and vengeance to a more compassionate and understanding mindset. She realizes that holding onto her grudge and seeking revenge only perpetuates pain and suffering. Through her experiences, she learns the value of letting go, extending forgiveness, and finding healing and reconciliation.

The forgiveness of Bishamonten in the Noragami anime series reminds us of the transformative power of forgiveness, the importance of surrendering our desire for revenge, and the need to trust in God's justice. It calls us to extend forgiveness to others, relying on God's guidance and grace as we navigate the complexities of human relationships.

"You are human, are you not? You are allowed to make mistakes." - Bishamonten

December 3

Oil and perfume make the heart glad, and the sweetness of a friend comes from his earnest counsel. Proverbs 27:9

Ninja Rivals

(Naruto)

In the series, Naruto and Sasuke initially have a complex and often tumultuous relationship. Sasuke carries a deep resentment and desire for revenge, causing him to isolate himself from others. Despite Sasuke's struggles and his pursuit of darkness, Naruto never gives up on him. Their friendship goes beyond mere companionship. Their support and advice to one another are sincere and heartfelt, aiming to guide each other in times of difficulty and confusion.

In Proverbs 27:9, we are reminded of the profound impact that genuine friendship can have on our lives. Just as the aroma of perfume and incense brings joy to the heart, the companionship of a true friend brings delight and happiness. The pleasantness of a friend lies in their ability to offer heartfelt advice and counsel.

Naruto and Sasuke's friendship exemplifies the transformative power of authentic relationships. They challenge and inspire each other to grow and become better individuals. Similarly, as Christians, we are called to sharpen one another through heartfelt counsel. We should strive to help our friends mature in their faith, encouraging them to pursue righteousness and godliness.

The friendship of Naruto and Sasuke in Naruto anime encourages us to cultivate genuine friendships that bring joy and offer heartfelt counsel. Their relationship serves as a reminder of the importance of seeking and providing wise counsel in our friendships, ultimately bringing happiness and growth to our lives. Ultimately, their friendship exemplifies the beauty and significance of godly companionship in our lives.

"If you don't like the hand that fate's dealt you with, fight for a new one." - Naruto Uzumaki

December 4

And I am sure of this, that he who began a good work in you will bring it to completion at the day of Jesus Christ.
Philippians 1:6

Monster Girl

(Magi: The Labyrinth of Magic)

Morgiana's journey in the anime is marked by transformation and the discovery of her purpose. She embarks on a journey of self-discovery and personal development, gradually transforming from a timid and oppressed slave into a strong and empowered individual. She becomes an instrumental figure in the battle against injustice and fights for the well-being of those she cares about.

The message of Philippians 1:6 assures believers that the good work initiated by God within them will be brought to completion. It highlights the idea that the process of growth and development is ongoing, and God is faithful to fulfil His work within us. The verse reminds us to have confidence that God's work in us will not be in vain. He is actively working to mould and shape us into the image of Christ. We can take comfort in the knowledge that God's work in us is ongoing, and He is faithful to bring it to completion.

Through Morgiana's story, we see the importance of perseverance and trust in God's plan. She faces numerous challenges and obstacles along her journey, but she remains resilient and determined. Her growth also emphasizes the significance of embracing our identity and purpose in God. Just as God used Morgiana's journey to impact the lives of those around her, He desires to use each of us to bring about His kingdom purposes.

The growth of Morgiana in the anime Magi: The Labyrinth of Magic reminds us of God's transformative power, the importance of perseverance, and the significance of embracing our identity and purpose in Him. May we trust in God's faithfulness as He continues His good work in our lives, knowing that He will bring it to completion for His glory.

"I will not hesitate anymore. I'll reach my destination, no matter where it is!" - Morgiana

December 5

The Lord your God is in your midst, a mighty one who will save; he will rejoice over you with gladness; he will quiet you by his love; he will exult over you with loud singing.
Zephaniah 3:17

Elite Net-Diver

(Cowboy Bebop)

In the anime Cowboy Bebop, the character Edward Wong Hau Pepelu Tivrusky IV, also known as Ed, brings a unique sense of joy and happiness to the story. She is a quirky and free-spirited individual who finds delight in the simplest of things and approaches life with childlike wonder. Her infectious laughter and carefree attitude serve as sources of happiness, not only for herself but also for the other members of the Bebop crew.

Zephaniah 3:17 reminds us that God takes pleasure in His children, just as He delights in Edward's unique personality and zest for life. This verse encourages us to find happiness not only in our achievements or circumstances but also in our relationship with God. When we embrace a childlike trust in Him, we open ourselves to experiencing the fullness of His joy.

Edward's character demonstrates a fearless and light-hearted approach to life, finding happiness in the simplest of things and approaching each day with curiosity and wonder. This serves as a reminder for us to embrace a childlike faith and trust in God's love and provision.

The happiness of Edward Wong Hau Pepelu Tivrusky IV in the "Cowboy Bebop"anime can be seen as a reflection of the joy and delight that God experiences over His children. This encourages us to embrace a childlike faith, finding happiness in our relationship with God and trusting in His love for us. Let us approach life with a sense of wonder and allow His joy to shine through us, impacting the lives of those around us.

"Everything has a beginning and an end. Life is just a cycle of starts and stops. There are ends we don't desire, but they're inevitable, we have to face them. It's what being human is all about." - Jet Black

December 6

Do you see a man skilful in his work? He will stand before kings; he will not stand before obscure men. Proverbs 22:29

Obsessive Inventor

(My Hero Academia)

Mei Hatsume from My Hero Academia is a determined and inventive character who consistently puts great effort and dedication into her work as a support class student. Her engineering skills and innovative ideas set her apart from others. Her hard work and commitment to constantly improving her inventions make her a standout talent in the field. Mei's relentless pursuit of excellence and her determination to push the boundaries of her abilities make her someone who is skilled in her work.

The verse Proverbs 22:29 reminds us that when we display skill in our work, we may have the privilege of serving before influential individuals. This can be understood as a calling to serve God's purposes and positively impact the world around us. When we diligently pursue excellence in our work, we open doors for opportunities to use our skills and talents for the greater good, influencing others and pointing them towards the light of Christ.

Mei's pursuit of excellence reminds us of the importance of stewardship. God has entrusted us with unique gifts and abilities, and it is our responsibility to develop and utilize them to their fullest potential. Mei's dedication to refining her engineering skills demonstrates good stewardship as she maximizes the talents she has been given.

Mei Hatsume's hard work in the anime challenges us to approach our own work with dedication, excellence, purpose, and stewardship. We must recognize that our efforts can have a significant impact. By emulating her commitment and using our skills for God's glory, we can fulfill our calling and bring about positive change in the world around us.

"If you want to cool your legs, all you have to do is just run with your arms!" - Mei Hatsume

December 7

No one who practices deceit shall dwell in my house; no one who utters lies shall continue before my eyes. Psalm 101:7

Wicked Tongue

(Naruto)

In the Naruto anime series, Zetsu is a complex character with dual nature, possessing both a white side and a black side, representing his contrasting personalities. He is known for his ability to blend into his surroundings, gather information, and deceive others. With his manipulative tendencies, he often engages in deceitful actions and conceals information for his own purposes.

Psalm 101:7 expresses God's righteous standards, stating that no one who practices deceit will stand in His presence. We are called to reflect the character of God, who embodies truth and integrity. Dishonesty and deceit are contrary to God's nature and His desire for His children. When we engage in dishonest practices such as lying, manipulation, or withholding the truth, we distance ourselves from God's presence.

The character of Zetsu serves as a cautionary example, demonstrating the negative outcomes of dishonesty. His actions are characterized by deception, betrayal, and a lack of genuine relationships. These characteristics stand in stark contrast to the values that Christians are encouraged to uphold, such as honesty, transparency, and treating others with respect.

Zetsu's example reminds us of the importance of striving for a life characterized by truthfulness and integrity, both in our relationship with God and with our fellow human beings. We are called to strive for truthfulness in our words, actions, and relationships, being people of integrity who reflect God's character. Through the grace of God and the guidance of His Spirit, we can avoid the path of deceit and instead embrace honesty, sincerity, and accountability.

"When you're sad and alone, the only one you can count on is yourself." - Zetsu

December 8

I lift up my eyes to the hills. From where does my help come? My help comes from the Lord, who made heaven and earth. Psalm 121:1-2

Revived Ace

(Haikyu!!)

In the Haikyu anime series, Asahi Azumane faces challenges that lead him to doubt his skills as a volleyball player. He becomes overwhelmed by his mistakes and the expectations placed upon him. However, through the support and encouragement of his teammates and his own determination, he begins to rediscover his passion for the sport and embraces his role as a vital member of the team.

The verses from Psalm 121:1-2 reminds us that our hope is anchored in the Lord, who is the Maker of heaven and earth. When we lift our eyes to Him, we find solace, strength, and assurance in His unwavering presence. He is the source of our help, offering guidance, wisdom, and the resources needed to navigate life's challenges.

The journey of Asahi mirrors the Christian concept of finding hope in times of doubt and uncertainty. In the Bible, we are reminded that our hope should not be placed solely in our own abilities or circumstances but in God. Asahi's transformation highlights the importance of relying on others and seeking support when faced with adversity.

Asahi Azumane serves as an inspiration to anyone who may be grappling with their own doubts and insecurities. His story reminds us that hope can be found in the support of others, the rediscovery of our passions, and the perseverance to overcome challenges. It also encourages us to find strength in our faith, knowing that God is with us every step of the way, guiding and empowering us to reach our full potential. Asahi's journey in Haikyu demonstrates that with hope, determination, and the support of others, we can overcome our limitations and achieve great things.

"To strike past all the obstacles… That's the Ace!" - Asahi Azumane

December 9

He leads the humble in what is right, and teaches the humble his way. Psalm 25:9

Philanthropic Doctor

(Monster)

Dr. Kenzō Tenma is a talented surgeon who has saved more lives than he can count. In the midst of challenging circumstances and moral dilemmas, he humbles himself, recognizing his own limitations and the need for guidance beyond his own understanding. He doesn't rely solely on his own expertise or intellect but seeks the counsel of others, valuing their perspectives and insights.

Psalm 25:9 reminds us that humility is the pathway to God's guidance and instruction. By humbling ourselves, seeking His wisdom, and being open to His teachings, we can walk in His ways and experience the abundant life He has prepared for us. In our own lives, embracing humility allows us to be open to God's teachings and transforms us into individuals who reflect His character.

Dr. Tenma's journey calls us to reflect on our own lives and consider how humility can deepen our relationship with God. Through humility, we acknowledge that our own understanding is limited and that we need His guidance to navigate life's complexities. Just as the doctor sought wisdom from others, we can seek God's wisdom through prayer, studying His Word, and seeking counsel from fellow believers. God's guidance helps us make choices that align with His will and lead to a life that brings Him honour and glory.

The character of Dr. Tenma in the Monster anime series reminds us of the importance of humility in our own lives. When we humble ourselves before God and others, we open ourselves up to His guidance and teachings. Like him, we can experience growth, transformation, and a deeper understanding of what is right as we embrace humility and remain open to learning from those around us.

"Even if you can forget, you can't erase the past." - Dr. Kenzō Tenma

December 10

You hypocrite, first take the log out of your own eye, and then you will see clearly to take out the speck that is in your brother's eye. Luke 6:42

Vengeful Freedom Fighter

(Avatar: The Last Airbender)

Jet's character in Avatar: The Last Airbender exhibits hypocrisy by condemning others for their actions while failing to recognize his own faults. He portrays himself as a freedom fighter fighting against the Fire Nation's tyranny, yet he resorts to violent and unjust methods in the process. He is blinded by his own prejudices and biases, often failing to see the consequences of his own actions.

Luke 6:42 reminds us of the importance of self-examination and humility before attempting to correct or judge others. It urges us to first address the larger issues within ourselves and acknowledge our own shortcomings. By doing so, we gain clarity and perspective, enabling us to offer genuine help and support to others. We are called to live lives of authenticity, integrity, and humility. We are to continually evaluate ourselves and seek God's guidance to remove the planks of hypocrisy from our own eyes. By doing so, we can approach others with humility, grace, and a genuine desire to help them grow.

Jet's hypocrisy calls us to reflect on our own lives and examine our motives, and actions. It challenges us to consider how often we may fall into the trap of hypocrisy, being quick to point out others' flaws while neglecting our own need for growth and transformation.

The reflection on Jet's hypocrisy in the anime reminds us that true transformation begins with self-awareness and a willingness to address our own faults. It prompts us to cultivate a spirit of humility, recognizing that we are all imperfect and in need of God's grace. By focusing on our own growth and allowing God to work in us, we can be better equipped to lovingly support and guide others, free from the shackles of hypocrisy.

"Sometimes the best way to solve a problem is to help others." - Iroh

December 11

Whoever is generous to the poor lends to the Lord, and he will repay him for his deed. Proverbs 19:17

Optimistic War Hero

(Fullmetal Alchemist: Brotherhood)

Maes Hughes, a character in Fullmetal Alchemist: Brotherhood, is known for being a warm and friendly military officer. He goes out of his way to help those in need, treating them with dignity and respect. His welcoming nature extends not only to his friends and family but also to strangers, making them feel valued and cared for. Hughes embraces Edward, Alphonse, and Winry, treating them as part of his own family. He offers them support, love, and a safe haven from their hardships.

Proverbs 19:17 emphasizes the significance of showing kindness to the poor and those in need. It assures that when we extend our kindness and support to those who are less fortunate, we are lending to the Lord. God sees and values our acts of compassion and promises to reward us for our efforts.

Maes Hughes' character reminds us of the importance of serving others with love and compassion, regardless of their social status or circumstances. His acts of kindness are not driven by personal gain or recognition, but by a genuine desire to make a positive impact on their lives. This challenges us to extend our kindness beyond those we know well and to actively seek opportunities to help those who are marginalized, oppressed, or in need.

By relating Maes Hughes' kindness in the anime, we are reminded of the importance of extending kindness to the less fortunate. Just as Hughes showed compassion to the Elric brothers and others in need, we are encouraged to treat others with love, generosity, and respect, knowing that our kindness is not in vain but will be rewarded by God.

"There are some things in life that will only be understood through words." - Winry Rockbell

December 12

If a brother or sister is poorly clothed and lacking in daily food, and one of you says to them, "Go in peace, be warmed and filled,"without giving them the things needed for the body, what good] is that? So also, faith by itself, if it does not have works, is dead. James 2:15-17

Magical Girl

(Puella Magi Madoka Magica)

Sayaka Miki's love in the anime is not merely expressed through words or intentions but through tangible actions and sacrifices. She actively seeks to address the needs of others, going beyond empty assurances and offering practical support. Her love is demonstrated by her willingness to step in and make a difference in the lives of those around her. She takes concrete actions to protect, help, and provide for her friends and those in need.

The passage from James 2:15-17 reminds us that love is not just about empty words or good intentions. True love is alive and transformative, moving us to actively engage with the needs and struggles of others. Sayaka's character embodies this principle, demonstrating that love requires tangible action.

Just as Sayaka's love brought comfort, aid, and hope to those she encountered; our love can have a profound impact when accompanied by practical action. By aligning our faith with deeds of love, we participate in God's transformative work in the world, bringing light and healing to those in need.

Sayaka Miki's character in Puella Magi Madoka Magica challenges us to go beyond superficial expressions of care and engage in tangible acts of love and support. Let her example inspire us to live out our faith through meaningful action, addressing the needs of others, and reflecting God's love in the world.

"I get to have a wish. But ya know, there's other people out there who deserve it a lot more." - Sayaka Miki

December 13

For my father and my mother have forsaken me, but the Lord will take me in. Psalm 27:10

Young Lordling

(Kotaro Lives Alone)

Kotaro is a brave and independent 4-year-old boy who lives alone in an apartment. Despite his young age, he can do tasks like cleaning, cooking, and taking care of himself. Kotaro's parents treated him poorly, but he holds onto the hope of being reunited with them and having a happy family life. He teaches us that no matter what challenges we face, we can overcome them and find happiness if we have a positive attitude and try our best.

Psalm 27:10 calls us to place our ultimate trust in God, to find solace in His presence, and to seek our identity and worth in Him. The beauty of this verse lies in its proclamation of God's unwavering love and faithfulness. Even when our earthly relationships let us down, the Lord stands ready to receive us with open arms. God's love is not conditional or fleeting; it surpasses the limitations of human love. He is a Father who never forsakes His children, a mother who always nurtures and cares for us.

As we reflect on Kotaro's journey, we witness his resilience and the strength he gains from discovering new relationships and connections. It is a testament to the redemptive power of God's love in our lives. When we feel abandoned, lonely, or unsupported, we can turn to God, knowing that He is always there to receive us.

In Kotaro's life, we see a reflection of our own journeys. We may have experienced brokenness, abandonment, or loneliness, but we are never truly alone. God, our Heavenly Father, is always present, ready to receive us and provide us with the love and comfort that we long for. Kotaro's story reminds us of the unchanging nature of God's love and His faithfulness in every season of our lives. Let us find our refuge in Him, allowing His love to heal our wounds and fill the emptiness within us.

"You do not want to be the reason someone you love becomes a bad guy." - Kotaro

December 14

Set your minds on things that are above, not on things that are on earth. Colossians 3:2

Mr. Honor-Roll & Teach

(The Quintessential Quintuplets)

Fūtarō Uesegi, the protagonist of the anime "The Quintessential Quintuplets,"begins as a diligent student primarily concerned with his studies and earning money for his family. However, as he becomes the tutor for the Nakano sisters, his priorities and perspective gradually shift. Initially, he approaches his role purely as a means to earn money. However, as he spends more time with the quintuplets and gets to know them individually, he begins to develop a deeper understanding of their unique personalities, aspirations, and challenges.

The verse Colossians 3:2 encourages believers to focus their minds and priorities on heavenly matters rather than being consumed by earthly possessions and desires. It challenges us to evaluate our desires and ambitions, urging us to prioritize spiritual treasures over temporary possessions. It also invites us to cultivate a mindset focused on heavenly values and the pursuit of righteousness.

As Fūtarō progresses, he starts to focus not only on the academic and financial aspects of his tutoring job but also on the emotional, personal growth, and relational dimensions. He learns to set his mind on the individual needs of the Nakano sisters, their dreams, and their well-being, going beyond the surface-level responsibilities of a tutor.

The character development of Fūtarō Uesegi in The Quintessential Quintuplets anime series reflects a shift in perspective from earthly concerns to higher, more meaningful matters. By setting his mind on the well-being and personal growth of the quintuplets, he demonstrates a transformation that goes beyond the pursuit of earthly gains, similar to the Biblical call of focusing on things above.

"The annoying thing about human relationships is that... you can't proceed with just one side's opinion." - Fūtarō Uesugi

December 15

Because of your little faith. For truly, I say to you, if you have faith like a grain of mustard seed, you will say to this mountain, 'Move from here to there,' and it will move, and nothing will be impossible for you. Matthew 17:20

Inspirational Pilot

(Gurren Lagann)

Kamina, from the anime series Gurren Lagann, is known for his unwavering determination, indomitable spirit, and charismatic leadership. His motivation stems from a desire to break free from the confines of an oppressive world and reach unimaginable heights. Despite facing countless obstacles and overwhelming odds, Kamina maintains a firm belief in the potential of humanity and their ability to transcend their limitations.

In Matthew 17:20, Jesus uses the analogy of a mustard seed, emphasizing that even the tiniest amount of faith can produce remarkable results. We are encouraged to have faith, not only in God's power but also in our own potential as vessels of His grace. By trusting in God's strength, we can move mountains and overcome the obstacles that stand in our way.

Kamina's motivation serves as a reminder that God has equipped us with the faith and determination to break free from self-imposed boundaries and reach new heights. Just as he inspires his comrades to rise above their circumstances, we are called to inspire others through our unwavering faith and belief in God's power.

Reflecting on Kamina's character in the anime, we are reminded to cultivate a faith that moves mountains. We are encouraged to trust in God's limitless power and to believe that, with even the smallest amount of faith, we can achieve extraordinary things. Kamina's character serves as a testament to the transformative power of unwavering faith, inspiring us to step out boldly, overcome obstacles, and bring glory to God through our actions.

"God gave us eyes at the front of our heads so we can look forward to the future." - Kamina

December 16

O Lord, God of vengeance, O God of vengeance, shine forth! Psalm 94:1

Preternatural Deal Maker

(Hell Girl)

Ai Enma, the main character of the Hell Girl anime series, has a tragic backstory. She was a young girl who suffered from constant torment and bullying in her village. The villagers eventually decided to sacrifice her to the mountain god, despite her parents' attempts to save her. Ai was buried alive and died a horrific death. After her death, she transformed into an evil being and sought vengeance by killing everyone in her village. As a consequence of her actions, the Master of Hell punished her by making her the first Hell Girl, forever bound to serve as a messenger of vengeance.

Psalm 94:1 reflects the cry for justice and vengeance found within human nature. It acknowledges God as the ultimate authority and avenger. It expresses a longing for divine intervention to shine forth and bring forth justice on behalf of those who have been wronged. It challenges us to reconsider our desires for revenge and to entrust the pursuit of justice to God. Rather than taking matters into our own hands, we are called to seek His guidance and trust in His ultimate plan for justice and restoration.

While Hell Girl portrays a distorted view of vengeance, the Bible provides a broader perspective on the concept. The Bible consistently teaches that ultimate justice and vengeance belong to God alone. He is the righteous judge who will ensure that justice is served with perfect fairness.

By reflecting on Ai Enma's character, we are reminded of the importance of entrusting justice to God. It prompts us to recognize that seeking personal vengeance often leads to a cycle of pain and darkness. Instead, we are called to rely on God's wisdom and timing, knowing that He will ultimately bring about justice according to His perfect will.

"The real hell is inside the person." - Ai Enma

December 17

The Lord is good to those who wait for him, to the soul who seeks him. Lamentations 3:25

Youngest State Alchemist

(Fullmetal Alchemist: Brotherhood)

Edward Elric is both intelligent and impulsive, with a mastery of alchemy and a knack for quick thinking. While his impatience can lead to unwise decisions, his ability to assess situations and think creatively sets him apart. His determination to restore his brother's body drives him. Despite facing setbacks and difficulties, he maintains a patient and determined attitude, never losing sight of his goals. His patience is not passive waiting but an active pursuit of knowledge, justice, and personal growth.

The verse Lamentations 3:25 encourages believers to wait upon the Lord and seek Him with their whole heart. It reminds us that God is good to those who patiently trust in Him and diligently seek His presence. It also invites us to align our hearts with God's timing and to seek Him earnestly.

Edward's character demonstrates the importance of perseverance and faith in the midst of challenges. His patience reflects a steadfast belief that there is a purpose and a greater plan behind the difficulties he faces. It reminds us that our own trials and waiting periods can be opportunities for growth, transformation, and a deeper reliance on God. Like Edward's pursuit of knowledge, we should diligently seek God's word to shape our decisions.

As we reflect on Edward's patience, we are encouraged to trust in God's goodness and faithfulness. We are reminded that even in the midst of uncertainty and hardship, God is working for our ultimate good. May we patiently wait upon Him, seeking His presence, and allowing His wisdom to guide our paths, just as Edward's patient pursuit led him to extraordinary revelations and transformation.

"Even when our eyes are closed, there's a whole world out there, that lives outside of ourselves and our dreams." - Edward Elric

December 18

Whoever walks with the wise becomes wise, but the companion of fools will suffer harm. Proverbs 13:20

Great Saiyaman

(Dragon Ball)

In Dragon Ball, Gohan learns valuable lessons from wise individuals like Goku and Piccolo, who guide him in embracing his true potential while staying grounded in his values. When his father, Goku, is killed before his eyes, Gohan's anger and emotions reach a breaking point, leading to his Super Saiyan 2 transformation. He displays incredible power and easily defeats the strongest enemy in the series at that time, called Cell. This surprising moment shows that even calm characters like Gohan can have a hidden, intense side to them.

Proverbs 13:20 teaches us about the significance of the company we keep. It emphasizes that our associations have a profound impact on our character and well-being. Walking with wise individuals who possess discernment and moral integrity can lead to personal growth and wisdom. Conversely, associating with foolish companions can lead to harm and negative consequences.

Just as Gohan benefits from the guidance of wise individuals like Goku and Piccolo, we are called to surround ourselves with godly influences who will positively shape our character and help us stay rooted in our faith. These relationships can provide accountability, support, and wisdom as we navigate the pressures of the world.

Reflecting on Gohan's experience in Dragon Ball challenges us to evaluate the influence of our relationships. We should actively seek wisdom and discernment, choosing companions who will uplift us spiritually and help us grow in our faith. By walking with the wise, we can become wise ourselves, avoiding the harm that comes from being a companion of fools.

"One thing I learned from my father is to never give up, even when the odds are stacked against you." - Son Gohan

December 19

For the foolishness of God is wiser than men, and the weakness of God is stronger than men. 1 Corinthians 1:25

Pirate King

(One Piece)

Gol D. Roger, the Pirate King in One Piece, achieved remarkable feats without relying on a Devil Fruit power. Despite facing a mysterious illness and having only his Haki abilities, he became the first person to reach Laugh Tale and became the most powerful pirate. He fought against formidable opponents like Whitebeard, Shiki, and Garp using his exceptional Haki skills. Roger's incredible achievements highlight the strength and determination of his character, proving that even without special powers, one can accomplish the impossible.

The verse 1 Corinthians 1:25 highlights the contrast between human wisdom and the wisdom of God. It acknowledges that even the most impressive displays of human strength and intelligence pale in comparison to the wisdom and power of God. We should remember that true power lies in surrendering ourselves to God's plan and relying on His guidance. It is through aligning ourselves with His wisdom and strength that we can find true fulfilment and make a lasting impact in the world.

Gol D. Roger's sickness in the anime serves as a reminder that even the most impressive displays of human strength and wisdom are ultimately temporary and limited. It is in recognizing the surpassing power and wisdom of God that we find true meaning and purpose.

The power of Roger encourages us to recognize the limitations of human power and seek God's guidance and power in all areas of our lives. By doing so, we can align our actions and aspirations with God's will and experience a true transformation of power and wisdom.

"Inherited Will, The Destiny of the Age, and The Dreams of the People. As long as people continue to pursue the meaning of Freedom, these things will never cease to be!" - Gol D. Roger

December 20

The wicked flee when no one pursues, but the righteous are bold as a lion. Proverbs 28:1

Uncrowned Undefeated Lioness

(Black Clover)

In Black Clover, Mereoleona's boldness is showcased through her relentless pursuit of strength and her willingness to take on any opponent. She never hesitates to step forward and protect those in need, even if it means putting herself in harm's way. Her lion-like bravery is a testament to her righteousness and unwavering commitment to justice.

In Proverbs 28:1, we see a contrast between the behaviour of the wicked and the righteous. It highlights the tendency of the wicked to be fearful and flee even when there is no immediate threat or danger. On the other hand, it portrays the righteous as bold, strong, and courageous, likening them to the noble and fearless lion. This verse serves as a reminder that true courage and boldness come from our relationship with God.

The character of Mereoleona reflects the lion-like courage that can only come from aligning ourselves with God's wisdom and power. It is by seeking His guidance and surrendering to His plan that we find the strength to face any situation with confidence. Through prayer, studying God's Word, and relying on the Holy Spirit, we can develop the boldness and fearlessness that Mereoleona embodies.

Mereoleona shows that true strength lies in facing challenges with courage and unwavering resolve. Her example challenges us to examine our own lives and question whether we are boldly living out our faith. She encourages us as believers to embrace righteousness, stand boldly for what is right, and rely on the strength and wisdom of God. By doing so, we can navigate life's challenges with unwavering courage, make a positive impact in the world around us, and ultimately bring glory to God.

"We might not be a family by blood, but we should treat all the teammates we're going to make in the future as family!" - Asta Staria

December 21

For the Son of Man came to seek and to save the lost. Luke 19:10

Violence Jack

(Devilman Crybaby)

In Devilman Crybaby, Akira takes on the role of Devilman to save humanity from the threat of demons. He demonstrates empathy and compassion by reaching out to lost and broken individuals, even when they reject and persecute him. His actions can be seen as an attempt to bridge the divide between humans and demons, seeking redemption and healing for everyone.

Luke 19:10 emphasizes Jesus' mission to seek out those who are spiritually lost and offer them salvation. It highlights His love, compassion, and desire to reconcile humanity with God. As Christians, we are called to follow Jesus' example by sharing the good news of salvation and demonstrating His love through our actions. We are called to seek out those who are lost, spiritually or otherwise, and lead them towards the saving grace of Jesus Christ.

Throughout the anime series, Akira seeks to understand the motivations and struggles of others, attempting to bridge the gap between different beings and find common ground. In doing so, he offers a glimmer of hope and a chance for redemption to those who may be considered "lost"in their own ways. Akira's journey involves personal sacrifice and selflessness as he willingly embraces his role as Devilman, risking his own safety and reputation to protect others.

By embodying qualities of empathy, compassion, and self-sacrifice, Akira's character can be seen as a reflection of the broader concept of a saviour who seeks to bring redemption and offer hope to those who are lost. While the anime's narrative and themes may differ from biblical teachings, they can still prompt reflection on the importance of reaching out to those in need and offering them a chance for transformation and salvation.

"Why do I run? When I run forward, maybe something behind me will change. Even if it's trivial, even if it's just a tiny bit." - Miki Makimura

December 22

For to this you have been called, because Christ also suffered for you, leaving you an example, so that you might follow in his steps. 1 Peter 2:21

Byakugan prodigy

(Naruto)

Neji Hyūga from the Naruto anime initially had a cynical outlook and focused on the rigid social structure of the Hyūga clan. However, during a battle with the Ten-Tails, Neji sacrificed himself to save Naruto and Hinata. He willingly took a fatal blow meant for them, dying with a smile on his face. Neji chose to die for his loved ones, allowing him to overcome destinies and shape his own fate.

The verse 1 Peter 2:21 highlights the suffering and sacrificial example of Jesus Christ. It encourages believers to understand that they have been called to a similar path of suffering and selflessness, following in the footsteps of Christ. It invites Christians to imitate His character and conduct, reflecting His love, patience, humility, and sacrificial nature in their own lives. By following Christ's example, believers are called to live lives that bring glory to God and exhibit the transformative power of His grace.

Neji's sacrifice reminds us that the call to follow Christ is not an easy one. It requires courage, perseverance, and a willingness to endure hardship. Neji's commitment to protect his friends in the face of danger, exemplifies love that Christ calls us to demonstrate.

In contemplating Neji Hyūga's sacrifice in the anime, we are encouraged to deepen our understanding of Christ's sacrificial love and its implications for our own lives. It challenges us to examine our motives, attitudes, and actions, and to strive towards selflessness and sacrificial love in all aspects of our lives. Neji's sacrifice serves as a poignant reminder of the transformative power of love and the profound impact we can have on others when we choose to lay down our lives for their sake.

"No one can determine another's destiny." - Neji Hyūga

December 23

Because you are precious in my eyes, and honoured, and I love you, I give men in return for you, peoples in exchange for your life. Isaiah 43:4

Loyal Delinquent

(Fruits Basket)

In the anime Fruits Basket, Arisa Uotani is initially portrayed as a tough and independent character with low self-esteem due to her troubled past. She harbours feelings of unworthiness and struggles to believe in her own value and potential for happiness. However, through her friendship with Tohru Honda and the support of others, Arisa begins to heal and grow, gradually developing a healthier sense of self-esteem.

Isaiah 43:4 reminds us of the profound truth that we are precious and honoured in the sight of God. God's unconditional love for us is the foundation of our self-esteem. He sees us as valuable and worthy of honour, regardless of our past mistakes or the opinions of others. This truth is echoed in the verse when God declares His love and willingness to exchange nations for our lives.

Arisa's journey can be seen as a reflection of God's transformative love. As she encounters the love and acceptance of those around her, she begins to recognize her own worth and value. This process aligns with our Christian faith, which calls us to embrace the love of God and allow it to heal our deepest wounds.

Through Arisa's life in the anime series, we are reminded that our self-esteem is intimately connected to our relationship with God and the love He lavishes upon us. As we embrace His love, we can find healing, restoration, and a newfound sense of self-worth. It empowers us to let go of past hurts, forgive ourselves and others, and live with confidence, knowing that we are cherished and honoured by the Creator of the universe.

"Hey, don't pick a fight over something stupid just cause your ego got bruised." - Arisa Uotani

December 24

Everyone who hates his brother is a murderer, and you know that no murderer has eternal life abiding in him. 1 John 3:15

Delusional Quirk Villain

(My Hero Academia)

Overhaul, also known as Kai Chisaki, is a villain from My Hero Academia. He is a yakuza boss who wants to get rid of quirks and sees them as diseases. He hurts and kills people without remorse, and his main goal is to use a little girl named Eri to create a drug that can destroy quirks. He only cares about his boss, but even when his boss refuses his plan, he puts him in a coma. Overhaul shows no regret for his actions and doesn't value human life.

1 John 3:15 boldly states that anyone who hates a brother or sister is considered a murderer in the eyes of God. This verse reminds us that hatred is not merely an emotion or a fleeting feeling; it carries significant weight and spiritual consequences. By equating hatred with murder, the verse underscores the severity of this sin.

Overhaul's hatred led him to commit acts of violence and harm towards others. His obsession with power and control blinded him to the intrinsic value of human life, resulting in a disregard for the well-being and dignity of his fellow beings. This serves as a poignant reminder that harbouring hatred not only damages our relationship with others but also separates us from God's life-giving presence.

In contemplating the sin of Overhaul, we are called to examine our own attitudes and actions. It challenges us to embrace the transformative power of God's love, allowing it to permeate our hearts and guide our interactions with others. By rejecting hatred and embracing love, forgiveness, and reconciliation, we can live out our faith in a way that honours God and reflects the life-giving message of the Gospel.

"A goal with no plan is called a delusion. You need a plan in order to achieve your goal." - Overhaul

December 25

Bless the Lord, O my soul, and forget not all his benefits, who forgives all your iniquity, who heals all your diseases, who redeems your life from the pit, who crowns you with steadfast love and mercy, who satisfies you with good so that your youth is renewed like the eagle's. Psalm 103:2-5

Blazing Fury

(Pokémon)

In the beginning of Pokémon, Ash's Charizard was initially abandoned and left to die as a Charmander. Ash rescued it, and it became his companion. As it evolved into Charmeleon and later Charizard, it developed a disobedient attitude that caused problems for Ash, even costing him a crucial competition. However, after Charizard's stubbornness nearly led to its demise, Ash stayed up all night to save its life. This act of care and dedication changed Charizard, leading it to stop disobeying Ash and become more loyal.

Psalm 103:2-5 calls us to praise the Lord and remember His benefits. It reminds us that God forgives our sins, heals our diseases, redeems us from the pit, and crowns us with love and compassion. When we express gratitude to God for His forgiveness, healing, redemption, and love, our hearts are transformed.

Just as Charizard's thankfulness strengthened its bond with Ash, our gratitude towards God can deepen our relationship with Him. It opens our eyes to the goodness and faithfulness of God in our lives, allowing us to experience a renewed sense of joy, peace, and purpose.

Charizar d's journey inspires us to cultivate a spirit of gratitude in our own lives. Let us continually remember and appreciate the benefits that flow from our relationship with God. By embracing thankfulness, we can experience transformation, a deeper connection with our Heavenly Father, and a renewed outlook on life.

"A caterpie may change into a butterfree, but the heart that beats inside remains the same." - Brock

December 26

As far as the east is from the west, so far does he remove our transgressions from us. Psalm 103:12

Tragic Pianist Prodigy

(Your Lie in April)

Kōsei Arima was born with an amazing ability to perfectly reproduce music he heard just once. Because of this talent, he faced intense pressure and mistreatment from his mother, who pushed him to practice the piano relentlessly. One day, in a moment of anger, he wished for her to die, never imagining it would actually happen. After her death, Kōsei felt overwhelming guilt and struggled with low self-esteem. However, with the help of Kaori Miyazono, he found the strength to overcome his past and move forward.

The verse Psalm 103:12 reminds us that God's forgiveness knows no bounds. When we seek God's forgiveness, our transgressions are completely removed from us, just as the east and the west never meet. This verse reflects the unconditional love of God, who extends His mercy and grace to all who turn to Him.

Kōsei's acceptance in the anime parallels divine forgiveness. Through the support and understanding of his friends, especially Kaori, he experiences a journey of redemption where his past mistakes and self-blame are gradually released. He finds healing and restoration, ultimately embracing a new chapter in his life.

The Christian reflection on Kōsei's acceptance highlights the profound truth that God's forgiveness is limitless and liberating. It teaches us that no matter our past, mistakes, or guilt, we can find acceptance and renewal in God's loving embrace. It encourages us to extend forgiveness and acceptance to ourselves and others, understanding that we are all in need of God's grace. Kōsei's story reminds us that through God's forgiveness and the acceptance of others, we can find healing, transformation, and a renewed sense of purpose in our lives.

"Maybe...just maybe, the light can reach even the bottom of a dark ocean." - Kōsei Arima

December 27

A fool gives full vent to his spirit, but a wise man quietly holds it back. Proverbs 29:11

Meat Master

(Food Wars!)

Ikumi Mito is a character from the anime Food Wars known as the Meat Master. She is a talented butcher who has a fierce temper driven by her intense competitiveness and desire to be the best. Her anger stems from feeling challenged or disrespected, leading her to respond with violence. She carries knives and knows how to use them efficiently, making her temper a cause for concern.

Proverbs 29:11 teaches us that giving full vent to our rage is unwise and characteristic of a fool. As followers of Christ, we are called to exhibit the fruit of the Spirit, which includes self-control and gentleness. The verse reminds us that our words and actions have consequences, and responding in anger can lead to harm and damaged relationships. Furthermore, it challenges us to examine our own hearts and attitudes toward anger. It prompts us to seek God's guidance and rely on the Holy Spirit to transform our responses, allowing us to embody the love, grace, and peace of Christ in our interactions with others.

Ikumi has a strong and competitive personality, often becoming angry when her skills are challenged or when she feels disrespected. Her temper can sometimes lead her to respond with aggression. However, she is also passionate about her craft and strives to be the best in the world of meat.

When contemplating Ikumi's anger in the anime, we are reminded of the Christian call to exercise self-control, seek calmness, and respond to challenging situations with wisdom and grace. By aligning our attitudes and actions with the teachings of Scripture, we can strive for healthier relationships and a deeper reflection of Christ's character in our lives.

"If you want to grow, just look above you. There are plenty of people perfect to serve as fodder for your growth." - Kojiro Shinomiya

December 28

For those who live according to the flesh set their minds on the things of the flesh, but those who live according to the Spirit set their minds on the things of the Spirit. For to set the mind on the flesh is death, but to set the mind on the Spirit is life and peace. Romans 8:5-6

Hyūga's Future Heiress

(Boruto)

In Boruto, Hanabi initially resembled her modest older sister, Hinata, but over time, she became increasingly obsessed with appearances. She often prioritizes how she looks, even in battles, and worries about aging. However, she still respects her sister and can be serious when needed. She invests her time, energy, and thoughts in pursuing physical beauty and seeking validation through her looks.

The verses in Romans 8:5-6 remind us that when we set our minds on the things of the flesh, such as physical appearances, external validations, and worldly standards of beauty, it leads to spiritual death. It hinders us from experiencing the fullness of life and the peace that comes from aligning our thoughts and desires with the things of the Spirit.

Hanabi places a high value on looking attractive and strives to maintain a polished image. However, as followers of Christ, we are called to cultivate inner beauty, such as love, humility, kindness, and compassion, instead of external appearance.

From Hanabi's character, we can learn to reorient our priorities and seek a mindset that aligns with the Spirit. It challenges us to pursue a beauty that comes from within, rooted in our relationship with God, and expressed through acts of love and service to others. By embracing this perspective, we can discover a profound sense of identity and worth that transcends the confines of mere appearance and leads to a more meaningful and fulfilling life.

"Bonds aren't about history or blood. It's something much stronger! Feelings of love. That's all you need." - Naruto Uzumaki

December 29

Cur sed be the day on which I was born! The day when my mother bore me, let it not be blessed! Jeremiah 20:14

Human Monster

(One-Punch Man)

Garou's attitude, as portrayed in the One-Punch Man anime series, reveals the depth of human brokenness and the consequences of a distorted sense of identity. He experiences profound despair and self-loathing, longing for a different reality. His rejection of societal norms and his desire to challenge the hero system highlight the flaws and injustices present in the world.

Jeremiah 20:14 expresses the deep anguish and despair of the prophet Jeremiah. In this particular verse, Jeremiah laments his own existence, wishing that the day of his birth had never occurred. Throughout the series, Garou battles with his own identity, feeling rejected by society and longing for recognition. He harbours resentment towards heroes and the systems they represent, leading to his desire to disrupt and challenge their authority.

While Garou's attitude may reflect the brokenness of the world, it also highlights the importance of recognizing our own shortcomings and seeking a path of healing and reconciliation. Rather than succumbing to bitterness and violence, the Christian faith calls individuals to strive for justice, mercy, and love.

The journey of Garou in the One-Punch Man anime can serve as a cautionary tale about the dangers of allowing our anger and frustration to consume us, leading us further away from the path of true transformation and reconciliation. It encourages us to seek a balance between acknowledging the brokenness of the world and actively working towards positive change, guided by the principles of justice, forgiveness, and restoration.

"If you don't want to get bossed around or mocked by the people around you... you just need to become stronger." - Garou

December 30

But the one who did not know, and did what deserved a beating, will receive a light beating. Everyone to whom much was given, of him much will be required, and from him to whom they entrusted much, they will demand the more. Luke 12:48

Void prince

(Guilty Crown)

In "Guilty crown," Shu Ouma is the protagonist who possesses a power called the "Power of the Kings." Initially, he is reluctant to take on the responsibility that comes with this power, as he fears the consequences of his actions and the burden of leadership. However, as the story progresses, Shu realizes that he has the ability to make a difference and must shoulder the responsibility that comes with his unique abilities.

In Luke 12:48, the verse emphasizes the idea that those who have been given talents, resources, or authority are expected to use them wisely and for the greater good. It highlights the principle of accountability and the notion that individuals who have been blessed with more have a greater responsibility to act justly and contribute positively to society.

Shu's ultimate realization that his power is meant to be used for the greater good reflects the Christian principles of stewardship and selflessness. It serves as a reminder that our talents, resources, and positions of authority are not for personal gain but should be employed to benefit others and bring glory to God.

When reflecting on Shu Ouma's circumstances in "Guilty crown," we can find lessons in recognizing and embracing God's gifts, the process of sanctification, and the call to selfless stewardship. It encourages believers to reflect on their own lives, evaluating how they can utilize their God-given talents and resources to make a positive impact on the world around them while remaining accountable to God and others.

"There are only two paths you can choose. You can sit quietly and be selected out of this world, or you can adapt and change!" - Gai Tsutsugami

December 31

Let each of us please his neighbour for his good, to build him up. Romans 15:2

Mischievous Brother

(Fruits Basket)

Ayame Sohma is a character from the Fruits Basket anime series who belongs to the Sohma family, which is cursed in the story. He is known for his flamboyant and outgoing personality, often striving to entertain and make others happy. Despite his own personal struggles, he goes out of his way to uplift and build up the spirits of those he interacts with, particularly his younger brother Yuki and his friends.

In Romans 15:2, the apostle Paul emphasizes the need for believers to consider the well-being and benefit of their neighbours. It encourages a selfless mindset where individuals seek to please and serve others in a way that brings about their growth and edification. The underlying message is to prioritize acts that contribute to the spiritual and emotional welfare of others, fostering a sense of harmony and encouragement within the community.

Ayame embraces his true self and encourages others to do the same. He is unapologetically himself, even when faced with societal expectations or criticism. Ayame's commitment to authenticity reminds us of the importance of being genuine and true to who we are, rather than conforming to societal pressures. This aligns with the biblical call to love our neighbours as ourselves and treat them with honesty and sincerity.

Ayame Sohma's commitment in the Fruits Basket anime series can be seen as he seeks to please others, build them up, demonstrate selflessness, and encourage authenticity. His actions reflect the Christian values of loving and serving our neighbours, prioritizing their well-being, and being true to ourselves. Ayame's commitment serves as an inspiration for believers to emulate these principles in their own lives and interactions with others.

"Strangely enough, when you get older... The things you didn't understand when you were a child... Start to make sense" - Ayame Sohma

About the Author

Rev. Sam T Rajkumar is an accomplished and energetic minister with a strong background in children's ministry. He has a solid history of achievements in counselling and ministering to children and youth, teaching them how to incorporate Christ into their lives as a means of navigating life's challenges.

Additionally, Sam has experience as an Engagement and Outreach Ambassador at Wattpad, where he engaged with the community, provided support, and encouraged new readers and writers to participate in the platform. He has also worked as a Music, Arts & Crafts Teacher at Candlefire Academy, where he focused on equipping children with creative skills in music, arts, and crafts.

The author is currently pursuing a Master's degree in Biblical Studies (Old Testament) at United Theological College, Bangalore. He has a wide range of specializations, including music production, singer-songwriting, public speaking, communication, writing, sketching, art, and design. He has several certifications, including an International Leadership Certificate Course (TCE-level-1), Grades from London Trinity Guildhall in Solo Piano, and local certificates for music and other artworks. He has also completed numerous certificate courses from Established Universities on various topics from platforms such as Saylor, Udemy, and Coursera.

Sam has written and published VBS syllabuses for teachers and all age groups of children and has also penned short stories and fictions. His recent theological Publication is titled "Resounding Faith: Embracing Modern Music in Children's Ministry."

Among his accomplishments, Sam has composed over 50+ songs that are available on major music platforms. As a music artist, he has collaborated with both national and international artists to curate his enriched soundscapes that distinctively outline his charismatic approach towards sound design. His music is now available on all major music streaming platforms like Spotify, YouTube, and Apple Music. You can follow him on Facebook, Twitter, and Instagram for more details.

www.ingramcontent.com/pod-product-compliance
Lightning Source LLC
LaVergne TN
LVHW041140150826
845673LV00001B/53

* 9 7 9 8 8 9 1 8 6 5 0 8 2 *